THE MAN BEHIND
THE MASK

ANDY MARTIN
Executive Editor
ContrarianCommentary.com

ORANGE STATE PRESS
Washington, DC – New York
London – Chicago

Published in the United States of America

Orange State Press
Washington, DC – New York – London – Chicago
www.orangestatepress.com

ISBN 978-0-96578124-4

Cover design and logo by Cindy Pardy
Author photograph by Leo Sorel
Book design and layout by Lee Lewis Walsh, Words Plus Design

First Edition, July 2008

Printed in the United States of America by Edwards Brothers, Inc., Ann Arbor, Michigan

Contents

About the Author

Andy Martin is one of the legendary corruption fighters and activists in Illinois political history. He began by exposing corruption in state government while still a law student at the University of Illinois over forty years ago. While still a student he also helped pursue and expose scandal at the Illinois Supreme Court. His investigations of crooked Cook County (Chicago) judges helped trigger federal prosecutions and sent guilty judges to jail.

In *Obama: The Man Behind the Mask*, Andy Martin examines Senator Barack Obama's character and questionable career in Illinois.

Andy started his career as an investigative author in VietNam and Southeast Asia in 1967-1971. In 2003 he served as a Baghdad bureau chief and was the first analyst to vigorously expose the incompetence and arrogance of Paul Bremer and the U. S. mission.

Andy holds a Juris Doctor degree from the University of Illinois College of Law.

Introduction

HOW THIS BOOK CAME TO BE

Five years ago I was living in Baghdad and working as a bureau chief gathering news and providing analysis and interpretation of the increasingly untenable situation in that country. I didn't know if President George Bush had an "enemies list." But if he did, my name was the first one in line. My controversial reporting and analysis from Baghdad incurred increasing ire. When I read in the Washington Post that President Bush and Baghdad impresario Paul Bremer had shared weight-lifting, movies and popcorn at the White House, and that the president had expressed a desire to discipline that profligate "internet journalist" in Baghdad I knew my name was on *some* list.

I returned to Illinois in late 2003, and started studying the candidates for United States Senator in the March, 2004 primary. Although I attempted to get on the ballot as a Republican, ultimately I was unsuccessful. But the race continued to hold my attention.

In March 2004 State Senator Barack Obama won the Democratic Party's nomination after a wildly improbable primary campaign in which his principal opponent was exposed and discredited because he allegedly abused his wife.

In August, 2004 State Senator Obama delivered a widely praised speech at the Democratic National Convention. By then, I had already begun to study Obama more closely, and on August 11, 2004 I held news conferences in New York and London to expose Obama's "autobiographical" book, "Dreams From my Father," as a fraud. I did not have any strong personal feelings for or against Obama then, and I don't have any now.

Rather, Obama was an interesting subject, and I wrote about him. But I came to believe that Obama was not genuine, and that he had fabricated a paper-maché resumé and personal history that was significantly at variance with the facts of his life.

Unlike United States news organizations, that were featuring Obama as a new face on the national political scene, while ignoring any questions about his past and personality, I was able to draw on my independent news sources around the world to shed light on Obama's unseen and unknown family history. Using our unconventional resources we were able to begin to beat the "mainstream media" on major aspects of the Obama story.

In particular, it seemed to me that the major news organizations in Chicago, the Chicago Tribune and the Chicago Sun-Times, had imposed a virtual wall of silence around Obama. The Tribune, most likely out of misplaced local boosterism and as part of the legendary Chicago inferiority complex about being the Second and now Third City, wanted desperately to promote Obama as a dynamic new national presence. Selfish business interests may have also played a role in the Tribune's silence.

The Tribune was then, as now, locked in an old-fashioned circulation battle with the smaller Chicago Sun-Times. The Tribune fancied itself as both a national and regional paper. The Sun-Times was indisputably a local operation, with its largest readership in minority communities where Obama coverage would energize circulation. And so, I believe the Tribune adopted a veil of silence over criticism of Obama as a competitive response to selling more newspapers in minority neighborhoods and being a credible alternative for reports on the future United States Senator. Obama's closest political adviser, David Axelrod, was also a former Tribune reporter.

As writers and analysts always do, I went on to other topics. Facing no rational opposition from the Republican Party, Obama was duly elected to the U. S. Senate in November, 2004 and ascended to the national stage. He promptly began building a political operation to campaign for president in 2008.

I continued to monitor and research Obama, but for a period wrote little about him. Others, however, had noticed my original research and commentary. Gradually my August 11th, 2004 piece became a cult document in the growing anti-Obama movement.

At the time I was unaware how my research and writing represented the only critical commentary about Obama. I was even less aware of how Obama's life and my own would become increasingly entwined over the last four years as public demand for original content concerning Obama began to grow exponentially, and the mainstream media continued to refuse to criticize the presidential aspirant.

Four years after my original research, "Barry O" as I have come to call him, is the Democratic Party's presidential candidate, and I am generally recognized as the founding father of the anti-Obama research and commentary movement on the Internet.

As Obama's presidential aspirations grew and expanded, we received endless requests for old information and for new commentary on the senator. Sometimes we prepared original research. We also took what had now been publicly revealed, and analyzed that new information, placing Obama in clearer context than the mainstream media were either prepared or willing to do.

But, my news organization, which had evolved into ContrarianCommentary.com, had one overwhelming advantage over any competing media: I have been involved in some form or fashion in Illinois politics since 1965. I have known the outlandish and outsized figures. I had helped trigger investigations that eventually led to criminal prosecutions of local judges, and sent them to prison. I had seen dynasties rise, fall and rise again. I had known some of the legendary reporters and writers of the era. Ironically, with the passage of time, I became something of a legend myself. Like the legendary Eliot Ness, who had battled Al Capone and introduced the anti-corruption "Untouchables" to the world, my relentless efforts against political corruption and public cynicism in Illinois marked me as someone who spoke the truth to power, and did not have to look over his shoulder before speaking the truth. I had developed into a modern, media-based "Untouchable" myself.

I was not a prosecutor, but prosecutors looked in the direction I pointed; some of my pointers led to prosecutions. While I was not a powerful media majordomo, the powerful stopped to ask, "What's he doing?"

And thus, as the Obama phenomenon continued to gain altitude, and the mainstream media became more and more reluctant to challenge Obama, I became the lonely voice of truth in Chicago, a voice that exposed, revealed, analyzed, interpreted and always presented the truth about Senator Barack Obama.

II.
WHAT THIS BOOK IS NOT ABOUT

Some of my readers have viewed me as a partisan. I am not a partisan. I am involved in political activity within the Republican Party, fighting cronyism and corruption. But I am probably as unpopular in some parts of the Republican Party apparatus, the so-called "Combine" in Illinois, as I am in the Obama camp. Some have suggested I am a supporter of Hillary Clinton. I have written admiringly of her, and encouraged her to persevere. I am not her partisan either.

But having been "in the arena" as an activist as well as an analyst in Illinois politics has given me a deeper understanding and unique insights into the process and personalities. By tradition, mainstream media have been barred from being involved in the very events they cover. My unique background, as a sometime participant and lifelong expert on the events I was reviewing, allowed me to interpret and explain them in a way that traditional reporters could not.

III.
WHAT THIS BOOK IS ABOUT

My research writing became and continues to be a form of performance art. I not only write columns, but I hold news conferences, I publicize important matters ignored by the media, and I focus attention where I believe attention needs to be focused. I am a performer as well as an observer.

This book is a continuation in that performance art involving Obama. Some of the topics I cover are virtually unknown to the national public; although they are no secret in Chicago, the mainstream media either passed over them quickly, or failed to understand their significance. I continue to bore in.

Because I am trained as a lawyer, I also have a relentless passion for organization and order (except on my own desk), and so I am constantly plowing, replowing and retilling again in the Obama pasture. I believed readers needed to have information about the very complex questions involving Obama organized and placed in coherent order.

This book had its origins in Palm Beach, where I was at a family dinner. I explained how I was constantly getting calls from the media, politicians and ordinary citizens; and how I kept having to repeat to them what I had written weeks, months or even years ago. Then, in a "eureka" moment as I stared at some winsome hibiscus plants weaving in the gentle breeze, I said "we need a book that collects my writings and takes a fresh look at everything. What can I see now that I did not or could not see then?"

This book is not a biography. Obama's anti-biography, his fictionalized "Dreams" from his "Father," served as a launching pad for my own investigations and commentary. But I felt readers needed a collection of commentary, a pathway through the past few years, an insight and understanding of how the Obama phenomenon had evolved, what his campaign team had concealed and sometimes begrudgingly admitted, and an occasional prediction of where all of this activity would lead.

With this orderly assemblage of the columns and commentaries, coupled with my latest analysis and interpretation, the reader is able to view the progression of the Obama chronicles over the past four years. I hope readers will find the evolution of my views helpful. Some of the early columns do not contain the details about Obama of which we are only now aware. As times passes and new details emerge, we are able to refine our analysis and interpretation. But it is precisely because the truth about Obama has only emerged slowly and grudgingly and fitfully that the process by which we dissolved the myths and discovered the underlying realities about Obama, in an ever-so-slow and frustrating process, that the reader will understand how investigative journalism and commentary operates in a hostile and resistant environment.

Ultimately, this book is not a scholarly work, it is not laden with footnotes and an intimidating bibliography. Rather, this book represents an understanding of Obama through the eyes of someone who has "lived with" the candidate for almost four years and who has in some sense "gotten under the skin" of the inscrutable Mr. Obama.

This book is a work of interpretation and synthesis. The book is written in the form of a casual conversation with the reader; how someone would explain Obama to us if we were just sitting down, informally, conversing about the man. What would you say? What conclusions and opinions about Obama would you want someone to take with them? What stuck in your memory? How would you begin to explain the Obama phenomenon to someone who was not familiar with Obama's life and recent political history?

How would you try to tell people that Obama had rubbed elbows with and done business with some very bad people in Chicago politics, a city legendary for corruption and greed? This book is intended to be a practical handbook, not an encyclopedia.

Ultimately, this book represents the author's conclusions about what makes Obama tick. Or, to use Budd Schulberg's classic study of relentless self-interest and self-promotion to the point of caricature and endangerment, and ultimately self-destruction, as a template, "What makes Sammy Run?," What Makes Barack Obama Run? What indeed?

Andy Martin
Chicago
June, 2008

Columnist Says Barack Obama 'Lied To The American People;' Asks Publisher to Withdraw Obama's Book

NEW YORK, Aug. 10 /PRNewswire/ — Out2.com's independent contrarian columnist, Andy Martin, will publish a column and hold simultaneous news conferences in New York and London on Wednesday, August 11th to disclose he believes Barack Obama is a political fraud who "lied to the American people." Martin has asked Crown Books to stop sales of Obama's book because of its fraudulent content. Martin says Obama may be a threat to the Jewish community.

NEWS CONFERENCE DETAILS

New York:
Time/date: Wednesday, August 11, 2004 11:00 A.M.
Location: Northeast Corner of Fifth Avenue and 65th Street (Temple Emanu-El)

London:
Time/date: Wednesday, August 11, 2004 4:00 P.M.

"I feel sad having to expose Barack Obama," says Martin, "but the man is a complete fraud. The truth is going to surprise, and disappoint, and outrage many people who were drawn to him. He has lied to the American people, and he has sought to misrepresent his own heritage.

"Obama's life story is vastly different from the one he portrays. My point: if he will lie about his mother and father, what else is he lying about? Can we expect 'bimbo eruptions?'

"Fiction: Obama stated in his Convention speech: 'My father ... grew up herding goats.' The 'goat herder' claim has been repeated endlessly. It is a lie. Fact: Obama's grandfather, Hussein Onyango Obama was a prominent and wealthy farmer. His son, Obama's father, was a child of privilege, not privation. He was an outstanding student, not a herdsman.

"Fiction: Obama was given an 'African' name. Fact: Obama is a Muslim who has concealed his religion. I am a strong supporter of the Muslim community, and I believe Muslims have been scapegoated. Obama has a great opportunity to be forthright. Instead, he has treated his Muslim heritage as a dark secret. His grandfather was named 'Hussein.' That is an Arabic-Muslim, not African, name. Hussein was a devout Muslim and named his son, Barack Senior, 'Baraka.' Baraka is an Arabic word meaning 'blessed.' Baraka comes out of the Koran and Arabic, not Africa.

"Barack Senior was also a devoted Muslim, and chose a Muslim name for his son, our own Barack Obama, Junior. Again, his name is Arabic and Koranic.

"Obama has spent a lifetime running from his family heritage and religious heritage. Would his father have given his son a Koranic name if the father was not a devout Muslim? Obama's stepfather was also a Muslim. Obama will be the first Muslim-heritage senator; he should be proud of that fact. There is nothing to be ashamed of in any of the three great Abrahamic religions.

"Fiction: Obama Senior was a harmless student 'immigrant' who came to the United States only to study. Fact: Obama was part of one of the most corrupt and violent organizations in Africa: the Kenyatta regime. Obama's father ran back to Kenya soon after the British left. It is likely Obama's father had Mau Mau sympathies or connections, or he would not have been welcomed into the murderous inner circle of rapists, murderers, and arsonists. I believe Obama's secret shame at his family history of rape, murder and arson is what actualizes him. Our research is not yet complete. We are seeking to examine British colonial records. Our investigation to date has drawn on information on three continents.

"And what about Obama's beloved Kenyan brothers and sisters? None of his family was invited to Boston to share his prominence. Are his relatives being kept in the closet? Where are they? More secrecy, more prevarication.

"It is time for Barack Obama to stop presenting a fantasy to the American people. We are forgiving and many would still support him. It may well be that his concealment is meant to endanger Israel. His Muslim religion would obviously raise serious questions in many Jewish circles where Obama now enjoys support," Martin states.

"Our investigation is continuing. In he meantime, Crown Books should stop selling Obama's novelization of his life. We have asked Crown to do that. Obama is living a lie."

CHAPTER ONE

The Many Masks of Barack Obama

M asks are essential to human survival. There are a vital part of a healthy human existence.

We all wear them.

They define us.

Sometimes the masks are visible. Halloween is an obvious example. People love wearing masks at Halloween; the post-Christian holiday, has become one of the biggest celebrations of the year, a nondenominational blockbuster. In Africa masks have been worn by warriors and witch doctors. Soldiers often mask their identity in battle.

We wear a wide variety of masks in our daily lives, when we are among workers, students, spouses, children and relatives. Almost every event in our interaction with others calls for a different response, a different reaction, a different mask.

Sometimes we mask our disappointment, at losing a job promotion, or a college acceptance, losing a critical game or a bad date.

At other times we mask our feelings to avoid disappointing others.

And there are gender divisions regarding masks. "Big boys don't cry" was a traditional expression for many decades. Mask your emotions or you are not a real man. Today men are allowed to unmask and express their emotions in a wider variety of circumstances and situations.

Some masks are only seen by a few. Unmasking can also be a semi-private affair. The way men (and increasingly women) react to combat and carnage on the battlefield is a unique experience usually seen by only a handful of individuals, those on the battlefield in the midst of chaos and death. The camaraderie of battle affords everyone who shares the experience a special mask. And a special protection against the aftermath of the experience.

We learn who we are when engulfed in hopelessness and conflict. No one wants to look themselves in the face when they have to kill, or may be killed. The mask is usually maintained, but not always. The mask also protects us from whom we are or whom we could become if we abandon self-control and revert to base instincts. The law of lawyers and judges is a mask applied sometimes only very loosely to the "law of the jungle."

And then there is the subject of this book: Senator Barack Obama, the Democratic Party's candidate for president in 2008.

Obama is a master of masking.

He masks his emotions towards adversaries and allies alike.

He masks his feelings about the possibly nonexistent marriage of his parents. He conceals his feelings about racial groups. Throughout his life he has masked his conflicted and convoluted feelings towards his rather colorful and confusing family situation; his white relatives, only one of whom is alive today, his Kenyan relatives and their families. He has applied a mask to his religious heritage.

This book was and continues to be a voyage of discovery. The author has spent four years studying Obama, trying to unmask the senator's feelings in all sorts of environments, towards all types of crises and personal attitudes. Trying to unmask Obama's past.

Has this book succeeded? Only the reader will be the judge.

As noted in the introduction, this book proceeds along two lines.

First, our conclusions and observations over the past four years are summarized. These are personal conclusions and analyses. They are opinions.

And, second, the questions we encountered along the way are reprinted, using the columns, commentaries and controversies that were generated about Barack Obama to understand him and to expose the man behind the mask. Often there was only partial or incomplete information at the beginning; only grudgingly and with great effort could the mask slowly be peeled away.

Because masks are an insight into a person's psyche, a rough read on their character and integrity, studying the many masks of a public figure is challenging, frustrating. Politicians do not like to reveal themselves; Obama is no different.

Except as he has revealed his life and feelings to us in his books, under his total control, he does not want us to know much about his personal trials, his true feelings, his conflicts and emotions. Obama has been willing to unmask himself, but only on a very limited, self-serving basis.

Voluntary disclosure, however, is only a partial revelation of character. Americans must demand a fuller picture of a man who would be their president. What is behind the masks of Barack Obama? Obama's self-revelation is only a very preliminary starting point in studying his identity. I have spent four years studying Barack Obama. Here is my point of view.

The Mask of Barack Obama:
A Psychological Profile

by the editors and contributors and analysts
of ContrarianCommentary.com

February 10, 2007

I.
THE HISTORY OF PSYCHOLOGICAL PROFILING

At some elementary, functioning, practical level we are all "profilers." Every human being is constantly reacting to other humans, profiling their likes and dislikes, their attractiveness and unattractiveness. The police detective at the crime scene is already creating his or her own profile of a possible perp.

Indeed, we use the colloquial term "read" to reflect efforts to probe deeper into someone's psyche. "Can you read him?" "Does she read me?" And so on.

Organized, governmental profiling came into general use in World War II. Initially, Great Britain's Special Operations executive (SOE) began to profile aspects of the Nazi regime and its demented leaders. Later, the US's Office of Strategic Services (OSS) also began to use profiling techniques to delve more deeply into the motivations of our enemies.

The advent of the Cold War and the CIA brought even more organized and expansive profiling techniques into use. These operations were later copied and extended by the FBI.

"Profiling" became controversial in 1964 when psychologists ran an ad in the New York Times claiming that Republican presidential candidate Barry Goldwater was psychologically unfit to be president because he was unstable and dangerous. They were issuing an expert opinion based on the profiling of the candidate.

Since the 1964 debacle profiling has come into general use by campaigns, media and other public projects. We also use the colloquial expression "What makes him tick?" to reflect our informal attempts to profile the motivation and character of potential customers, competitors and others with whom we come into conflict.

Finally there was a barrage of profiling analysis during the period of Bill Clinton's impeachment proceedings. Thus, we are on solid ground in seeking to analyze and create a psychological profile of presidential candidate Barack Obama.

II.
THE METHODOLOGY/TECHNIQUES OF PSYCHOLOGICAL PROFILING

Psychologists use the Diagnostic and Statistical Manual of Mental Disorders (DSM) as a matrix for profiling and diagnosing mental illness. This study is not limited by the DSM which, in any case, has limited application to a study of political personalities.

A profiler will use what is available; the value of the profile will depend on the input. During the Cold War, for example, the CIA successfully profiled Russian and Chinese leaders using published materials as well as media reports. There was little else to go on and the profiles were still remarkably accurate.

Personal interviews and views are obviously the gold coin of psychological profiling a political candidate but they were unavailable in the case of Mr. Obama.

More significantly from a profiling approach, his personality lends itself to planting subtle nuggets of self-revelation in his writings. His earlier writings, moreover, were prepared at a time when the prospects of a presidential campaign were probably not even an idle dream. So these early statements are especially helpful to a personality examination and identification.

III.
PROFILING BARACK OBAMA

Initially one can ask: why profile Obama? Is a psychological profile really needed? The answer is, understanding a public figure's psyche and psychological motivation is no less critical because that person is in the public arena. It may be even more important. We can see an example of the need for constant review and evaluation of a person's mental state ripped out of the headlines, in the saga of the astronaut who went berserk and sought to stalk her romantic rival.

NASA is now reviewing its external psychological profiling procedures, to see if changes are necessary, as well as internal evaluation protocols to see why it was that no one was aware and recognized Capt. Lisa Nowaks's mental deteriorating. So it is essential not only to profile Obama, but to keep profiling him as more information and more self-revelation become available.

A review of Obama's public speeches, campaign materials and especially his writings reflect that Obama's personality has been remarkably consistent from childhood through adulthood.

In his book "Dreams From my Father," Obama lays out the foundation for an examination of his character and personality. That seminal work reveals much, and almost all of what it reveals is truthful and applicable to his presidential prospects.

Obama's life began with loss, hurt, confusion, alienation, frustration. Out of these he constructed a psychological "mask" that still endures.

Every individual wears a mask. It is a part of reality and a part of a healthy personality and psyche.

But Obama's pain still controls his personality. Like Dr. Strangelove's arm, that can't help rising, Obama's sense of loss, exclusion, frustration and fantasy still overarch his personality. He authored a book "Dreams From My Father," when in reality he got no dreams from his father. Obama created his father's "dreams" in his own fantasy world. The fantasies associated with the "missing parent" are among the most powerful, the most enduring and occasionally the most devastating in human experience.

He was "Barry" until he went to college. Then he became the tribal Barack. But on his first visit to his "roots" in Kenya, he once again succumbs to "Barry," because that is what his father and family called him.

He apparently held and still holds Kenyan-American dual nationality, but has scrupulously avoided any discussion of his "dual" status. Duality is not what Obama craves: he craves the singular, the linear, and the straight and narrow, to compensate for his own confused and winding initiation into the hardship of life and family, of creating a personality and mask consonant with his troubled feelings.

Over and over again, Obama returns in his speeches and in his writings to a sense of loss, alienation, detachment. He is a skillful promoter, and he manages to overcome his mask, to gild it with soft statements and lofty promises. He sells his weakness as a new paradigm of strength, security and clarity when there is little strength and no clarity in his mind.

Indeed the very essence of his personality is the perpetual, eternal promise unfulfilled. Obama's "Hope" is the absence of reality, the unattainable in his own life scaled up to a national fantasy which he hopes to peddle to unsuspecting voters and especially young people. When he fails, they will feel betrayed.

While decrying the "smallness" of our politics he resorts to the smallest dimensions himself. Is he seeking to control foreign policy, or is he a frustrated local school board member? Should our schools be run from Washington, as he suggests, by the president, or should local people have final authority? Should the federal government have a bigger role in local schools, or is he just engaging in the casual blather that he decries in others? What is he going to do about teacher salaries? Nationalize or federalize them? And, oh, the teachers' unions. In Obama's fantasyland all of these conflicts and contradictions dissolve into "hope." He is for more pay and perks, but which teacher's union supports strict accountability and expedited procedures for dismissal of incompetents?

Does Obama really believe that we need to revive the role of "labor unions" in his "digital economy," or is that merely another sop to leaders that might support his candidacy? The very things that Obama condemns, he is in the process of becoming.

Bill Clinton reduced the presidency to worrying about school uniforms. Before long, Obama may be promising "healthy snacks" for school children as part of his "hope" for the future. Where does the smallness end? Obviously not with Obama, the newest champion of the same, the secure, the warm and fuzzy and ultimately the same escapist fantasies as every other career politician.

In Iraq? Obama wants to "cut and run," by 2008. "We can't wait, till 2008." It will succeed marvelously as political policy in the Democratic Party primaries, but it will bring collapse to or failed policy even worse than that engendered by George Bush.

While Obama claims to be moving along Robert Frost's "road not taken," in reality he is on the same road, seeking the same fund raising contributors (tens of millions of dollars), seeking to stimulate the same media hysteria and ultimately seeking to run a traditional campaign while claiming he is doing precisely the opposite. In short, a bunkum artist who is fully capable, because of his "Mask," of convincing himself of the truthfulness of his delusions. The same way children are.

Can his personality stand the stress? Probably not.

The media will get tired of Obama's same old tired message, he substitution of hope for reality. And, ultimately, he will get tired of himself.

Politically Obama will become cannon fodder for the Republicans. Goofy Republicans wanted Hillary; they may get Barack, a dream come true. Giuliani (whom I don't particularly like) would rip him up. Ultimately, Obama's personality matrix left Obama weak inside, weak under the surface, "all sail and no anchor." He learned to avoid conflict, not fight. His mother raised someone who would run away, not stand his ground. And in Iraq that could prove fatal.

Obama says his campaign is "not just about me." But in his mind it will always be just about him. Righting the wrongs he perceived and experienced as a child. Strengthening the powerlessness he reviled. Restoring his role, the one his siblings called his father's "Obama" attitude, in the pantheon of politics. He will strive to be a strong leader on the surface, using powerful language and images; but inside he will still be the pied piper of powerlessness. And know it.

Obama has succeeded largely by his successful concealment at the margins. Obama's natural tendency, his default state of mind, is to evade, conceal, avoid—and escape. He managed to hide his middle name in 2004; he can't any longer. Questions of family background will still plague him. As Democrats raise the volume of their demands for withdrawal, our adversaries will seek to stroke those fears with renewed attacks of their own in Iraq.

War is war, but war is also psychology. Obama's psychology is weak. His presentation today was weak, and his approach to dealing with his adversaries will ultimately come to be seen as weak. Obama is still the outsider, still the one who needs to justify himself, and still the one who still needs to create a fantasyland to compensate for the void left by his absent father.

IV.
SUMMARY AND CONCLUSIONS

The conflicts inside Barack Obama's soul played out today in Springfield, where he alternated between jive and reality.

As much as Obama might try to change his face, to abandon his "old" Obama for a "new" persona, he cannot do so. His growth is limited by the demons within him. The mask is rigid, hardened.

He approached the American people as though he were speaking to a college audience, casual and insufficiently serious for someone who asks for the right to put his hand on the nuclear button as well as Washington's bible.

Obama's 2004 Democratic National Convention speech was so powerful and so memorable precisely because he was constrained by format and content. Today's display was free-form Obama, and he won't travel well and sell well outside a narrow spectrum of the electorate.

As Obama comes to realize he may have finally overreached, and perhaps even exceeded his level of incompetence, he may withdraw into himself, withdraw from the battlefield, and plan to return again in a later campaign.

The Mask, however, will remain. It can never be removed. He hasn't learned how. All of the inadequacies and frustrations he perceived as a child still drive him and still control his personality. He won't learn how to remove the Mask because he continues to be afraid there is nothing behind it.

CHAPTER TWO

The Obama Family

I.
BARACK OBAMA'S TROUBLED ORIGINS

Barack Obama was conceived in the licentiousness of a bigamous "marriage." He has carried the burden of his lack of legitimacy throughout his life. No one knows for sure, except Barack, when he first learned that his father was a rake, a fraud and a bigamist.

Barack Obama, senior ("his father") was also a habitual con man, alcoholic and, apparently, a serial polygamist.

Obama claims that his parents were "married" in Hawaii, although no lawful marriage was possible because his father already had a valid marriage and children in Kenya. The Dunham/Obama marriage appears to have been what used to be called a "shotgun" marriage. Obama was born six months after the marriage.

No one has provided a copy of a valid "divorce" decree of the Obama/Dunham "marriage." Whether Ann Dunham was even aware that her marriage had been a legal nullity is not clear.

Obama may have learned the cruel facts of his parents' self-indulgence and prevarication from his grandmother. That would explain why he manifested both extreme antagonism and warm affection for his sole remaining white relative. Madelyn Dunham was the practical and steady member of the family. Most likely she sat her grandson down one day and said, "There are some things about your parents you probably wonder about, and would like to know about, so here goes."

Obama was desperate for the truth, but no less angry and frustrated when he learned and had to digest the unpleasant facts about his family. The grandmother/grandson conversation probably came just before or just after Obama's only visit from his father at the age of 10.

Obama at some point came to accept the truth about both of his troubled parents. He has carried the burdens of his mother and father every day. Unconsciously, he is always frustrated, powerless, angry and anxious to move on from the unpleasantness of his origins. Moreover, it is likely that his frustration with the reality of his conception and birth has fueled his relentless passion for power and self-promotion.

II.
OBAMA'S FATHER: BARACK HUSSEIN OBAMA, SR.

Throughout his early life Barack Obama maintained and presented a fantasy image of his father. Barack senior was not the "goat herd" that Obama mendaciously suggests *ad nauseam*. Rather, Barack senior was a child of privilege, a child of an educated and sophisticated father who wanted no part of the Dunham's white bloodline in the Obama family tree.

Barack Junior's grandfather had traveled the world and had risen from the primitiveness of colonial era Africa to sophistication, knowledge and success. Barack Senior, his son, was the beneficiary of his father's (Obama's grandfather) accomplishments and wealth. Why Barack Junior stubbornly continues to portray his father in a false and diminutive light is unknown.

Indeed, suspicions about Obama's disinformation concerning his Kenyan relatives originally prodded this writer to investigate Obama's Kenyan origins in 2004. Why was U. S. Senate candidate Obama lying about his family and what were his motives for doing so?

Instead of being proud of his accomplished father and even more so of his successful grandfather, Obama has always sought to minimize these men in the public's perception. This is a radically different attitude towards the past than that of Senator John McCain, who proudly reminds Americans he is the son and grandson of Navy admirals.

After his parents' separation at age two, Obama met his father only once, in Hawaii when he was 10. His father died before Barack Junior would have much contact with his African relatives.

The truths that Barack eventually had to accept about his father were extremely painful ones: (1) His father came to Hawaii as a married man with a family in Kenya; (2) He claims to have entered into some sort of void and bigamous marriage with Ann Dunham. That marriage was absolutely a nullity under Hawaiian law.(3) He dumped his wife and son and went to Harvard, where he began yet another affair, eventually leading to another bigamous "marriage." (4) Obama, Senior, a product of the war for Kenyan independence in the Mau Mau era, returned home to Kenya where he never became part of the future leadership of his homeland. Instead, he took refuge in alcohol, licentiousness and anger.

Published writing appears to confirm that Barack senior was a committed African socialist and someone who had morphed from his hostility to colonial rule into disaffection with his second homeland in the United States.

Barack Junior was abandoned by his father. That abandonment has weighed heavily on Barack's entire life.

III.
STANLEY ANN DUNHAM OBAMA SOETERO

Barack Obama usually claims his family is from Kansas. But his mother, while born in Kansas, spent her formative teenage years in Washington, and graduated from high school in Mercer Island, Washington.

Ann appears to have begun her teen years as a delightfully rebellious and unconventional young woman, the kind that parents might describe as a "handful." Although she reportedly was not anxious to move to Hawaii with her parents, she appears to have adapted rapidly to the lack of conformity and bohemian existence of the college crowd in Hawaii. She went to college just before the explosive social upheaval of the mid-1960's.

Ann was unusually bright, and in the free and loose society of island academic life she took a heady attitude towards her own freedom. Her exaggerated sense of security led her to disastrous results.

Ann became pregnant by the Kenyan hustler Barack Senior. She was later abandoned by this man, a potential bigamist who probably concealed his existing family from the young woman he impregnated. Ann likely learned about Obama's Kenyan family in a letter from Obama Senior's father, who condemned the proposed union.

Whether Stanley Dunham pushed for the shotgun union of his daughter, apparently unaware that the marriage would be void under Hawaii law, is unknown [see *Baehr v. Lewin*, 74 Haw. 530, 852 P.2d 44 (Hawaii 1993); *Tagupa v. Tagupa*, 108 Haw. 459, 121 P.3rd 924 (Hawaii App. 2005].

No doubt Ann felt victimized by a man who impregnated her, "married" her, and then abandoned mother and child to start yet another romantic adventure in Massachusetts.

Ann appears to have inherited the decency of her parents. She probably shielded young Barack (then known as "Barry") from the reality of his unfortunate origins.

Sadly, Ann herself later abandoned Barry, and sent him "home" from Indonesia to Hawaii for uncertain reasons when Barack was 10 years old.

The fact that both of Obama's parents abandoned him is important to understanding the development of his "mask," his relentless pursuit of power and his self-aggrandizement as a palliative for childhood impotence.

None of this sad family background is meant to "blame" Barry/Barack for his parents' indignities and indiscretions. Nevertheless, no one could realistically assess Barack the man without knowing the frustrations, inconsistencies and helplessness felt by Barry the child. It would be humanly impossible for Obama not to have been deeply affected and disaffected by his parents' self-indulgent shenanigans.

IV.
OBAMA IN INDONESIA

Obama's years in Jakarta have generated some of the most sensational accusations against the senator, and some of the most vehement defenses by his media admirers.

Obama's religion while in Indonesia is covered in a separate chapter.

V.
OBAMA'S HAWAII YEARS

Why Ann Soetero (Obama's mother had married Lolo Soetero, an Indonesian citizen, before moving with her new husband and son to Jakarta, Indonesia) sent Barack back to live with her parents in Hawaii is unclear. The only person alive who knows the facts is Obama's white grandmother; she has never been allowed to speak with the press without handlers present.

Obama was enrolled in the prestigious Punahou School, where the children of Hawaii's leading families were educated in a traditional prep school environment.

By the time he retuned to Hawaii, Obama felt abandoned by both parents. His father was absent; his mother had separated herself from her son to ensure that Barry's obtained an adequate education. But even a logical or legitimate separation can create feelings of abandonment and anger.

Obama's mother occasionally returned to Hawaii. During one of her return periods, she applied for and received welfare. Obama seems to take great pride in the fact his mother accepted welfare, but he has never explained why she qualified or would have wanted to accept public assistance. He constantly reminds audiences his mother received food stamps, but the facts of her financial condition have never been clear.

Her son was in an elite private school; Obama's grandmother was an officer at a bank. In short, Ann does not appear to have been a candidate for welfare. Although he has never admitted it, it must have been embarrassing for him to have a parent on welfare while he was attending an expensive private school.

Obama has never explained the questions that linger about his mother's lifestyle. These patent inconsistencies point to highly questionable family values, all of which negate his TV commercial claims that he grew up surrounded by "strong values."

VI.
OBAMA'S TRAGIC LOSS

There is no doubt that Barack Obama deeply loved his mother. Even the most peculiar parents engender absolute love and often loyalty from their children. A similar dynamic exists with parents who have emotionally abused and confused their children. Ann Dunham Obama Soetero appears to have been the type of person who retained the deep love of her son. Ann's death must have been very difficult for Barack to accept.

There is no doubt Obama also felt extreme anger and alienation towards is mother. After all, he dreamed about his father, and relegated his mother's role and influence in his young life to a less-exhaled position. Obama has never felt comfortable showing public admiration or affection for his white relatives.

Still, the loss of his mother in 1995 when she was only 54 must have devastated for Obama. He was not with his mother when she died; some guilt must have come to the surface. Ann died with her parents at her side, not her son.

Even though Ann may have been an indifferent parent she was still a loving mother. By separating herself from her son, and sending him to live with his grandparents, Obama's mother made perhaps the single-most critical decision affecting his success later in life. His graduation from the elite Punahou School in Honolulu was his ticket to college and beyond.

Thus there were copious amounts of love, hate, frustration, affection, adoration and confusion in the mother-son relationship. Obama carries those scars and those unanswerable questions with him every day. Because he was not with his mother when she died, Obama will never be able to obtain the answers that he probably seeks.

VII.
MICHELLE OBAMA AND HER FAMILY

Michelle Obama and her family are the unsung heroes of Barack Obama's life.

Barack Obama found Michelle and pursued her. Although Mrs. Obama has become controversial for "running her mouth," she and her family have given Senator Obama a steady foundation. In Michelle's family, he has found a real family and a stable group of individuals who relate to each other on a consistent basis.

Michelle's family is ordinary, Chicago, African-American working class. They have benefited from the political system, through public employment, and they have advanced in status through the accomplishments of their bright children.

Michelle's family is the only solid foundation in Senator Obama's life.

VIII.
OBAMA'S KENYAN RELATIVES

Obama's Kenyan relatives played two very different roles in his life.

The first role, while he was a growing boy, revolved around the fantasies created by his mother to explain the circumstances of his absent father and Kenyan relatives. Obama's mother concocted an elaborate fairy tale world to confirm his father's exalted role in the world. Unwilling to concede that she had made a colossal mistake by becoming pregnant by a married man—a fact that she continued to conceal from her vulnerable son—Ann Obama Soetero Dunham instead created a "pretend" world where Barry's father lived and served with majesty and importance.

Whether lying to your son is the correct parental approach is a question this author is not qualified to decide. However, as a purely personal opinion, his mother's decision to fictionalize the life story of her former "husband" may have made Obama's ultimate confrontation with reality even more difficult and even more painful when he visited Kenya.

Although Obama apologized in the foreword to his 2004 edition of "Dreams From My Father" for not writing more about his mother, he may have still felt angry about being deceived when he was growing up. "Why didn't, why wouldn't my mother tell me the truth?" is a fair question Obama may have asked himself.

Obama had reason to be angry with both parents. Each in their own way had abandoned him.

His father had abandoned his family in Hawaii to accept a more prestigious opportunity at Harvard, when his father had also been offered an alternative option to move his wife and child to New York. Barack Obama, Senior was finished with Ann Dunham when he left Hawaii for Harvard.

His mother eventually abandoned Barry and sent him to live with his grandparents. Later she rejoined him, and later still moved back to Indonesia. Barry's was an up-and-down, back-and-forth childhood that left lifetime scars.

IX.
THE ULTIMATE ELEPHANT IN THE ROOM:
OBAMA'S ABSENT FATHER

As this book was in its final editing stages, Juan Williams of National Public Radio wrote a column for the Wall Street Journal in which he discussed "America's disappearing fathers." Williams summarized all of the handicaps experienced by children who grow up without a father. (http://online.wsj.com/article/SB121340023355173717.html?mod=opinion_main_commentaries)

Some of the handicaps Williams lists are practical and ordinary; others are deeply emotional.

Barack Obama has often referred to himself as being raised by a "single mother on food stamps." (http://www.time.com/time/magazine/article/ 0,9171,1546302,00.html)

As it turns out, Mrs. Obama-Soetero was married much of the time her son lived with her. Why she chose to accept public assistance as a graduate student seeking a Ph.D, while her son was apparently living with her temporarily, is problematic. He was attending an expensive private school while his mother was accepting public assistance. Nevertheless, Obama wraps himself in the gauzed-up mantle of "single parenthood."

Obama and all of his media sycophants seek to exploit the "bonus" of "welfare" sympathy without accepting the "onus" that absent fatherhood imposed on Barack Obama's psyche. We are perfectly willing to reflect on the problems of fatherless African-American children in Juan Williams' abstract discussion; we refuse to confront the reality that Obama fits squarely in that model.

It is impossible to calculate the emotional and psychological impact that Obama's absent father had on him; and how Barry felt when he learned the truth about the father who discarded him, barely communicated, showed no interest, and ultimately was killed in an auto accident. Senator Obama's early years closely parallel that of the misspent youths in Juan Williams' column. With one exception.

When his father left him, Obama's white relatives stepped in to fill the void. Thus, beneath the surface, Obama labors under two deep emotional conflicts: first, the conflict of his father's abandonment, and his son's desperate efforts to invent and glamorize the absent father; and, second, the fact that while Obama has chosen to portray himself as a "Black man," he survived and prospered only because his white relatives rescued him and assumed the burden of raising their grandchild.

Is it any surprise that Obama feels deep conflicts about his white grandmother, whom he has to date refused to allow to appear in public during the presidential campaign? No surprise at all.

Every day of his life Barack Obama will continue to suffer the emotional consequences of both an absent and abandoned parent and the fact that his "blackness" was allowed to survive and prosper solely because of the generosity and stability of his white relatives. We ignore Obama's conflicted early years, tumultuous family life and absent mother at our own peril.

Much that lurks beneath the surface of his public persona is obscured by Obama's glibness and the willingness of the media and Democratic primary voters to ignore the obvious risks in electing an emotionally damaged and deeply conflicted man to the presidency.

Rationally speaking, no one could seriously suggest electing any person to the White House whose emotional stability and very character had been so undermined by his formative years. We can ignore Obama's "family" and his pre-college upheavals, confusion and alienation, but we do so only at great national peril.

X.
OBAMA'S "DREAMS"

Obama's great opus, Dreams From my Father, was originally claimed as an "autobiography." The book is far less than an autobiography. "Dreams" is more of a fictional work, and a psychological self-portrait, than it is a straightforward recollection of a life lived to the age of 30.

First, Obama did not receive dreams "from" his father. Rather, he dreamed about his father, and created a fictional world.

Second, even at the age of 30 when he began writing "Dreams" he reflected a mild form of emotional disturbance. Obama was steadfast in "remembering" an incident at the American consulate in Jakarta, where he was allegedly shattered by an article and photographs in Life Magazine depicting someone who had been devastated by seeking to bleach away his skin color.

Although Obama has presented this imaginary incident as fact, and did so even after he was challenged on the point, the Chicago Tribune did an exhaustive search of the literature and could find no factual foundation for the "Life" claim (Chicago Tribune, March 25, 2007).

Why would a grown man lie about an incident that never happened in his childhood? Either Obama still believed his fantasy, or thought he could get away with the fib without being caught

Using my own sources in England and Africa in 2004 I began exposing the imaginary life Obama presented as fact in "Dreams." But the most devastating critique of Obama's imaginary "autobiography" was presented on January 27, 2007 in the Daily Mail of London. The Mail writers, who had used a local researcher in Kenya, labeled Obama's claims about his family "largely myth," and branded Barack Obama, Senior "an abusive bigamist, an egomaniac, whose life was ruined not by racism or corruption but his own weaknesses." The Mail stated that Obama's mother "divorced" his father after she discovered that her "husband" was a bigamist.

Barack, Senior apparently never "divorced" his original Kenyan wife and continued to produce children by her even after he had "divorced" Ann Dunham, married a third "spouse," and maintained other relationships. Obama's own half-siblings referred to their father's polygamous behavior as "part of life."

It is undeniable that children with absent parents, particularly absent fathers, fantasize about the missing parent and create elaborate justifications for the absent parent. Obama's mother added to this fantasy by refusing to tell Barry the truth; he only discovered who his father really was later in life.

Significantly, Obama does not disclose how he discussed "family matters" with his mother after he returned from his journey of discovery to Kenya where he learned the truth about his father. Obama was unwilling to share this crucial moment in his life with us in "Dreams." But then he virtually wrote his mother out of the book, which should tell us something.

Second, Obama uses his Kenyan relatives as a prop and photo op. He managed to confuse the Chicago Sun-Times for many months; the newspaper had a picture of his "granny" on SunTimes.com. Only the "granny" on the web was not his real Kenyan grandmother. She was a subsequent wife of his grandfather, and not Barack, Senior's mother.

The use of the Kenyan relatives to create a ruse, namely that his white relatives were no longer significant, is dealt with in the next section of this chapter. Obama has resolutely tried to "white out" modern references to white relatives, and sought to use the Kenyan branch of the family as his "true" family.

Third, Obama's "autobiography" was not only a work of fiction, in later years he could not even remember whom he had used as the basis for his fictionalized characters.

When challenged by Lynn Sweet, a Chicago Sun-Times writer, (August 8, 2004) to disclose the identities of the "colorful characters" in "Dreams," Obama said "I don't remember what Smitty's real name was. I think it was Wally." So much for lasting lifetime impressions.

The man who created the imaginary existence of a Life magazine article could not remember the actual existence of people he had converted into fictional figures. Imagination anyone? For a man now in his 40's to be so overwhelmed by fantasy figures is a serious psychological symptom that has been largely ignored by mainstream media.

It does not take someone learned in psychiatry or psychology to be suspicions of a man who can't tell the truth and can't remember the truth. Placing such a man in the White House is an invitation to disaster. When his "campaign research director Devorah Adler" (Chicago Sun-Times, February 20, 2007) tried to prepare a reply to a Los Angeles Times article questioning whether Obama had inflated his role in an asbestos battle, Lynn Sweet wrote "Adler had to dig up the real identities by herself even though it would have seemed simpler for her to ask Obama." Obama had no recollection of the true identities of his "autobiographical" persons even though "He also kept a journal."

Over the years, Lynn Sweet morphed from a sycophant of Obama to a skeptic.

Despite the fact that Obama's "autobiography" had been exposed as a work of fiction and fantasy, Obama was still using the book to encourage gullible New Hampshire voters to support him through "book clubs" (Chicago Sun-Times, July 11, 2007). How do you spell *chutzpah*?

In yet another sleight-of-hand to Sweet, Obama told her in 2004 "Marty Kaufman" in "Dreams" was a composite based on Gerald Kellman. Three years later, Obama morphed "Kaufman" into someone based on Michael Kruglik.

Does Obama even know what the truth is any more? Does he care? He has shown utter contempt for reality, facts, family, and "autobiography." Anyone who confronts him over his fantasies and inconsistencies is labeled a "smear artist."

Mr. Obama's inability to distinguish fact from fiction will prove devastating and create chaos if he should succeed in catapulting himself into the White House.

XI.
WHAT'S IN A NAME? BARRY VS. BARACK

Newsweek Magazine devoted a cover story on the dichotomy between the names "Barry" and "Barack" Obama. (http://www.newsweek.com/id/128633)

Throughout most of "Dreams from My Father," Obama's family refers to him as "Barry." But it was perhaps during Obama's turbulent late teen years that he crossed over the line: someone with parents of two races became someone who identified himself as exclusively Black or African-American.

Shortly thereafter, he went to Africa to meet his Kenyan relatives, where he discovered for himself the truth about the man his mother had misidentified as a virtual "Lion King." Obama admitted his shock at the revelations.

Barry may have also felt that Barack sounded more "ethnic," thus allowing him to participate in affirmative action programs.

Ultimately, however, the Barack Obama of 2008 is based on the confused and frustrated Barry Obama of his childhood years, not the later period when he was a rebellious college student. As the poet William Wordsworth wrote, "The Child is father of the Man." Indeed.

XII.
OBAMA'S MISSING WHITE GRANDMOTHER

Obama's supporters attacked me for calling on Obama to "free" his white grandmother. Obama's last remaining white relative has not appeared in public in years. Still, Obama manages to shamelessly manipulate her as well.

Toot, as he called his grandmother, Madelyn Dunham, was the foundation of the family. She worked, advanced and became a bank officer in Honolulu. She was a solid midwestern woman.

Because of Madelyn's advancing years, it is not surprising that she might be frail. Most people in their 80's are not ready for a touch football game.

Still, Obama has sought to exorcise any living presence of his white grandmother.

In 2008, Obama went beneath contempt when he sought to justify the racism of his pastor by equating it with his "racist" white grandmother. Once again Obama was dealing in altered reality that he converted into malignant fantasy. In "Dreams," Obama relates an episode where Mrs. Dunham was harassed by a Black panhandler who demanded money rather persistently and caused her to be concerned for her own safety. So she asked her husband to drive her to work.

Obama's grandfather discussed the incident with his grandson, Barry. Obama was wounded because his grandmother had reacted to a Black man who tried to panhandle her by asking for money. Obama then used his grandmother's completely justifiable behavior decades ago to create the fantasy that his white grandmother was a racist who avoided Black men and who could be compared and equated to his racist preacher, Reverend Jeremiah Wright in 2008.

Perhaps stung by the public reaction to his abuse of his infirm grandmother, Obama then discovered that Granny Madelyn was well enough to tape a TV commercial. Although Obama had not made an issue of praising his absent white grandmother before, in June 2008 he reversed himself and opened his campaign acceptance of the nomination with profuse praises for the absent woman. In short, Obama views his grandmother through the same frame of reference as he views everyone and everything else in his life, as malleable instruments to be used and abused as he sees fit for his own selfish enrichment and advancement.

A man who would shamelessly manipulate and abuse his self-less grandmother, a woman who by his own admission repeatedly sacrificed for him, is no one that any loyal American would want controlling the White House.

The real world in Barack Obama's life serves solely to support the fantasy world, and the fantasy world exists only to advance and exalt Barack Obama's march to power and glory.

In the conclusion to this book, I refer to "Dreams" as Obama's Mein Kampf. I do not mean to suggest that Obama proposes any plan to exterminate a racial group or start a war. Rather, "Dreams" like Mein Kampf, serves as a blue print and window into the troubled psyche of the author, Barack Hussein Obama, Jr. Hitler warned the world what he planned in Mein Kampf.

Obama has signaled to us what kind of a leader he would be, if we simply read and reread "Dreams From My Father."

We have been warned.

Barack Obama:
Please Let Your White Relatives Out of the Closet

Where's Barry's white grandma?

Is Obama guilty of racism?

"Hey Sis!"

(CHICAGO)(January 3, 2007) During the recent campaign I wrote about Senator George Allen of Virginia ("Bubbe is Bupkis"), who had hidden his grandmother to conceal his Jewish roots.

When is Barack "Barry" Obama, the itinerant hustler-senator, going to bring his grandmother out of the closet?

Grannies are special. They offer unconditional love to grandchildren. They overlook family troubles and try to bring peace to domestic disturbances. They are a treasure.

The way Obama treats his white relatives is scandalous and racist.

Barack Obama nominally represents the People of Illinois. I say nominally because he does everything he can to avoid Illinois and, when he appears, he appears clueless. He claims "his staff" actually represents Illinois. Obama represents only himself.

Last month Obama was on the road to New Hampshire and other points far away from Illinois. When he had a chance to go home and at least spend Christmas with his fellow Illinoisans, he chose to go off to Hawaii to "visit family." Well.

Obama "visited family" last summer. He went to Kenya and posed as a Kenyan-American. He prominently featured distant cousins and half siblings, all of whom were African-African.

For Christmas he went to Hawaii, with a totally different approach. He ignored any public displays of connection to his white relative; his white grandmother was kept out of press view. Likewise his sister. He made no disclosure of any family contacts and media were forced to rely on second-hand information. There were no photo-ops with his white relative. (Check Google and Obama + sister or grandmother under Images)

Obama's sister spoke with the Associated Press, but it is not clear if that conversation was in person or on the phone. His sister, Maya Soetoro, said she was discussing presidential politics with her brother so there is a natural interest in who she is and what she is advising.

If the closeting of Obama's white relative is not blatant racism and contempt for the intelligence of the people of Illinois and America, I don't know what is. Hiding your relatives because they undermine your racial politics? That's what it looks like.

I have stated in the past Obama is a deeply conflicted human being. Under the veneer of what Washington Post writer Donna Britt last week called "cool," there is burning conflict and contradiction. Is he angry with his white relative? Ashamed of her? Why does he treat her differently than his Kenyan clan? Why are the blacks publicized and the whites ostracized? Why? Where's Granny?

Mr. Obama, you have a lot of explaining to do. And it ain't cool. I can't believe anyone would feature one side of his family and hide the other, but that's what you are doing.

Where's your white grandma? And your sister?

Or don't they want to be seen in public with you?

Answers please.

Chicago Tribune Plays Catch-up with Andy Martin and ContrarianCommentary.com; Will the Sun-Times Be Next?

Wall Street Journal also joins the piling-on

"It ain't so lonely anymore," says Andy Martin. "Cock-a-doodle-doo. I'm crowing. And someone is eating crow. Guess who?"

Contrarian Commentary for March 23, 2007

(CHICAGO)(March 23, 2007) Friday evening March 23rd the Chicago Tribune announced it will join Andy Martin and ContrarianCommentary.com in placing Senator Barack Obama's early life under a spotlight. In a banner headline the Tribune blares: **Coming this weekend: Barack Obama's not-so-simple youth.** [http://www.chicagotribune.com]

Why the sudden interest in Barack Obama's past, a topic ContrarianCommentary.com has been pursuing for 2-1/2 years?

"I think it is finally sinking in that Contrarian Commentary.com has been on to something for a long time, something the so-called 'mainstream media' ignored and tried to pretend did not exist," says Executive Editor, broadcaster and media critic Andy Martin.

"I have been vilified by DailyKos.com, and other media for writing about Obama's fabricated past. I have been credited, in a negative sort of way, with many stories I wrote and some I did not. But the consistent refrain always was: why are you telling the truth about Obama when we would rather believe a lie?

"The Democratic National Committee has even given some deranged Obama backer a blog to slime me.

"Well, who's laughing now? Who has been saying all along that there was more to Obama than he wanted us to know? More than the fictional life Obama had created for himself, more than the imaginary world that the Tribune and Sun-Times had accepted as true?

"Today's front-page story in the Wall Street Journal about a former Obama BFF who apparently tried to extort the senator finally blew the dam.

"I don't think all of the truth will come out this weekend in the Tribune, or the Sun-Times. It will be a gradual process.

"But our historic and pioneering effort to expose massive political fraud by a presidential candidate has borne fruit. Obama's past has been rouged up more than Anna Nicole Smith's corpse. People were offended when I told them 'Obama's truths' were not the real truths.

"Well, I say to the Chicago Tribune, and to the Sun-Times when they join the parade, 'Welcome to the truth.' Cock-a-doodle-doo.

"Now that the media are finally paying attention, we will be moving shortly in court to block Obama and Random House from marketing his book 'Dreams From my Father' as an 'autobiography' or 'biography.' It is fiction, plain and simple. The 'dreams' didn't come from his father; the dreams came from Obama.

"Not long ago someone mocked the claim that my commentary represented the work of the 'man who brought down Obama.' I hope those nut cases are still looking, but their eyes are probably too flooded with tears to read. I am still the 'man who brought down Obama.' It took a lot of hard, old-fashioned newspapering, research and legwork. But we kept at it. We published the first psychological profile of Obama the day he announced February 10th.

"Our columns are archived (see below) and someone can now go back and track and trace our efforts to simply tell the truth about Barry Obama," says Martin.

Obama Supports Gays,
but Keeps His Grandma "Closeted"

Chicago Tribune says "The Obama campaign declined to make Madelyn Dunham" available to the media

Well, why?

What goes here, as Obama keeps his white grandmother locked away in a dungeon?

Contrarian Commentary for March 26, 2007, Part II

(CHICAGO)(March 26, 2007) If anyone else running for president locked his granny away and refused to allow her to be seen, would the media complain? You betcha.

But America's media have supinely allowed Barry Obama to pretend he has no white relatives. He has paraded his step-grandmother in Kenya, who never saw him until the 80's, as his "granny," and locked the grandmother who actually raised him away in a closet.

Today the Chicago Tribune said "the Obama campaign declined to make [his white grandmother] available."

Is she sick? Not apparently. Bedridden? Hospitalized? Not apparently. She is the "Prisoner of Obama," and of Obama's racist myth that he is "Black" and not "Black and White."

What a disgrace.

And like whimpering puppies the media do not protest, complain or demand access.

FREE GRANNY MADELYN DUNHAM [OBAMA]!!!

Barack Obama is one of the most racist politicians in America today. And we let him get away with it. We are afraid to confront Obama's reality, so we pretend that reality is not there, even though it is staring us in the face. Anyone remember "Miss Lillian?" Or Barbara Bush? Or Bill Clinton's mom, drinking, gambling card-playing gal that she was?

No one else but Obama could get away with pretending that his paternal grandfather's second or third or fourth wife was his "granny" when she wasn't.

Maybe that's the core of the antipathy between grandson and grandmother. Maybe that's why Obama's white grandmother is locked in purda. She is offended that Obambi shamelessly highlights his black relatives in Kenya and equally shamelessly pretends his white relatives in Hawaii who actually raised him do not exist. It would hurt me.

No one could get away with pretending his white grandmother didn't exist except a media witch doctor such as Obama.

I have been attacking Obama for months because of his racist exclusion of his white relatives from the campaign trail. (http://www.contrariancommentary.com/community/Home/tabid/36/mid/366/newsid366/59/Default.aspx)

We finally smoked out a picture of Obama's sister in the Chicago Tribune. She had said she was his "adviser" but refused to be photographed. Did she plan to enter the White house with a paper sack over her head?

But the "segregation" of Madelyn Dunham, Obama's white grandmother, and only real grandmother, has to be one of the cruelest and most mendacious political kidnappings this nation has ever seen.

Mrs. Dunham lives alone in the same apartment where she has lived for many years. Thus, it is reasonable to assume she is not incapacitated or an invalid.

Granny Dunham told the New York Times she was not well enough to speak, but in reality the Obama campaign maintains Stalinist "control" over potential interviewees. Obama's minions tried to control access to Obama's friend who was recently released from prison. Since he became a candidate for U. S. Senator, Obama has locked his remaining white relative away in his racist closet.

Madelyn Dunham raised Barry Obama. It was probably her money that got him admitted to the prestigious Punahou School in Hawaii and paid his fees. Her efforts were formative, perhaps even more so than those of Obama's mother Ann, Madelyn's daughter. And yet Madelyn is being hidden away.

All because she is white and Barry Obama is a "black" candidate for president.

What a lie. What hypocrisy. What cowardice. And this man wants to sit in the oval office?

Ironically, locking Madelyn away is going to hurt Obama more with African-Americans than with whites. Whites delight in drinking Obama's Kool-Aid. Reason and reality will only gradually descend on them.

But Blacks are a lot smarter than whites when it comes to slights, because they have felt racial slights all their lives. Blacks know who Obama is, and they know how he is trying to "pass" and ignore his past.

During the decade when crack devastated the African-American community it was "Black Grannies" who were and are the backbone of the community. These grandmothers helped stabilize disintegrating families ravaged by drugs. Black grannies will not like the fact that their white counterpart is being treated badly by Obama. Black and White grandmothers? My guess is they will stick together on this one. They will be offended by the way Obama is treating the woman who really raised him and was the stabilizing factor in his life, Madelyn Dunham.

I repeat: FREE GRANNY MADELYN DUNHAM [OBAMA]!!!

Associated Press and CNN Continue to Distribute Disinformation about Senator Barack Obama's Relatives in Kenya

Why are American media incapable of printing accurate facts about the presidential candidate?

(CHICAGO)(January 9, 2008) There has been a great deal of disinformation about Senator Barack Obama on the Internet and in mainstream media. One of the reasons for this confusion is that United States news organizations that champion the accuracy of their facts continue to convey disinformation about Obama's family ties.

The latest disinformation was released today by Associated Press and CNN:

http://news.aol.com/elections/story/_a/obama-family-in-kenya-watches-us-vote/20080108163509990001?ncid=NWS00010000000001.

Both Associated Press and CNN claim that Sarah Hussein Obama is Barack Obama's "grandmother." CNN refers to her as "granny," which is only an honorific title, not a statement of relation. Sarah Obama was married to Obama's grandfather, but she is a subsequent wife and is not the mother of his father Barack Obama, Sr. Many cultures refer to "aunties" and "grannies' as honorific titles, assigned to other relatives and sometimes even

39

friends, neighbors, and stepparents, when they in fact have no basis in blood relation.

Yet AP and CNN continue to avoid disclosing that the "grandmother" to whom they are referring is not the senator's grandmother in fact.

Mrs. Obama's picture has appeared in media, erroneously listing her as the senator's grandmother. Despite all of the controversy over erroneous descriptions in 2007, Associated Press and CNN negligently continue to convey false facts to their audiences in 2008.

Is it any wonder the public will believe anything about Obama, when media are feeding their audiences outright distortions?

Concerning the religious beliefs of the Obama family, it is noteworthy that the uncle quoted in the AP's Obama story also has a Muslim name. Said Obama. I fully accept that Barack Obama is a practicing Christian today, but why has he gone to such lengths to obscure the religious origins of his family? He could have put all of this confusion to rest last year if only he had made a simple and straightforward disclosure of the undisputed facts.

Finally, although AP was not under any duty to do so, it could have disclosed that Senator Obama said nothing about the chaos in Kenya until he was prompted to do so by ContrarianCommentary.com. Not one word appeared anywhere reflecting Obama's "concerns" until we chastised him for his prevarication on the post-election breakdown in Kenya.

During the past several days ContrarianCommentary.com has received a bevy of e-mails from persons either claiming to be or seeming to be close to the Obama family or the campaign. It is obvious that ContrarianCommentary.com continues to drive the news agenda where questions about Senator

Barack Obama's past and family background are concerned, and that the Obama operation pays intense attention to our reporting and opinion commentary.

CHAPTER THREE

Barack Obama's Religious Roots

Nothing has so bedeviled Obama as his religion. Is he a Muslim? Is he a Christian? Both Obama and his detractors have sought to confuse the issues. Obama has created a web site, FighttheSmears.com to defend against widespread accusations and beliefs that he is a Muslim.

But the facts are relatively straightforward and do not favor either side. Here they are.

I.
THE UNDISPUTED FACTS ABOUT OBAMA'S RELIGION

Obama's grandfather was a devout Muslim. He raised his family under Islam. He gave his son, Barack Hussein Obama, Senior, an Arabic-derived name. His family gave Barack, Junior's father a Muslim funeral when he died. All of the evidence points in one and only one direction.

Barack Hussein Obama, Junior, took his Muslim father's name. We also know that most of Obama's father's siblings adhered to Islam.

When Obama was taken to Jakarta as a child, he initially attended a Roman Catholic school where someone (probably his mother or stepfather) registered his religion as Muslim.

Later, Barack Jr. moved to a state school in Jakarta, where he was again identified as a Muslim. He was given Islamic instruction.

One writer (**not** this author) attempted to sensationalize Obama's Jakarta education by using the currently inflammatory term "Madrassa" to describe Obama's state school. There was no evidence that Obama ever attended a school whose primary focus or orientation was religious, that is a madrassa.

Nevertheless, years later, Obama still remembers the Muslim call to prayer and can recite the words in Arabic. He learned that repetition in school.

II.
THE BOTTOM LINE: OBAMA WAS A MUSLIM, AND IS A CHRISTIAN

Christianity is an open religion. Almost every denomination and almost every church is free to set its own criteria for membership or attendance. We do not know what baptismal records, if any, exist for Barack Obama at Trinity United Church of Christ. But his mere "association" with the parish would and could have made him a member.

Obama's claim that he attended Trinity UCC for twenty years and yet had no idea about the incendiary sermons of this pastor, mentor and friend Reverend Jeremiah Wright is not believable.

Obama now says he is a Christian, and therefore he is a Christian, although the date of his conversion and level of his commitment to Christian principles remains somewhat uncertain.

"I Told You So," Part Four:
The Man Who Brought Down Barack Obama

Madrassa Madness explodes, but CNN won't put out the fires

[Editor's note: With "I told you so," Part One, Andy initiated a beginning-of-the-year series of comments on some of his columns, predictions and projections that have stood the test of time and continue to generate intense public interest.]

(CHICAGO)(January 23, 2007) Two and a half years ago, in August 2004, I held news conferences in London and New York to expose Barack Obama as a complete fraud. My news release is posted on the web, http://www.freerepublic.com/focus/f-news/1189687/posts, so there is no doubting the date or authenticity or content of our original research.

Since then, all opposition research on Obama has relied on our seminal work from the London Bureau, working through our special contacts in the Foreign and Commonwealth office for Kenya analysis and Chicago headquarters for political insight.

ArchPundit.com, a site that identifies itself as "the best blogger on the Illinois political scene," now states that "Andy Martin is the guy who seems to have gotten all this started." I should point out that ArchPundit.com is no friend of mine and gives credit only grudgingly and venomously.

When the history of the Obama fall-from-media-grace is written, our columns will have been the fuse that exploded the Obama myth and stripped the mask off Barack's face.

Chicago Sun-Times columnist Neil Steinberg [http://www.suntimes.com/news/steinberg/221436,CST-NWS-stein21.article] refers to some of Obama's opponents as "crazies" and "nuts" who live in an "intellectual wasteland."

I can't speak for other writers and other groups, but for myself I just write the news as I see it. At Contrarian Commentary.com we go where other media are too lazy or incompetent to tread, perhaps including Mr. Steinberg.

We broke the original Obama stories in 2004 because we conducted the international investigative reporting concerning Obama's invented family history that Chicago newspapers had failed to perform. We did the same from Baghdad beginning in 2003; those columns were the first to predict the chaos and collapse of Paul Bremer and the Coalition Provisional Authority; many can still be found on the web. It is an enviable track record of impartial accuracy and unerring analysis.

I don't bear Obama any animus as a person or as a politician, any more than I take media criticism of myself personally. Neither Mr. Steinberg nor ArchPundit are drinking buddies on Friday afternoons.

Nevertheless, while people are entitled to their own opinions, they are not entitled to their own facts. We deal in facts and even those who disagree with us can't dislodge our facts. So let it be with Obama.

So, as ArchPundit states: "Andy Martin is the guy who seems to have gotten this [Obama controversy} all started." Well.

CNN claims it has extinguished the "Madrassa Madness" about Obama with a report from Jakarta supposedly exploding the myths about his Indonesian education, but don't bet on it.

We will have more to say, of course. (Question for Barry: Do you still speak Bahasa?)

COMING: a CIA-style psychological profile of Barack (Barry) Obama.

And thank you ArchPundit for stating the truth. We have "gotten this all started" and we will keep adding fuel to the fire. Keep reading the controversial truth, only at ContrarianCommentary.com. "Just the facts, mam'm."

Obama "Swift Boats" the Truth
to Hide His Religious History

Barack gradually and grudgingly admits to little facts while still denying the larger reality

Andy Martin once again punctures "The Audacity of Obama"

(CHICAGO)(January 25, 2007) "Swift boating" is a term that came into use during the 2004 presidential election to reflect Senator John Kerry's flaccid response to attacks on his wartime record in Viet-Nam. The term, a noun, adjective and verb, has entered the political lexicon and is usually invoked when liberals and Democrats are stung trying to defend themselves against unpleasantly truthful accusations hurled by conservatives.

Well, "swift boating" is obviously a two-way street in politics. Democrats are equally adept at hurling painful accusations at Republicans and conservatives.

I have no problem with people bringing the truth to light, digging up unpleasant facts and seeking to raise legitimate issues. For the record, ContrarianCommentary.com has never "swift boated" anyone. Our mantra is: "Just the facts, mam'm."

Well, what are the facts? When you penetrate Obama's smokescreen you see that he is completely paranoid about investigation and accusations concerning his religious past.

Obama lined up a gaggle of trained geese yesterday, portraying them as "religious leaders." They promptly condemned any investigation into Barry's religion as "despicable," a violation of "values," "moral standards" and "malicious." The "religious leaders" said they were "set[ting] the record straight," but then admitted they accepted Obama's version of the record "at face value." No inquiry or investigation there. Trained parrots would have been more communicative than Obama's geese.

Two and a half years ago we reported that Obama *had been* a Muslim and that his family was Muslim. Today Obama admitted as much while still trying to deny the same truth. If Jack Ryan had been as slick as Obama at hiding in plain sight, Ryan and not Obama would be in the senate today.

Obama's parents registered him as a Muslim *at a Catholic school.*

It is absolutely true that Obama did not "choose" to be a Muslim when he registered as such at a Catholic school. Parents make those choices for their children. But those decisions nonetheless reflect family facts and practical reality. Parental choices also have developmental significance.

Obama later transferred from a Catholic school, where by his own admission yesterday he studied the "catechism," to an exclusive public school where the children of Indonesian leaders were enrolled and where he began to study Islam as a mandated part of his instruction. Free will? No. Fact? Absolutely.

All of these small truths were admitted yesterday by Obama and his communications meister Robert Gibbs. Contrary to what Obama claims are "scurrilous" accusations, he has confessed to the core of the Insight article and my own seminal research 2-1/2 years ago on which all subsequent articles about Obama have been based. Even Hillary Clinton began with my research. No surprise; because I was right.

Notably absent from yesterday's dog and pony show on Obama's religion was any mention of his quickly forgotten father and grandfather, both of whom were lifelong Muslims and both of whom named their sons Hussein, a very honorable Muslim tradition.

The bottom line: all of the factual material I disclosed in 2004 has been proven 100% correct, grudgingly and gradually admitted, or silently conceded by Obama and his staff.

But ultimately what interests me about Obama is not his religion or lack thereof. I could care less. Rather I am drawn by the fact that Barack continues to fictionalize large portions of his life, including his religious history, and steadfastly denies reality. No man with such a rich fantasy existence can be trusted in the Oval Office.

My political affiliation is not a secret. I am a Republican and generally conservative to libertarian on governmental issues while liberal on social issues. As the late Governor Adlai Stevenson would have put it, "I'll stay out of your bedroom if you stay out of mine." And my research manages to offend almost all shades of the political spectrum. I drive both "conservatives" and "liberals" batty. Read my past columns and decide for yourself.

In 2003 in Baghdad I performed similar psycho-surgery on Paul Bremer. He didn't like it either. Nor did George Bush. They attacked me. But I was right and they were wrong. As a result, I probably get more than my fair share of hate mail.

Nevertheless, while my opinions and conclusions are clearly my own, as an Internet editor and investigative journalist I adhere scrupulously and impartially to the facts I unearth. And, yes, small facts can be assembled to disclose larger truths. I have been doing that all of my life.

In the case of Obama, conservatives and even liberals fail to see the critical trees for the mesmerizing enchanted forest Obama he presents as his persona: way into adulthood Barack maintained a rich fantasy life about his past, and he continued to do so when he wrote his first book, fictionalizing characters and dialog. Lynn Sweet of the Chicago Sun-Times castigated him for these fabrications in a review dated August 8, 2004.

As a psychoanalytic case study, I believe Obama will prove to be a basket case. But because of the therapeutic culture in which we live, the media and public are willing to ignore Obama's dysfunctional reality in preference to his fictionalization about his history and himself. Inconvenient facts that intrude on Obama's fantasy life are summarily erased (Father and Grandfather Muslims? Nope. Name Hussein? So what. White relatives? "Book'em Danno." And so forth).

Investigative journalism is still about investigation; people such as Obama do not like to be either investigated or analyzed. That is why the "religious leaders" presenting themselves as Dancing Bears for Barack are apologists for his "ask no questions" approach to research and analysis concerning his background. (Their letter can be found at the New York Times blog "The Caucus.") What will Mr. Obama place off limits next?

Yes, there is "swift boating" going on here. But the swift boats have been launched by Obama to torpedo the truth about his past.

There is much, much more to Obama's fantasy life. As Barack struggles to place his lies about religion in a concrete crypt he opens himself to accusations concerning other fabrications and fantasies in his life. During Obama Week leading up to February 10th, we will release our CIA-style psychological profile on him; that analysis will cast more light on Barack's supple psyche and his ability to seamlessly deny objective reality.

In the words of the Psychoed by Hughes Mearns, "As I was going up the stair, I met a man who wasn't there. He wasn't there again today. I wish. I wish he'd stay away. Mr. Obama is both the man going up the stair and the man who isn't there. Obama wishes the real Obama would disappear so the fictional fantasy Obama can prevail. But that will not happen. Barry keeps seeing himself on the stair. And he doesn't like what he sees.

Or, if you prefer to move from psychology to boxing, as Joe Louis might have put it, "Obama can run, but he can't hide."

Stay tuned. Obama Week is only a few days away.

Obama Cover-up Reflects
Mainstream Media Mendacity

Washington Post betrays its Watergate heritage
Somewhere, Richard Nixon is smiling

(CHICAGO)(January 28, 2007) When Barack Hussein Obama was born he was given a Muslim name, identical to that of his father and grandfather. His mother married two (2) Muslims, Barry's father and a second Muslim who brought her and Barry to Indonesia. In Indonesia, Obama's parents identified him as a Muslim, and he studied Islam. All of these are facts on which no one disagrees and everyone agrees.

So why the media frenzy to cover-up Obama's Muslim heritage?

I broke the Obama/Muslim story 2-1/2 years ago. Obama had indeed casually mentioned his Muslim contacts, but he had carefully avoided any details. I was troubled and intrigued by the lack of specificity in his explanations. I launched an international investigation.

And, as I told a reporter for the New York Times who contacted me last week, we are still actively pursuing the "Obama's religion" story and will have more during "Obama Week," which we have planned for February 5th.

As someone who is known worldwide as a friend of Muslims, as well as Christians and Jews, and has been identified on conservative web sites as a Muslim supporter, I bore Mr. Obama no animus, and bear him none today.

Others picked up on my research. No doubt Hillary Clinton used my reporting as a starting point. My disclosures of Obama's fabricated past have been an outstanding piece of investigative journalism because all of the facts I reported 2 years ago have eventually either been confirmed or conceded.

So why the frenzied attacks on reports concerning factual information about Obama's religion?

The webzine Insight referred to Obama's Jakarta school as a "madrassa." What is known is that Obama's stepfather was a Muslim, and that he removed the child from a Catholic school and placed him in an institution where Islam was part of the curriculum. Insight's use of the word "madrassa" was probably overstated; I had never used that term in my writing (except in quotation marks) and I have been careful not to. Nevertheless, although I had no direct contact with Insight, the facts of their story were substantially true.

How can the Chicago Tribune then call the issue of Obama's Muslim background the "Anatomy of a False Story?" Jake Tapper of ABC referred to the Obama's story as a "fuss" over an "ordinary" school. Ordinary, perhaps, by Muslim/Indonesian school standards but not ordinary at all by ordinary main street education in the United States. Liberal lapdog Jonathan Alter at Newsweek called the "madrassa" story a "hoax." Monday, January 29th, the Times reporter who contacted me has a story calling Insight's Obama reporting "false." What's false?

The only "hoax" in all of this has been the way the "mainstream media" have been trying to tamp down any coverage of Obama's religion. They will not succeed.

The lowest blow was struck Sunday by the Washington Post of Watergate fame. Somewhere, Richard Nixon must be smiling.

The Post called reports on Obama's religion "juvenile," "scurrilous" and "contemptible." The Obama reporting was none of those. Maybe the real motivation for the Post's hysteria was that the paper was badly beaten on this story, as was the rest of the mucky muck media establishment.

I don't find it at all suspicious that someone in Hillary Clinton's camp could have leaked the Obama story. Thanks, Hillary. Indeed, it was probably the imprimatur of legitimacy conferred by Clinton's negative research that finally ignited the hothouse reporting.

The Post was incorrect in stating, "Mr. Obama has never tried to hide his past or his family name." That's a real hoax and a real media lie by the Post itself. Obama has done everything he can to craft a fictional reality for himself on national television. Never in recent American politics has there been such a spurious, self-invented "Music Man" candidate who literally conjured up most of his family history.

And Obama continues to dish lies at every opportunity (of which we will have more to say in later columns). Suffice it to say as early as 2004 I disclosed based on our original research in Kenya that Obama's presentation of his family history was somewhere between grossly disingenuous and a complete fiction. Obama came from Kenya's black colonial aristocracy and any livestock held by his family was a sign of wealth, not poverty. How's that for Barry flipping the truth, and the media sucking it up? Baaaaa.

Over and over again Obama has distorted and invented his family history. It is disgraceful. It prompted us to begin a CIA-style psychological profile of this deeply disturbed public figure that will be released during Obama Week.

In the meantime, the Washington Post, Chicago Tribune and lefties such as Mr. Alter love it and lap it up as Obama hides his past in plain sight. Once again the media are being lapdogs. The Post suggested Barry's "multicultural" background was a plus. On the contrary, Obama's complete and continuing confusion about his "culture" is what makes some people view him as a "Manchurian Candidate."

The Washington Post created the modern era of investigative journalism (although I was a skilled investigator long before Watergate). Now the Post says, imperiously, "If we say it's investigation its investigation, and if we say it's scurrilous its not investigation." But facts are facts.

And they wonder why people don't trust the mainstream media. The only contemptible aspect of this entire Obama controversy—-which is not going away—is the outrageous behavior of newspapers.

Way back in 1978 I broke a story on my then-Opponent Alex Seith, who was preening over his morality but was scheduled to be a character witness for a Chicago Crime Syndicate hoodlum. I still remember the surprise on the reporter's face. He said "How did you discover that; it's our job." I had used plain, old investigative journalism. (Full disclosure: I also hold a law degree from the University of Illinois and one thing good lawyers are taught to do is investigate, investigate, investigate. My primary training in investigation has come out of law and government, not working for a newspaper.)

For shame, Washington Post. You tarnish your own legacy of Watergate fame when you seek to "take down" people who are forcing Barry or Barack Obama to slowly and grudgingly tell the truth about his past.

Bottom line: Barry Obama is still living in a dream world and still lying about his family history and his religious history. And no one, not anyone, is likely to stop the people of this country from being given access to basic facts before they are called to vote on the suitability of this master con artist for national office.

If you wonder why the print media and particularly newspapers cry they have no future, look at the way they have tried to cover-up Obama's life and the way they have sought to excoriate anyone telling the truth. Who wants to pay to read a pack of lies?

President Nixon, at least they don't have you to kick around any more.

Obama's "Religion" in the News – Again

Barry's "secret sister" surfaces to deny Muslim "roots" as Los Angeles Times breaks "Barry O" news from Indonesia

(CHICAGO)(March 15, 2007) You just have to wonder why people want to hide the obvious. Barack Obama's "religion" was in the news again today, with a new round of Obama denials, prevarications and a new "modified, limited hang-out."

Obama no longer denies he was a Muslim. Now he says he wasn't a *"practicing"* Muslim. Well, I guess Obama learned something at Harvard Law School. How to lie with a straight face. Hey, "practice" makes perfect.

People in general, the general public, will accept most anything from public officials as long as they don't lie about it. I knew former U. S. Rep. Mark Foley was gay fifteen years ago. Who cared? South Florida is a liberal place and if Foley had only come out at some New Years' party his private life would have been a forgotten issue, not a guided missile that helped give Democrats a majority in Congress.

I am sometimes asked, "Have any skeletons in your closet?" My answer, "I have so many skeletons in my closet I can't close the door. Which ones do you want to hear about?"

I have been lambasted by crooked judges, attacked by the Bush Brothers (Jeb and George) and generally beaten up by the power structure that I have spent a lifetime exposing as corrupt.

The Chicago Tribune unleashed a three-man "smear squad" on me last year, and published a pack of lies. The only thing missing was a female reporter to lure me into a "compromising" position. The Tribune ambushed me on the streets, reported untruths and half-truths and shaded the truth; and generally sought to smear me because one of their employees (Rick Pearson) has an obsession with me. Yup, one of those. But it didn't hurt me and no one really cares. Sticks and stones.

Now Obama's people are peddling thirty-five year old smears about me, and they won't get any more traction than the Tribune. The public knows I'm honest, and the public knows I fight the bad guys. I have the scars to prove it. As a journalist, I try to be scrupulously impartial and honest. Just read my columns.

Which is all by way of introduction to "Barry" Soetoro's past, I mean Barack "Barry" Obama's secret life in Indonesia.

Obama has a half-sister. Anyone seen a picture of her? She says she's an advisor, but she's kept securely locked in a closet, and only allowed to be heard when she is needed to deny Obama is a Muslim.

Today the Los Angeles Times published original research from Jakarta that confirmed my original research two and a half years ago. Yes, in 2004 I reported that Barack Obama had been a Muslim. I'm glad the L.A. Times finally caught up with my August, 2004 writing. I'm also glad all of the mainstream media around the world have, piece-by-piece, confirmed my original, and very controversial, reporting in 2004. Why did I have the story then, and they didn't?

Now I don't really care one way or the other whether and why Obama was a Muslim in Indonesia. It's an interesting footnote. But every time the truth oozes out, as it did again today, Obama's staff goes crazy and flies into full Clinton-style "war room" damage control.

The Times reports that Obama was registered as a Muslim student all the time he was in school in Jakarta. Obama's sister, Miss Soetoro, denies her family was Muslim and says her relatives only went to the Mosque for "big communal events." Well, Ms. Soetoro, have I got news for you.

There are millions of Jews who only go to synagogue for "big communal events," such as Passover and Rosh Hashanah. And they're still Jews. And tens of millions of "Christians" flock to churches for Easter and Christmas. And they would slap you down if you told them they were not Christians merely because they only appear twice a year for "big communal events." And I am sure Muslims have their "twice a year" Muslims too.

So Obama's family was just as Muslim as many Jews are Jews and many Christians are Christians. What's the big deal?

Yesterday Obama's press secretary trashed Obama's childhood friends, stating according to the Times that they were telling stories "40 years old, and subject to four decades of other information." Well, guess what. I still remember where I went to church fifty years ago, and longer. I remember going to church in Manchester, New Hampshire when I was five (!) years old.

Obama's says he's now a Christian, and I believe him. We Christians accept everyone who professes and steps up to be baptized. But what kind of a Christian is he? Obama asked his minister to give the invocation on February 10th, and then dumped him because the minister is too "controversial." Barry, I have news for you too: Christ was *very* controversial. A real troublemaker. Still is. And he wasn't a coward. You chickened out.

Maybe you should read about St. Peter this month as we approach Easter Sunday. Will you deny your minister three times? I will be watching. So, what kind of a Christian are you? Really?

There is a little amusing sidelight to all of this Muslim-denial on Obama's part. Until last year, Obama always reached out to the Muslim community. He sashayed around religious differences and was well thought of. As I noted in an earlier column, some of my Muslim, pro-Palestine friends were unhappy when I exposed Obama. They thought that Barry O was one of them.

That is until last week, when Obama drank the AIPAC Kool-Aid and said Israel could do no wrong. End of Muslim love affair with Obama. Obama had sold out to the highest bidder, and it wasn't Muslims. Palestinians, to the back of the bus! Israel comes first, last and only. Especially when Hillary is watching.

So why won't Barry just fess up (he was known as Barry Soetoro in Indonesia) and admit he was a Muslim and let the truth wash away his veneer of lies? No one will hate him for it. No one really cares except his campaign operation. And him.

But the longer he keeps denying the truth about his past the more people will remain interested. If you don't believe me just go to today's L. A. Times story and see for yourself: http://www.latimes.com/news/nationworld/la-na-obama15mar15,1,26632.story.

And while you're at it, just remember I had that news 2-1/2 years ago. Obama lied then; he denied then. He's lying now, and denying now. What's wrong with the guy?

Now about the skeletons in my closet.

The Obama Scandals, Part Two:
Obama Continues to Lie about His Religion

What else is he lying about?

Why does Barry do it?

(CHICAGO)(December 11, 2007) Three and a half years ago I stunned the world by disclosing Senator Barack Obama's family ties to the Muslim religion. Well, "stunned" is not exactly the right word. No one cared. Illinois political writers were asleep at the switch, or perhaps saying "Shhh, we want him to win to make Illinois relevant again." Whatever.

The truth about Obama's Muslim history was there to be discovered, but through masterly inactivity the media ignored what was staring them in the face.

I didn't write about Obama because I hated him or hated Muslims or hated anyone. I saw a good story that the mainstream media was ignoring. Someone who lied about their past religion.

For myself, I am a Christian, and an Episcopalian. In my church, all are welcome. We welcome "newcomers" four times a year. Holy Baptism is all it takes and, presto! you're a Christian. We are inclusive religion. We have no interest in who your mother is or was, or who your father is or was, or anything except your own belief structure.

I was baptized into the Greek Orthodox Church of my mother, which made me "Greek" as a kid, but eventually gravitated to the Anglican (Episcopalian) church of my father. It wasn't much of a shift. I feel at home in both. I can still pray in Greek. During the 1980's I studied with a thought to holy orders (ordination) in the Episcopal Church, but decided there was more good to be done fighting secular demons than praying. Plenty of people were ready to pray; not so many knew how to fight the bad guys the way I had been trained in Champaign-Urbana and Chicago.

And so I began to research Obama's past, and his past religious practices as well as his family's religion. Based on exhaustive research around the world, ContrarianCommentary.com documented Obama's religious practices from childhood to adulthood, from the Muslim faith to the Christian faith. Lacking any agenda or obsession with the topic, I moved on to other subjects as columnists/editors usually do.

But I found myself in the focal point of media scrutiny when Obama began to run for president and when some people circulated e-mails attacking Obama's religion based on my research and editorial writing. *The Nation* magazine published an attack article claiming I was at the center of a "Right-Wing Smear Machine," when I was not smearing anyone. I was just telling the truth and laying out the facts.

In 2007, as the Obama charade escalated into a political cult, ContrarianCommentary.com continued to publish new research and new insights into Obama's character (q.v.). And I continued to be blamed when people published articles about Obama's religion. One anonymous article in Washington triggered calls asking "Did you write it," to which I simply replied they all based their claims on my writings and research, and then embellished to suit themselves. But no, I didn't."

As 2007 progressed my own campaign for the U. S. Senate has claimed more of my time, and gradually I left Barry (as Obama called himself until he left Hawaii) to the "mainstream." From time to time I notched another article about Obama's prevarications but mainly I focused on my own race and my efforts to reform the corrupt politics of the Illinois Republican Party.

But Obama keeps calling me back. Although I don't practice law, I was trained as a lawyer, and I was trained in cross-examination by a federal judge, the late Judge Prentice Marshall who was my law school professor. I know how to examine a witness. Central to cross-examination, or the "search for truth," is a sense of when and what a witness is hiding. It was the fact that Obama was hiding his religious past that drew me to research the issue in 2004, and I am back at the same stand for another installment as a result of Obama's latest lies.

Barry can't keep from lying, on and on.

In Monday's New York Times (December 10), Obama told new York Times columnist Roger Cohen that "[I] had relatives who practiced Islam." (http://www.nytimes.com/2007/12/10/opinion/10cohen.html?_r=1&oref=slogin)

Note Obama's passive voice. Notice the disconnect between relatives he "had" and cousins he "has." There is no active connection there. But family is one and the same, as Barry may not understand due to his convoluted background. You can't claim some of your relatives all of the time, or all of your relatives some of the time. Family doesn't work that way. Love 'em or hate 'em, we are stuck with family.

What makes Obama fascinating, and perhaps confusing to the inexperienced and unprepared cross-examiner such as Mr. Cohen, is that Obama lies within the same conversation and almost within the same sentence. "Slick Willie" meet "Obama the Obfuscator."

Fact: Obama's father was a Muslim. Fact: Obama's grandfather was a Muslim. Fact: Obama's stepfather was a Muslim. Fact: Obama went to mosque with his stepfather and worshipped there as a child. Fact: Obama was registered at a state school in Indonesia, *as a Muslim student* (not a Christian). Fact: some of Obama's relatives in Kenya are still Muslims. Fact: Obama's father was buried in a Muslim ceremony, suggesting he was a Muslim to his death.

So why can't Obama just come out and come clean and tell the truth, he was born a Muslim due to his parents' choice, and later during either his childhood spent with grandparents in Hawaii or in his adult years, he converted to Christianity. But for Obama it's all politics and all prevarication. Obama is terrified to use the "M" word, which is why he "had" relative who were Muslims.

Barry, your dad is not someone you "had." He is still your dad, even though he died. Barry, Lolo Sotero is still your stepfather, and the father of your sister, even though Sotero was Muslim. Sotero took you to the mosque with him. Your mom registered you as a Muslim student in the state school in Indonesia. (CNN made a great deal of its vacuous "investigation" in Jakarta that tried to debunk nonexistent accusations, in the process missing the obvious facts about Obama's religion as a child.)

And may I be permitted to remind the good reader of the belief of some in the Roman Catholic Church, where they claim "give us a child until age 7, and we have him for life?"

Like most kids, I am sure Obama did not understand much about religion. I am sure I didn't at the age of 8 or 9, although I wanted to be a priest even then. But what makes Obama's brazenness and mendacity so irritating is that he treats his personal family facts as chess pieces, able to be moved and repositioned for maximum political effect. First he says he "had" relatives, and then simultaneously he wants to use his "cousins," who are probably still Muslim, all in the same act. Hello?

Obama tells Roger Cohen that Obama can be a potential world statesman because of his family history, and then denies his family history and suggests that some part of it is in the past tense. It just can't be.

Ultimately, Obama is consummate huckster, playing Three Card Monte with the truth and playing Three Card Monte with his family history. Sad but true. Obama claims to be brave enough to tackle world terrorism, but he is not brave enough to admit he worshipped at a mosque as a child, or that he father and stepfather were Muslims. How brave is he really? Really?

Obama fooled Roger Cohen. Who else is he trying to fool? Why only the American people he claims to want to lead. Oprah? Naw.

Is Barack Obama brave enough to be our commander-in-chief? Not so long as he denies the religion of his father and family.

Postscript: No one denies that Obama is a Christian today. But it is obvious from the undisputed facts he was not always a Christian. And, for all of us, all of whom were children once, our religion and religious practices are usually chosen for us by our parents. That our parents choose for us does not make our religion any less real, or dilute its impact on our psyches. So, the issue is not what Barack Obama is, the issue is what he was and members of his family who he cites as "cousins" still are.

Andy Martin's "Right Wing Smear Machine" Strikes Again – Or Does It?

Miami Herald portrays Martin as "chief rumor-monger" against Barack Obama

Mainstream media disinformation services go into overdrive to protect Obama from the facts and the truth; Washington Post, Miami Herald latest to join Obama's fantasy parade

Who is really telling the truth, and who is really publishing "rumors", Martin asks

Question: When was Obama baptized as a Christian?

(CHICAGO)(December 17, 2007) A reporter from the Miami Herald interviewed me last week. We had a long, substantive discussion, in which I pointed out that I had only published facts and original research about Barack Obama since 2004. All of my factual claims had been found to be true, and all of my opinions based on my facts were accurate.

Sunday the Herald portrayed me as a "chief rumor-monger" concerning Obama. Previously I had been called the kingpin of a "Right-Wing Smear Machine" by The Nation magazine.

What's going on here? Me? Rumor-monger? "Smear machine?"

I submit that it is the mainstream media, and not ContrarianCommentary.com, that are the real peddlers of rumors, fantasies, half-truths and disinformation from Obama Central.

First, a little background. Way back in August 2004 I published original research on Obama's religious past. At the time, the Illinois media were soused on Obama's Kool-Aid, and pretended the facts were not as I presented them. Fast forward to 2006. Obama is running for president, and I am still doing original research. Some people started paying attention.

The Nation magazine suggested I circulated anonymous e-mails about Obama; but my name is my brand, and my name is on anything I have ever issued about Barry O. I do not do anonymous. Not many publishers and columnists do. So why the attempt to snarkily suggest I do "anonymous" postings about Obama?

The mainstream media can't face the truth, and they are engaged in a massive disinformation campaign to sell Obama to the American people.

Fact: In 2004, I debunked Obama's myth that his father was a "goat-herder." But there was Obama's lie, published in Friday's Washington Post (http://www.washingtonpost.com/wp-dyn/content/article/2007/12/13/AR2007121301784.html: "Barack Hussein Obama Sr. grew up herding goats...")

This claim is a crass distortion and misrepresentation of the Obama family's history. Obama's father was a rich boy, who came from an educated and affluent family.

In Kenya, where a great deal of wealth (not unlike Illinois where I live) is measured in land and livestock, Obama's grandfather had some goats, and his son helped care for them. Guess what? We have prosperous farmers in Illinois, and no one calls them "goat-herders" even though their children come to the State Fair to display their prize animals. Barack Jr. has slandered his father by calling him a "goat-herder," and the media lets him get away with this lie. Do they fact-check at the Post?

The Post was right about one, thing, however: Obama has never wanted to know the truth about his father, because he has been so successful in selling the media a lie. One of Barack Senior's friends tied to engage Obama about his father but "[Barack, Junior] did not want to pursue it.""Not even a little bit." Strange. Or is it? If you are selling the public a myth, why muddy the waters with the truth?

The Miami Herald claims the "real story" is told on Obama's own web site. Puhleeeze. The Herald claims Obama's parents "did not practice any religion." Oh yah?

Then who registered Obama as a "Muslim" at primary school in Jakarta? Why did Obama's father receive a Muslim burial and, no doubt, a Muslim wedding in Kenya?

Instead of digging beneath the surface of Obama's fantasies, the Herald resorted to trying to undermine my credibility by citing a 34 year-old court opinion, where I was attacked by the Illinois Supreme Court for successfully being part of a team that forced two crooked judges off the court. I have always been committed to the truth. Obama has not. If Obama would just go back 34 years in his own life, and start telling the truth, instead of telling 34 year old lies about me, we could get somewhere.(Full disclosure: I am very unpopular with lawyers and judges, for successfully exposing decades of corruption both in Illinois and nationally. And I am very proud of that fact.)

And just exactly what "rumors" have I published? None whatsoever. My writings are all there to be seen, and all of my commentary has stood the test of time. [See ContrarianCommentary.com, as well as other sources on the Internet.]

I have always accepted the fact that Obama is a Christian. But the Herald muddied the waters as to *when* Obama became a Christian. Has Obama ever presented a baptismal certificate?

Of course not. That would date his acceptance of Christianity. He just focuses on the "is." "It all depends on what your definition of what "is," is. Bill Clinton meet Barack Obama.

Should religion be an issue? Obama thinks so. That is why he constantly uses African-American churches as a backdrop for his photo-ops. When you play the religion card, isn't fair game to ask when you were baptized? Or don't you want the public to know? Notice I am not questioning Obama's current Christianity, or seeking to slander his church. My doorman is a member of the same congregation. Rather, I am asking a simple question: when did you become a Christian? Do you have a record date for your acceptance? Conversion? A certificate? Something. So far as I am aware, there is nothing.

Bottom line: my commentary stings Obama precisely because I print the facts and lay out the truth, and no one can impeach me on the facts or the truth. So Obama's "disinformation doctors" have to resort to calling me names, such as "rumor-monger" and "smear machine," and fall back on 34 year-old court opinions in a desperate effort to debunk me. It hasn't worked, has it?

I correctly predicted earlier this year that the issue of Obama's religion would not go away, and that questions would not disappear, until the truth came out. All of it. I'm still waiting. The mainstream media thought they had buried Obama's religion in January. Now who was right and who was wrong?

Who are you going to believe?

I think it is time for full disclosure from Barack Obama. It is time for his "Mitt Romney Moment." Or are Democrats who traffic in religious allusions when they want to profit politically, and otherwise want to stonewall, held to a different standard of disclosure?

You be the judge.

Obama's Muslim Religion Causes New Explosions on the Campaign Trail, Part One

Did Obama's step-grandmother switch religions since 2007?

Andy Martin continues to explore Barack Obama's Muslim "roots."

Did the Associated Press report Obama's grandmother has converted to Christianity? Andy follows up on this unusual story: did Barack Obama's "grandmother" abandon Islam for Christianity? The reports are not clear; contradictory facts mandate an explanation from the candidate.

(CHICAGO)(March 6, 2008) I have been writing about Barack Obama's religious roots since 2004. It was my news conferences in Chicago and London that first presented the original research concerning Obama's father's religion (Barack Obama, Sr.) as well as his grandfather's religion and overall family heritage within Islam. Obama's hesitancy to openly and honestly discuss his religious roots intrigued me, and I have pursued the topic for four years.

But lately, it almost seems as though Obama's religion and his strenuous efforts to conceal his religious heritage are pursuing me. The topic has become so bizarre and so convoluted and so fascinating that I am now returning to Obama's religion with a two-part analysis and commentary.

Part One concerns Obama's step-grandmother, who may be experiencing sloppy reporting by the Associate Press, or failing memory, or bad translation. In any event, the facts are out there to see. Obama and his family owe voters a frank and uncomplicated explanation.

When last heard from, "Granny" Sara Obama was demanding cash ("outstretched palms") for interviews, from Nick Kristof of the New York Times. (http://www.nytimes.com/2008/02/24/opinion/24kristof.html?scp=3&sq=Kristof&st=nyt)

In an extended story on Obama's religions beliefs, the New York Times in 2007 reported a statement by Obama's step-grandmother, "Granny" Sarah, in which she stated:

"I am a strong believer of the Islamic faith," Ms. Obama, 85, said in a recent interview in Kenya. See: http://www.nytimes.com/2007/04/30/us/politics/30obama.html.

March 5, 2008, the Associated Press posted a story by Katharine Houreld, datelined, Kogelo, Kenya, in which Sara Obama is quoted as saying:

Obama's grandfather had converted to Islam from Roman Catholicism and taken the name Hussein, Sarah Obama said, but his children had inherited only the name, not the religion. Each person should be able to choose how they worshipped, she said...In the world of today, children have different religions from their parents," she said. She, too, is a Christian. See: http://www.washingtonpost.com/wp-dyn/content/article/2008/03/05/AR2008030501503.html.

With all due respect, the news that Barack Obama's step-grandmother has possibly converted to Christianity is blockbuster news. Barack calls her "granny" and Obama's half-sister states:

Sarah Obama was the second wife of the candidate's late grandfather, so she is not his biological grandmother. But Auma Obama said: "By our definition, in our culture, she is his grandmother," she said.

What is the truth? Obama owes us an answer. He has shamelessly exploited his Kenyan relatives for political advantage, claiming a "family visit" in 2006 is part of his "foreign policy" experience. I have previously asked why millionaire-Barack does not send his "granny" the money to connect indoor plumbing and electricity, and the response was that Sarah wants to live under primitive conditions.

So what has happened? Is Sarah losing it? Is AP guilty of sloppy or erroneous reporting, for not even bothering to fact-check the Sarah Obama story? Did AP use an incompetent translator? Or is it true that Sarah has abandoned Islam for Christianity?

Senator Obama, and/or Associated press, you have some explaining to do. The Chicago Sun-Times' editors recently posted their phone number in an editorial asking for a call to discuss Tony Rezko. Barry O has my number; I'd like a call on what gives with AP and Granny Sarah.

If the Associated Press and the Obama campaign are going to use Granny Sarah to launch attacks on people who question Obama's background and religious heritage, we have a right to know if she is mentally competent at this time or if the AP is guilty of sloppy reporting (which has been picked up by virtually every major American newspaper web site).

CHAPTER FOUR

Obama's Brief and Insignificant Legal Career

O bama frequently makes muscular statements that he was a "civil rights lawyer," but the reality is that he had a pitifully meaningless and insufficient legal career. This chapter will thus be mercifully brief.

Obama's sole distinction as a lawyer is that he was hired at Tony Rezko's law firm. He was apparently kept on the payroll as "Tony's guy," despite his modest legal accomplishments. To be sure, this is "The Chicago Way" of doing business.

Consider the following:

Obama never filed a lawsuit that he signed as counsel of record for the firm.

He argued one very basic federal appeal; his entire appellate career appears to consist of a single appellate argument (if I am in error on this point, my error is also insignificant, because I do not err by much). I do not believe he ever argued an appeal in the state appellate court.

Obama argued a paltry number of motions, all of them routine and pedestrian. There is no evidence he ever sat as a "second chair" in a major trial or became a member of the "trial bar" of the federal court.

In short, Obama's "legal career" is a far cry from the "civil rights litigator" that he describes himself to be. His view of his legal accomplishments is, frankly, delusional.

This from a Harvard Law School graduate?

Well, yes.

It is not at all unusual that law graduates possess "book knowledge" but lack the practical skills to be an effective lawyer. As a friend of mine used to say, every law firm has "finders, minders and grinders." "Finders" bring in the client. "Minders" watch over the client's legal affairs at the firm. "Grinders" grind out the quotidian legal product that is the output of every law firm.

Obama interviewed at Rezko's law firm. He was hired, and they kept him on until he was later elected to local office. Based on the available circumstantial evidence, his hiring at Rezko's law firm could have been the result of a Rezko/Obama understanding, what is sometimes called business done "The Chicago Way."

What of Obama's career as a "law professor?" Obama was a "Lecturer," a professional designation that describes a contract employee with no tenure rights to stay on the job. He was never an actual "Professor."

Obama taught "constitutional law," which is a basic first year course to acquaint new law students with major decisions of the U. S. Supreme Court. "Constitutional law" could as easily be taught by a historian as a lawyer, because "con law" does not delve deeply into the mechanics of being a lawyer. By all accounts Obama was a popular lecturer. More importantly, his status as a Lecturer allowed him entrée into the society that flourishes around the University of Chicago. It is entirely possible that Obama took the teaching job precisely because it would confer status at the University of Chicago and in the Hyde Park neighborhood community.

Because of the progressive history of the State of Illinois, African-Americans became prominent members of the legal community decades ago. Obama is not remotely comparable to any of the lions of the African-American bar.

Obama also appears to have a speaking problem. He delivers a previously written, teleprompter speech beautifully. But I find him irritating to listen to in an unscripted environment. He hems and haws and hedges; his speech is not fluid when he has no teleprompter in front of him. A lawyer such as Obama who can't speak effortlessly in an unscripted and spontaneous environment is not likely to become an outstanding attorney. Obama never did.

Rather, Obama appears to have been used as an "office" lawyer to do routine tasks usually handled by a junior and inexperienced lawyer. He began in that status, as a new law graduate; but he does not appear to have ever moved beyond that status, even in his very small and intimate law firm. He was always "Tony's guy."

Obama's denied in 2007 that he had any knowledge of the business connections between his senior law partner and Rezko. True or false? It's hard to say. How could he work in a tiny law firm with a handful of lawyers and not know what was going on? How could he vote, as a foundation board member, for actions that benefited his former law partner, and be unaware of the partner's overall scheme of activity? Hard to believe.

If there is one facet that characterizes lawyers and law offices, it is gossip. Lawyers are talkers. They get paid to talk. They love to gossip, chat, kibitz. Obama would have us believe he never gossiped, never learned anything and was totally clueless about what was going on in his tiny law firm. He is hardly credible. More delusion.

During the controversy over Tony Rezko's deteriorating (slum) apartment buildings in 2007, Obama's frequent defense was that he had never done any substantial work on Rezko's cases. However, there is no evidence that Obama ever did much billable work on any legal cases; at least he has never claimed that he handled any sophisticated client work. Rather, like so much of Obama's gossamer life history, he employs fantasies and exaggerations such as "civil rights litigator" to conceal the insignificance of his legal career.

But there is one highly unusual and notable aspect of Obama's legal career that raised my eyebrows: his manner of expeditiously exiting the profession. He was in a hurry to surrender his law license and to terminate his status as an attorney and member of the bar.

When I researched Obama's current legal status, I was stunned to learn that both he and his wife had cancelled their law licenses. They do not contemplate practicing law in the future. Lawyers are usually very jealous and highly protective of their law licenses. President Bill Clinton was subjected to discipline by the Arkansas judicial system because his law license was still active. Clinton was suspended because of his false testimony. But, notably, Clinton's law license was still active while he was serving in the White House.

Obama's law license and Michelle's law license no longer exist. They have surrendered their status as members of the Illinois bar.

What does the license surrender suggest? That Obama knew and knows he was never much of a lawyer, and even after a career in public life he has no future role practicing law.

More importantly, I believe that, learning from President Clinton's experience, Obama surrendered his law license before he could be subjected to professional discipline.

Discipline for what? We don't know, yet.

But I have an idea.

Sadly, in summary, Obama's law license and legal career appears to have fallen on the same trajectory as Tony Rezko's business empire. Without a boost from Rezko, Obama was apparently never able to build a substantial legal career. And as Rezko's fortunes declined, so did Obama's legal income. With one notable exception.

Perhaps Obama feared professional discipline for money laundering. I will deal separately with Obama's use of his law firm to launder money in 2001. At a minimum, Obama's use of his former law firm to launder and conceal a suspicious payment—apparently an outright bribe—may have been what Obama feared could trigger a review by the Attorney Registration and Disciplinary Commission of the Illinois Supreme Court. Indeed, Obama's money laundering and potential bribery schemes merit a separate chapter, The Illinois Legislature and The Blackwell Affair.

Barack Obama Charged with Possible Bar Admission Fraud

Obama quietly surrenders right to practice law in Chicago

(CHICAGO)(March 13, 2007) Internet Editor Andy Martin disclosed today that he has submitted a formal complaint to the Illinois Board of Admissions to the Bar, and Attorney Registration Commission, asking for an investigation concerning whether Senator Barack Obama obtained bar admission based on false representations.

Last week, Obama paid 17 year old parking tickets. Illinois agencies require that any outstanding parking tickets be paid prior to bar admission. It does not appear based on the available circumstantial evidence that Obama answered his bar admission questionnaire truthfully.

"Once again we see 'Mr. Ethics' shading his own ethics," Martin stated. "I think that if the circumstantial evidence is corroborated, Mr. Obama faces a sanction for his fraudulent admission to the Illinois Bar. We are also investigating whether Obama holds any other bar admissions.

"Interestingly, in the course of the investigation, we learned that Mr. Obama, who styles himself a 'constitutional lawyer,' had quietly surrendered his right to practice law in Illinois. Obama did not announce that fact and it came as a surprise to us as, indeed it will come as a surprise to many others."

The Obama Scandals, Part One:
National Media Bury Conflict of Interest by Obama, Law Partner

Mike Royko, meet Barack Obama

(CHICAGO)(December 3, 2007) During the 1970's I had several good friends in the Chicago Sun-Times (and Daily News) newsroom. I'd often stop by to chat when I walked home. Off in one corner of the newsroom was the legendary Chicago columnist Mike Royko. Royko had his own cube, as well as an assistant. He was newsroom royalty and he probably kept the Daily News from folding sooner than it did.

Royko was not an easy man to know, and we never became close, but he had Chicago street smarts that came from the City News Bureau as well as the Bureau of Hard Knocks (and Bureau of Hard Drinking). I can say without fear of contradiction that Royko would have loved writing about our own homegrown presidential phony, Barack Obama.

Royko would have fulminated at the way an outstanding Sun-Times expose last week was buried by the national press. (http://www.suntimes.com/news/watchdogs/672314,CST-NWS-watchdog29.article)

Sun-Times reporter Tim Novak unearthed not only a new Obama scandal on November 29th, he unearthed the arrogance and "L'etat c'est moi" demeanor that characterize Obama's real attitude towards ethics in government: "If I do it, there's no conflict of interest."

One of Royko's favorite expressions was "if you lie down with dogs, you catch fleas." When I began writing about Obama three years ago I had Royko's maxim in my mind. Obama had been too close to too many sleazy Chicago politicians for him to be clean. Indeed. Mike Royko, meet Barack Obama.

Obama worked for a law firm in Chicago. One of the name partners (Allison Davis) in the firm of Davis, Miner & Barnhill left the firm to enter "real estate development." Davis' partner? Indicted wheeler-dealer Tony Rezko, who later financed part of Obama's million dollar residence.

Davis came in front of Obama when Obama sat on the board of the Woods Fund. Obama voted to give his former law partner $1 million, for which there has been no accounting. Part of the money may have been funneled into a deal where Davis cleared $700,000 in "development fees."

When Novak asked Obama's campaign about the Woods Fund grant, there was no response. Except.

Except the defense that Obama now claims that "It's not a conflict of interest to do what's right for your community." Royko would have gone into orbit over that remark.

Barry Obama, meet the late Mayor Richard M. Daley, who always felt corruption in the service of "community" was a good deed. And if you didn't agree with him you could "kiss [the late Mayor's] mistletoe." Christmas was always, and always is, in season where "honest graft" is concerned in Chicago.

And so, Royko would have written, Obama hung around with bad characters in Chicago politics, and he became tainted beneath the surface, even if they allowed him to prance and preen as pristine on the surface.

On the matter of public integrity, there is no "good for your community" exception. A conflict of interest is a conflict of interest. The very reason we have conflict-of-interest laws is because individuals tend to have clouded vision when acting on business issues where they are related to the principals or participants.

Despite being a self-styled "constitutional scholar," Obama still hasn't learned that a conflict of interest—especially a $1 million conflict of interest—is a conflict of interest and should have been disclosed.

When the Daily News folded, Royko eventually moved to the Chicago Tribune. He died early. But his spirit lives. And, in so far as Obama is concerned, if I were able to wander into Royko's cube-in-the-sky, I know exactly what he would growl. "If you lie down with dogs, for sure you're going to catch fleas. Obama's caught more than a few."

Amazingly, the national media have completely ignored the Sun-Times' story on Obama's sleazy conflict of interest involving his former law partner. I guess where Obama is concerned, he is allowed to be the sole judge of his conflicts of interest. Or, as Bill Clinton once said, "it all depends on what your definition of 'is' is." I guess it just depends on what your definition of "conflict" is. And "interest" is. Obama and Clinton. Perfect together. Over to you, Mike.

Barack Obama was an "Arm Candy Attorney," Says Andy Martin

Chicago Sun-Times reports that Obama practiced law without ever filing a formal appearance in any lawsuit

"Law professor" who was not a law professor is exposed as an "attorney" who was never able to take a case to trial

(CHICAGO)(December 18, 2007) Today I work off and comment on the original research by Abdon Pallasch of the Chicago Sun-Times. (http://www.suntimes.com/news/politics/obama/700499,CST-NWS-Obama-law17.article)

What follows is my opinion and reaction to the story about Barack Obama's grossly inflated legal career as a "civil rights attorney." There was "no there, there."

When a lawsuit is initiated, or when a new attorney enters an existing case, an attorney files an "appearance," a formal legal document which notifies the court and, more particularly the clerk of the court, that counsel has "appeared" in the case.

Obama has made a career of defrauding the American public about his legal "career." Obama, a Harvard Law School graduate, never filed a single appearance in a single case all of the years he was "practicing" law.

Obama was an "Arm Candy Attorney." Or, to put in a Palm Beachy sort of way, he was a "Walker." In other words, he was almost always paid to show up in court, and do nothing more than be there.

The Chicago Sun-Times reports during the years Obama was affiliated with a law firm, he never formally was counsel of record in any lawsuit. I have a friend, a retired airline pilot, who has tried more cases than Barack Obama. One.

Obama describes himself as a "law professor," but he was actually a Lecturer, who is a contract employee paid to teach courses on a semester-by-semester basis. He was never on a "tenure track" to become a permanent part of the law school staff. I was an adjunct professor of law, akin to a lecturer but usually with fewer courses.

Obama's former partner says Obama "wrote lots of substantial memos, but he didn't try any cases." Obama would usually show up in court, and then let other lawyers do the talking. He was the legal equivalent of what people in the social pages call "arm candy," someone basically hired to appear in public and make the holder "look good." In Palm Beach we used to call these people "Walkers," because they were asked to squire ladies of a certain age and walk around with the lady in tow. You get the idea.

Obama was an arm candy attorney. A make believe civil rights attorney.

Legal memos are assigned by lawyers to junior attorneys. Indeed, Obama's vacuous legal career almost perfectly tracks his vacuous career as a national candidate. Barry O is brilliant at getting up and speaking in a situation he controls (compare to writing a memo). But when he has to enter the rough and tumble of political debate (compare to a courtroom hearing or trial) Obama is absent and ineffective. He can't cut the rigors of a courtroom. Couldn't then. Can't now.

I first walked in to the United States Courthouse in Chicago in 1969. I saw lawyers who would "practice" for days to appear in front of a federal judge for a couple of minutes, and argue with passion and vehemence—all for a two day extension of time, or for permission (leave) to "file instanter" (instantly). Eventually many graduated to presenting cases before a jury. Obama never graduated. Why?

Democratic Presidential candidate John Edwards was a real attorney. He tried real cases and he made piles of money for his clients, and for himself. He didn't only achieve the American "dream," he became American "reality." Sadly, Obama is still in the dream stage. He is a wonderful dream merchant. But reality is another matter altogether.

Small law firms such as Obama's, with only a few attorneys, usually send young counsel into the courtroom to fight just as quickly as possible. Obama was never up to the task.

In all fairness, Hillary Clinton also has a grossly inflated legal resume. I remember when she was "ranked' as one of the top 50 lawyers, or something like that, in America. Another fraud artist. Clinton was not much better than Obama. Hillary was basically a bagman (bagwoman?) for Bill.

By comparison, Republican Fred Thompson was also a "real" lawyer. He actually went to federal court and tried cases before a jury, as an assistant federal prosecutor.

To be sure, everyone who was contacted and quoted in the Sun-Times article was exceedingly polite about Obama's legal endeavors. They should be. He could make them federal judges if he wins the White House. And lawyers as a group are polite. Or perhaps imbued with a sense of politesse.

In fact, as I read Abdon Pallasch's article I had a sense that Obama may have performed one of he worst sins of an attorney: he may have inflated his billing hours to bilk the opposing party. The bank paid. Over billing is a crime, and lawyers have gone to jail for bilking their clients or opposing parties (in some cases, a party has to pay the bills of an opponent). Obama billed almost three hours of legal time for a routine court appearance that may have taken a few minutes, as well as "reviewing documents." I submit Obama's billing records need much more scrutiny, searching scrutiny. No doubt they have been or will soon be destroyed. Like his state senate files and records.

"Professor" Barack Obama, meet "Professor" Harold Hill, of "The "Music Man." The Music Man was a Broadway hit and later a big movie about a con man who shows up in—of all places—Iowa. Maybe history is repeating itself. First as fiction, and this time as fact. Or is Obama's "civil rights career" just another one of his many fictions, that he has merchandised so successfully to the gullible American public?

I'd say "You be the judge," but then Barry Obama never tried a lawsuit in front of either a judge or a jury. I invite you to read the Sun-Times article and e-mail me with your responses. Obama and Hill, perfect together. Perfect fictions. Hey, they even sound like a law firm, "Obama & Hill."

Obama was sure no Johnny Cochran. Or, if I met Obama I could say, "Barry, I knew Johnny Cochran, and you're no Cochran. Not at all. You're an 'arm candy attorney.'" Lordy, lordy. I don't envy the Democrats having to pick between two "arm candy attorneys" and a real trial lawyer, John Edwards.

Ok, you win. You be the judge. Iowa, are you listening?

CHAPTER FIVE

Obama and Tony Rezko

Many have identified The Reverend Jeremiah Wright as Barack Obama's surrogate father. Wright has certainly been a critical influence on Obama; undoubtedly the pastor helped Obama become comfortable in the racial identity Barack adopted to resolve his personality conflicts.

But I believe a stronger case can be made that Antonin "Tony" Rezko was really Barack Obama's "stepfather."

Obama's cover story has been that Rezko noticed Obama when he was a young Harvard Law Student. Obama is often vague about critical moments in his life. It is doubtful Rezko was following the student body of Harvard Law School with great care. Rather, it is a fair surmise that Rezko met Obama in Chicago before Obama left for Harvard. Obama's time line of his Rezko relationship seems to obscure the length and depth of the relationship.

Over the years, Rezko became Obama's biggest booster. Thus the cold and calculating way in which Obama repeatedly denied any close association with Rezko rivals Jesus' prediction that the Apostle Paul would deny the Lord before the crack of dawn.

Deep down, Obama must feel very lonely and very sad at Rezko's fall from power. Or Obama may be just as cold and calculating as he appears to be in his efforts to rival the mythical Sammy Glick in his reach for the presidency.

Rezko arranged Obama's first job. Obama's employment wasn't with just any law firm. Rezko got Obama a job at Rezko's own law firm, the firm that represented Rezko's own business interests. Obama later tried to minimize his role in Rezko's transactions at the law firm, pretending he did little work for Rezko & Co.

As always, Obama was trying to conceal the truth. The amount of time Obama spent on Rezko's legal business was meaningless; Rezko had arranged Obama's job with the law firm that hired the new graduate.

People at the law firm knew Obama as "Tony's man."

How would any of us feel towards the person who arranged our first job out of college or professional school? Deep loyalty and an appreciation of the sort that we reserve for father-like figures.

Obama has gone to extreme lengths to conceal his relationship with Rezko, and to provide incomplete, false or misleading information about the Rezko connection.

In an exchange of questions and answers with the Chicago Sun-Times on April 23, 2007, Obama sought to mislead the newspaper and was in full damage control mode, see http://www.suntimes.com/news/metro/35d3786,CST-NWS-rezquestions23.article#.

The Sun-Times asked: Had Obama ever referred to Rezko as a "political godfather?" Obama denied that he had.

Obama tried to draw a distinction between representing Rezko's companies and "Rezko, personally." Obama claimed that he was completely unaware of Rezko's financial problems.

As to Rezko's decrepit buildings, Obama claimed he merely followed" up on constituency complaints about housing as matter of routine," (sic) despite the fact that Rezko's real estate investments were centered in the geographic area of Obama's state senate district; it would have been impossible for him not to have known of Rezko's deteriorating buildings.

Despite the fact that Rezko and Obama's senior law partner were business associates, Obama's response to whether Obama had discussed Rezko's financial problems ***with anyone*** at the law firm" was that " ***The firm*** advises us that it is unaware of any such conversations." Obama said he "did not know about a business relationship between [his senior law partner] Allison Davis and Tony Rezko…"

In a giant law firm with hundreds of lawyers it is reasonable to believe that not every lawyer knows what other attorneys are doing. In a tiny law firm such as Obama's, with a handful of attorneys, his denials are laughable.

Obama misstated professional ethics when he indicated that a law firm must conceal whether it represents someone ("the fact of representation"). That is simply not the case. The fact of representation is not privileged information. See *In Re Grand Jury*, 969 F.2d 995, 997 (11th Cir. 1992); In Re Grand Jury, 204 F.3rd 516, 522 (4th Cir. 2000). Thus, even Obama's carefully prepared responses to the Chicago Sun-Times were false statements of and about the law.

When asked whether he "still considered Rezko a friend," Obama was evasive and stated "The Senator is troubled by the accusations…"

Obama's biggest lie to the Sun-Times was reserved for the open-ended question, "Is there any other information the senator would like to provide…"? Obama's reply was "No. The senator has answered all questions here to the best of his knowledge."

On March 14, 2008, Obama met with the Chicago Tribune and Sun-Times and held long discussions in which he disclosed extensive new information about his connections to Rezko. Thus, it is evident that Obama had concealed the truth from the Sun-Times almost a year earlier in 2007, as he has continued to dissemble since his "full disclosure" in 2008.

It is clear that Obama has lied persistently, lied repeatedly and lied boldly about his Rezko connections. When the Chicago Sun-Times asked if a Rezko "straw donor" had secured an internship in the senator's office, Obama replied, "That was not something that was ever brought to my attention." Obama blames his own staff for selling internships to a Rezko straw donor. Of course.

But why? Well, Obama's persistent and very public denial of Rezko stems from the close father-son relationship between the two men.

Rezko nurtured Obama over the years, and stood by him when logic compelled a different conclusion, another form of parental loyalty. In 2000, Rezko raised substantial money for Obama's quixotic campaign for congress against an established African-American incumbent. The political thing for Rezko to have done would be to have declined to assist Obama and to discourage the state senator from challenging the incumbent congressman. Rezko stuck by Obama.

Over the years, Rezko was Obama's first and one of his biggest fundraisers. And Rezko's most dramatic "fund raising" for Obama may have occurred when Obama purchased his mansion at 5046 S. Greenwood Street. Rezko appears to have borrowed money from a London-based Iraqi billionaire, Nadhmi Auchi.

Obama has done his best to obscure the connection between himself and Rezko in their tangled transaction.

First, by 2005, Rezko was facing severe financial pressure. Rezko appears to have borrowed money from Auchi to fund his part of Obama's mansion transaction.

Second, although Obama denies any connection, he bought his home for a $300,000 reduction in price ($1,650,000 reduced from $1,950,000) on the same day as Rezko, through his wife, purchased the adjacent lot for the "full price" ($625,000).

Third, the fact that Obama obtained his own mortgage from Rezko's lead bank, Northern Trust Company, has always been ignored by the media. Rezko appears to have brought Obama to Northern Trust as a customer.

Fourth, although the sliver of land that Obama later purchased from Rezko's lot was appraised at $44,000, Obama paid a full 1/6 of Rezko's purchase price. This calibrated top-off payment is consistent with a structured transaction in which Rezko was "banking" the admittedly financially overextended Obama to gain control of both pieces of real estate.

Were Rezko's financial machinations on Obama's behalf crimes? Did he intend to? Ironically, if we apply the stretched interpretation of federal criminal law that was applied in Rezko's own criminal trial, Obama appears to have engaged in a rather high-toned form of influence peddling. A crime. When Obama denied that hiring "interns" for his staff was linked to Rezko's straw donors," it is clear that Obama may have been selling influence for financial assistance.

Money did not change hands. Favors did.

Likewise, Obama appeared at social functions arranged by Rezko. The evidence was disclosed at Rezko's trial. (http://www.suntimes.com/news/metro/rezko/894559,CST-NWS-rezko15.article; http://www.chicagotribune.com/news/local/chi-rezko-obama-15apr15,0,3178018.story)

As usual, in all matters relating to Tony Rezko, Obama's memory failed him. Obama did not remember meeting Auchi at Rezko's event. How is it that Obama, the man who parlayed his modest legal skills into an ascent to the nation's highest realms, and who cultivated wealthy donors assiduously, could not remember meeting one of the richest men in the world?

Why would anyone vote for this man, Obama, with such a consistently poor memory?

Mr. Auchi was loyal to his friend Tony Rezko. Rezko was loyal to Obama.

Auchi was also accused by some intelligence sources of being a financial conduit and enabler for deposed Iraqi dictator Saddam Hussein.

Thus, in an ultimate irony, Obama may have purchased his Chicago mansion with money provided by a former confidante of Saddam Hussein.

My own relationship with Obama and Rezko began when Rezko was indicted. I was stunned that Obama told the media he had no real knowledge or connection with Rezko. In Obama's words Rezko was just a casual campaign donor. My own research had indicated Obama's remarks were a sham and I notified federal authorities on November 16, 2006, see e.g. http://contrarian-commentary.wordpress.com/2007/04/25/andy-martin-asks-for-grand-jury-probe-of-barack-obama/; http://jaxhawk.blogtown-hall.com/2007/11/23/front_runners_have_lots_of_baggage.tht ml.

With these introductory remarks, you can read my writing on the details of the Rezko-Obama relationship in context.

At the end of the day, and when all of Obama's links to Rezko are connected, I believe my thesis that Rezko was really Obama's "stepfather," and provided the kind of support parents often do, is the correct conclusion.

Obama's pretense that his friend Rezko was not his surrogate "dad" reveals yet another obvious source of emotional conflict. Obama could feel that Rezko, yet another father substitute, had betrayed him. Rezko had done for Obama what Obama's father never cared, tried or wanted to do, nurture and assist Barack Obama. Obama must be saddened that he now has claim he "does not recognize" the Rezko of 2008 in the criminal proceedings. (http://blog.washingtonpost.com/channel-08/2008/06/rezko_topic_of_gops_latest_ant.html)

Internet Editor and Republican Corruption Fighter Andy Martin Requests Criminal Investigation into "Deal" between Senator Barack Obama and Indicted Influence Peddler Tony Rezko

NEWS CONFERENCE DETAILS:

WHO: Internet journalist/editor Andy Martin
WHERE: Southeast corner of Wabash and Superior Streets, Chicago, (St. James Cathedral)
WHEN: Thursday, November 16, 2006 11:00 A.M.

WHAT: Andy Martin will hold a news conference to announce that he has filed a complaint with the Public Integrity Section of the Criminal Division of the U. S. Department of justice seeking a criminal investigation into the financial links between U. S. Senator Barack Obama and indicted Illinois influence peddler Tony Rezko. The complaint also names U. S. epresentative Luis Gutierrez. After his news conference, Martin will go to the U. S. Attorney's office to leave a letter for the foreperson of the U.S. Grand Jury.

MARTIN STATEMENT:

"Mr. Obama says he made a 'mistake' when he entered into a deal with Tony Rezko," Martin will state. "On the contrary,

Obama committed a crime, and he knew it. Rezko was engaged in influence peddling, plain and simple. Obama was not some unsophisticated jerk. He had served as an Illinois State Senator, a body that has been a fulcrum of corruption for decades. He knew the 'players.' What Obama did is no different than the same kind of 'honest graft' that has sent Illinois politicians to jail since Governor Otto Kerner. Now that the election is over, it is time to focus attention on what I believe was Obama's criminal conduct."

MEDIA CONTACT: (312) 440-4124

BIO: Chicago-based Internet journalist, broadcaster, critic and corruption fighter Andy Martin is the Executive Editor and publisher of ContrarianCommentary.com. Martin has forty years experience covering nationaland international politics. Martin has been fighting political corruption in Illinois since he was a law student at the University of Illinois. Columns also posted atpoliticalgateway.com.

Comments? E-mail: AndyMart20@aol.com.
Media contact: (866) 706-2639. Web site: AndyforIllinois.com

ANTHONY R. MARTIN, J.D.
Professor of Law (Adj.)
Suite 4406
30 E. Huron Street
Chicago, IL 60611-4723
Tel. (312) 440-4124
Fax (312) 440-4125
E-mail: AndyMart20@aol.com

November 16, 2006

Mr. Edward Nucci
Acting Chief
Public Integrity Section
Criminal Division
U. S. Department of Justice
950 Pennsylvania Avenue
Washington, DC 20530-0001

With copy to:

SAC Robert D. Grant
FBI – Chicago
2111 W. Roosevelt Road
Chicago, IL 60606
Via fax (312) 829-5172

Re: Possible criminal investigation of U. S. senator
    Barack Obama

Dear Mr. Nucci:

I am writing to you to suggest a possible criminal investigation of U. S. senator Barack Obama.

I have been engaged in fighting official corruption in Illinois since I was a law student at the University of Illinois, over forty (40) years.

I am in the process of organizing I-CAN (Illinois-Corruption Action Now) to continue the fight against corruption. I believe the modern remnants of the Chicago Crime Syndicate continue to seek to penetrate legitimate state offices and businesses. I have previously filed a complaint directing your attention to very suspicious links involving tens of millions of dollars in questionable "loans" between State Treasurer-elect Alexi Giannoulias' Broadway Bank and an organized crime figure.

Mr. Tony Rezko is under indictment in Illinois for seeking to extort money from potential state vendors. Rezko is a close associate of Governor Rod Blagojevich and Rezko has done "real estate business" with Blagojevich's wife, Patti Blagojevich.

Corruption, of course, involves two different approaches: (i) extorting/taking money from people, and (ii) paying money or giving tangible benefits to public officials to obtain access or influence. Sometimes people buy influence for an immediate project or need, and sometimes they just buy influence to bank it or to project the aura of access and influence in their business dealings. My complaint against Senator Obama falls into the second category.

Before being elected to the U. S. Senate, Mr. Obama served in the Illinois state senate. The Illinois senate has been a cesspool of corruption for decades. Back in the 1960's they censured a member, Senator Paul Simon (then serving as a state senator), for being too honest and exposing senate corruption. Matters have not changed much.

Mr. Obama was well aware of the culture and climate of corruption when he began his business dealings with Mr. Rezko.

Reduced to its essentials, Obama and Rezko engaged in a structured real estate transaction where they coordinated the purchases of adjacent parcels of real estate. Rezko claims he paid "full market price" and Obama apparently received a "discount" of several hundred thousand dollars for his parcel. Rezko then improved his parcel to benefit Obama.

Obama recently said these related and structured transactions were a "mistake." With all due respect I believe they were a federal crime and constituted a conspiracy.

I believe a grand jury could find a pattern of criminal activity. Instead of handing cash to Obama, Rezko handed Obama a preferential price for property. This is the same form of "honest graft" and preferential treatment that sent former Illinois Governor Otto Kerner to jail over 30 years ago, see United States v. Isaacs, 493 F.2d 1124 (7th Cir. 1974).

Taken in isolation, the Obama episode might be explainable, but I doubt it. Why would Rezko be buying land next to Obama and coordinating his actions with Obama if not to confer a benefit on Obama? Why?

More importantly, there appears to be a pattern of similar influence peddling by Mr. Rezko. The Chicago Sun-Times recently reported that Mr. Rezko, around the same general period he was wheeling with Obama, also provided a preferential price for a property purchase by U. S. Representative Luis Gutierrez. There is a pattern here. Instead of transferring cash to buy influence, Rezko was engaging in structured property transactions and preferential treatment of public officials to confer significant financial benefits on them, far above the legal limits of any legitimate political contribution permitted by federal law.

Most respectfully, I would urge you to consider allowing a grand jury to examine this series of suspicious transactions. I am sending a letter to the foreperson of the grand jury, through the U. S. Attorney's office, seeking to testify as an expert witness in this matter if the grand jury wishes to pursue this investigation.

Please feel free to contact me if you have any questions.

Respectfully submitted,
ANDY MARTIN
AM:sp

The Democratic Party's Dictatorship of the National Media

An extreme-left, taxpayer-subsidized Web site smears talk show hosts Rush Limbaugh, Bill O'Reilly and Andy Martin

The Obama cover-up confirms that nation's media are controlled by supine liberals who fear ferocious counterattacks by extremist elements in the Democratic party

Where is Spiro Agnew now that we really need him?

Obama receives "white glove" treatment from national press

(CHICAGO)(April 30, 2007) Something happened last week that illustrates why people have lost faith in the so-called "mainstream media."

For almost forty (40) years the liberal bias of the nation's major media has been a flash point. On November 13, 1969 Vice president Spiro Agnew attacked the nation's liberal media elite. He triggered a firestorm of controversy with his comments. Those fires are still burning.

Last week, Agnew's charges were once again corroborated by a national cover-up of Senator Barack Obama's defective memory and embarrassing corruption as a young attorney.

While investors decry the decline of print media, and broadcasters bemoan dropping nightly news audiences, the rise of the Internet has created a new and even more potent left-wing monster.

The silence of the nation's media where news of Obama is concerned also reflects extreme racism-in-reverse. Obama is allowed to bellyache that the "bar is higher for a Black candidate" when exactly the opposite is true: no white candidate could even remotely expect to receive the "white glove" treatment meted out to Barry O.

Last November Tony Rezko, a sleazy Chicago politician, was indicted by a federal grand jury. At the time I asked for a more extensive grand jury investigation of both Obama and Rezko, since I was aware the links were more expansive than reported. I also filed a complaint with the FBI. I sent a request to testify before the Grand Jury to Chief Judge James Holderman, who has not yet responded. (I will be contacting him again, soon. Stay tuned.)

Last week something truly bizarre happened in Chicago. The Chicago Sun-Times published an 8 page expose on the same Mr. Rezko. Prominent among the "usual suspects" in the Sun-Times coverage was Obama. Given Obama's status as a leading presidential candidate, the Sun-Times' disclosures should have been front page news across the United States.

What happened? An iron curtain of silence descended on Obama's outrageous evasiveness and blatant corruption while a lawyer and local politician in Chicago.

The Sun-Times pursued Obama for five (5) weeks and Obama evaded the paper because he knew that reporters wanted to ask questions about Rezko. If a candidate such as John McCain dodged a newspaper for over a month, and tried to avoid questions about links to an indicted supporter, would that be national news? Come on.

Here is what the Sun-Times reported:

Rezko had received over $100 million from city and state agencies for what soon became slum housing. Rezko had thirty (30) slum buildings.

Eleven (11) of Rezko's slum buildings were in Obama's geographically compact state senate district. (Obama served in the Illinois Senate from 1996 to 2004.)

In a large urban area such as Chicago state senate districts are not very large. They encompass several compact and contiguous neighborhoods. If you walked the district even occasionally you would know, you should know, almost every large building in the district.

How did Obama respond to the Sun-Times' disclosures? He invoked the Sergeant Schultz (on Hogan's Heroes) defense: "I know nothing; I see nothing and I say nothing." Obama professed total ignorance about the slum tragedies literally on his own doorstep.

How could a state senator in a poor neighborhood not know about eleven (count 'em) slum buildings in his own district?

Especially when the state senator's own law firm represented the slum landlord?

Yes, Obama's law firm represented Rezko in his sleazy slum landlord dealings.

A presidential candidate works in a law firm that represents a major slum landlord and he "knows nothing" about the client? The slum landlord client has slum buildings in the then-state senator's district and the presidential candidate has no idea?

That's the truth about Barry Obama.

Only the truth never reached the American people last week.

A veil of complete silence was imposed on Obama's sordid scandal.

Chris Cillizza, a blogger for the Washington Post, had a mention on his blog. But the Washington Post made no mention in its print editions. The silence in the New York Times was also deafening. There was no headline coverage anywhere.

Outside Chicago, this devastating expose of Obama's corruption and incompetence was completely suppressed. Even inside Chicago, the Tribune tried to pooh-pooh the story because the Sun-Times had beaten them on these devastating disclosures.

Of course during the period when Obama saw nothing, heard nothing and said nothing, he did received $50,000 from Rezko in "campaign contributions." Maybe he didn't learn about Rezko's contributions until later as well?

Obama's dirty dollars from Rezko were blood money. Tenants were suffering a few blocks away while Obama was collecting money to suppress any governmental relief. It's called "honest graft," and legal fees are one of the quintessential forms of honest graft in Chicago.

Obama brags about his work as a private citizen removing asbestos at the Altgeld Gardens housing project. In reality he was a minor player in that program, except in his fictionalized autobiography where he stars.

But when he was actually a public official, a sitting state senator, he covered up massive slum holdings of his Fifty Thousand Dollar Man *contributor*. And he knew nothing?

And the nation's media took no notice last week?

I said the Sun-Times was courageous. It was. The Sun-Times has a large readership in minority neighborhoods, where the Obama virus has been the strongest. The Sun-Times came close to alienating its core audience by telling the unpleasant truth about a local huckster who has managed to parlay media indolence into a serious bid for national office.

And, oh, what about Obama's claim that the "bar" is higher for him? What nonsense. No other candidate could get away with representing a slum landlord who had slums in the candidate's own district, and the candidate saying that as a local public official he had no idea what was going on in his own backyard. Who would believe that?

The national media are every bit as evil as Spiro Agnew said they were 38 years ago. They start with evasion, move to suppression and end with corruption of the information channels.

Agnew went on to attack the New York Times and Washington Post. Who suppressed the Obama shenanigans? The same Times and Post. Then as now the Times and Post were highly influential in setting the national news agenda.

Today the situation is even more dangerous than in Agnew's day. Liberal Democrats are funding a left-wing attack dog, Media Matters for America, led by former Republican Conservative and now liberal Democrat David Brock. Brock attacks me, Bill O'Reilly and Rush Limbaugh as an unholy trinity of conservatives.

But what is more critical is not Brock's attacks on conservatives. Rather, Brock is dangerous because he stands ready to smear *liberals* who stray from his left-wing orthodoxy. In other words, the extreme left has created a climate of fear in the nation's newsrooms: if you tell the truth about Obama, or other Democrats, you face the prospect of being smeared. The extreme left has begun to drive media coverage by the moderate left in the nation's national media.

Republicans and conservatives have not yet adjusted to the emergence of the extreme left-wing smear machine in this country. Wake up America.

If an incompetent but visually appealing candidate from Chicago who worked as a lawyer representing a slum landlord, and who now claims to know nothing about the slums that existed either in his own law practice or on the streets of his own local senate district, can rise to national prominence, then the power of the *extreme* left has exponentially increased from what it was in 1969.

Barack Obama is the avatar of the extreme left's growing power in American life.

The Emperor Caligula made his horse pro counsel of Rome. Media Matters, and the fellow travelers on the extreme left who support Media Matters, are on the verge of making a radical Chicago politician with a record of taking dirty dollars from a slum landlord a serious candidate for president: Barack Obama.

And they tell us the Democrats are ready to govern?

Putting Obama in the White House would be worse than putting Caligula's horse in power. We are horse's asses for even tolerating the dictats and suppression of the truth by the so-called "mainstream media." And now the mainstream media are increasingly falling under the indirect influence of the extreme left.

Spiro Agnew, rest in peace.

The Brazen Lies of Barack Obama

(CHICAGO)(May 17, 2007) Lynn Sweet of the Chicago Sun-Times has been a "true believer" in Barack Obama since at least 2004. She has chronicled his rise to national prominence. But today's column in the Sun-Times indicates that Sweet's tolerance for Obama's insatiable appetite for lying and distortion is ending. "Sweetie," we hardly knew ye.

Likewise, when I began to write about Obama's lies three years ago, no one was interested. They wanted to believe in the "dream." The truth didn't matter. One of these days the truth is going to come crashing down on these true believers. In the meantime, the extreme left of the Democratic Party has viciously attacked me, and forced me to become the point man in a conservative counterattack against Democratic media distortions.

Sweet is sending Obama a message today: Stop Lying! Will he heed, or even receive, Sweet's *cri de coeur*? Good question. Sweet, of course, is a good deal more polite than I am. I have relentlessly hammered away at Obama's links to indicted Chicago swindler Tony Rezko. But Sweet's remarks today indicate that Obama's endless litany of lies is wearing thin for his supporters in the Chicago media. When will the national media catch up?

Indeed, Sweet was much too polite. She limited herself to Obama's lies on George Stephanopoulos' program Sunday. She didn't tie the entire *oeuvre* of Obama's mendacity together. I will. Sweet points out that Obama lied when he said that he went to influence peddler Rezko for help buying a "first" house. In reality, Obama lied because he had already purchased a house and his latest mansion was not an innocent first purchase by an unsophisticated rube. He wanted Rezko's juice, and he got it. There was no "boneheaded" mistake as Obama claims. Obama, moreover, was a practicing lawyer who was familiar with real estate law and financing.

Stephanopoulos, of course starts from a prepared script and lacks the ability to zero in on Obama's lies. Obama went on to tell Stephanopoulos Obama didn't take money from "lobbyists." Sweet pointed out that he had, regularly. In his presidential race, Obama even has a lobbyist on his New Hampshire team.

It appears that Michelle Obama is also addicted to untruths and half-truths. Sweet was miffed when Michelle misled Sweet by removing campaign appearances from the "public" calendar because Michelle's stops were "private." Apparently it all depends on your definition of "private" and "public." When is a presidential campaign fund raising stop "private?" Bill Clinton would be proud. He has a way with words too.

What Sweet left out, unfortunately, was the sinew that ties all of Obama's Rezko lies together. Obama was collecting massive "campaign contributions" from Rezko at a time when Rezko had slum tenements in Obama's own state senate district. Obama claims he had no idea Rezko's slums were in his own district, a few short neighborhood steps away. If Obama didn't know what was going on in his own tiny state senate district in Chicago (before being elected to the U. S. Senate) how can we count on him to keep track of the world? How?

Barry Obama has risen to great heights by alternatively playing the race card and brazenly lying about obvious facts, and always hoping that the truth won't catch up with him. So far, it hasn't. It will be a great fall when the truth finally does catch up. And he will then play the race card, again.

Tony Rezko faces serious time in jail. He can cut a deal and "drop the dime" on Obama. Here's predicting Rezko "rolls over" and implicates Obama in some of Rezko's criminal activity. Even if Rezko doesn't, Obama will be a feature at Rezko's criminal trial, just in time for the primary season.

Barry, or Barack, Obama, are you listening? Do you even care? Or are you so addicted to lying you will keep on manifesting contempt for the media and the American people?

Three years and counting I have been telling the truth about Obama. When will they ever learn? When will they ever learn?

Obama's Deals with Tony Rezko
Come Under Scrutiny by ABC News

Internet storm begins to build over Obama's real estate deals with Daley Machine swindler

Is "the real wheeling and dealing" about Obama set to begin between Rezko's attorneys and federal prosecutors?

(CHICAGO)(January 10, 2008) Andy Martin, Executive Editor of ContrarianCommentary.com and Republican candidate for U.S. Senator, noted today, Thursday, January 10th that ABC News was now following the Obama-Rezko real estate connection.

"Since 2006 I have been pointing at Barack Obama and Tony Rezko and stating that as Rezko came closer to trial, Obama would be in greater jeopardy. In a 'perfect storm,' Rezko's trial is set to start in February, just as the primary season is reaching a climax.

"Obama's excuse that he was not aware of Rezko's shady politics is an insult to the intelligence. Obama has also said he had no idea that Rezko had slum properties right inside Obama's state senate district, a few blocks away.

"And Obama's law firm was doing Rezko's legal work.

"Does Obama think we are all dumb?" Martin asks.

"Moreover, Rezko's assistance to Obama in acquiring his home took place after Obama was already elected to the U. S. Senate. Obama knew then who he was dealing with, a Daley Machine fixer. Some people are confused and have told me they don't think Rezko helped finance Obama's home purchase. Indeed he did. Rezko provided financing for part of the package of two parcels of property. If I am buying two parcels of adjacent property, and a person helps me buy one of the parcels, he is helping me acquire the entire package.

"You heard it here first, but I predict Rezko will try to 'give up' Obama as part of a plea deal to avoid trial, and offer to testify against Obama as an influence-peddling newly-elected U. S. Senator. After thirty-five years of fighting Chicago corruption I have learned something, and when a crooked pol faces the pen, then the real wheeling and dealing begins," Martin states.

LINKS:

http://abcnews.go.com/Blotter/story?id=4111483&page=1
http://abcnews.go.com/Blotter/story?id=4115565&page=1

Andy Martin Explains Basis for Accusation that Chicago Influence Peddler Tony Rezko Paid Senator Barack Obama an Illegal Bribe in Housing Transaction

(CHICAGO)(January 11, 2008) Andy Martin will hold a Chicago news conference Friday, January 11th at 4:00 P.M. to explain the factual and legal basis for his claim that indicted Chicago influence peddler Tony Rezko paid and intended to pay a bribe to Senator Barack Obama.

"There has been a great deal of confusion over what Obama did and what Rezko did, and how their combination and action in concert to purchase Obama's home in Chicago constituted a federal criminal offense," Martin will state. "I am here today to clarify and explain the legal theories behind the accusations and behind their structured and coordinated real estate transactions.

"It is also critical to place the Rezko-Obama relationship in context. Obama sent letters on his Illinois State senate stationary on Rezko's behalf. Obama cannot take refuge in what federal courts call the 'Ostrich defense,' where Obama merely says he was 'boneheaded' and gets away with criminal actions.

"But while the machinations of Obama and Rezko may be confusing to a lay person, they are nothing out of the ordinary to experienced criminal and political investigators in Illinois," Martin will state. "I stand by my view that Tony Rezko is going to try to implicate Barack Obama in criminal activity as a means of escaping punishment for his own behavior."

Andy Martin Explains the Significance of the Chicago Sun-Times Story (January 20 Editions) Identifying Barack Obama as the "Political Candidate" in the Tony Rezko Criminal Trial

"As I predicted at a news conference a week ago," Martin will state, "federal prosecutors are putting squeeze on both Rezko and Obama"

Since 2006, Andy Martin has led the way in exposing the criminal implications of Obama's links to Tony Rezko

(CHICAGO)(January 19, 2008) Andy Martin will hold a Chicago news conference Saturday, January 19th at 7:00 P.M. to explain the context and significance of the Chicago Sun-Times' story in Sunday's editions identifying Senator Barack Obama as the "political candidate" in the forthcoming Tony Rezko criminal trial.

"A week ago I held a news conference and disclosed that Barack Obama was linked to Tony Rezko's criminal trial. No one paid attention. It took the somnolent Chicago media a week to pick upon my scent. Sunday's Chicago Sun-Times confirms my claim that Obama was linked to the forthcoming Rezko trial.

"For the past fourteen (14) months I have been both breaking news and making news concerning Barack Obama's links to the corrupt criminal syndicate that controls Chicago and Illinois politics. Some columnists call it a 'Combine.' Is it is in effect a crime syndicate (though not directly part of the 'Outfit' or 'mob').

"Tonight I will put the Sun-Times Sunday story in context, both with my prior disclosures at my news conference last week, and the overall context of what is unfolding at 219 S. Dearborn. I will disclose that the 'squeeze is on' both Rezko and Obama, directly and indirectly, to deal with federal prosecutors.

"In November, 2006 I sent a communication to the foreperson of the U. S. Grand Jury and outlined why further investigation was necessary.

"A few days ago the Chicago Tribune called me a 'crusader' who takes action against 'perceived wrongdoers.' Thank you Chicago Tribune. For fourteen months I have been exposing the Obama/Rezko links and leading the way with links and analysis to the criminal trial. Tonight I will follow up on my commentary and analysis," Martin states.

"It is a biblical proposition that there are 'none so blind as those who will not see; none so deaf as those who will not hear.' The Chicago media have tried to ignore and avoid what I have been disclosing, but the developments and actions of federal prosecutors are gradually revealing the dimensions of the case I have been making since 2006.

"Obama's local boosters in the media can try to ignore me in the short run; they can't ignore the coming explosion in the long run. The Rezko case is a time bomb that is coming closer to exploding."

Andy Martin has been an expert in Chicago criminal law and trials for over thirty years and previously taught criminal law as an adjunct professor.

Andy Martin Says Barack Obama is "Feeling the Heat" of Relentless Investigation and the Upcoming Federal Criminal Trial of Supporter Tony Rezko

After an Andy Martin news conference Saturday disclosing new scandals involving Obama and Rezko, Obama told the Chicago Tribune he is coughing up more tainted 2004 campaign cash

"What took him so long?" Martin asks

Martin says media boosterism and a sense of Chicago's inferiority have led local media to fail to vet Obama properly and thoroughly

(CHICAGO)(January 20, 2008) Andy Martin will hold a Chicago news conference Sunday, January 20th at 12:00 noon to comment on Senator Barack Obama's latest disclosures in the Sunday Chicago Tribune that Obama is disgorging over $40,000 in tainted campaign cash. Martin will also disclose new pieces of the Obama-Rezko puzzle. Obama acted to disgorge campaign within hours after Martin announced a Chicago news conference disclosing new links between Obama, indicted influence peddler Tony Rezko and Rezko's forthcoming federal criminal trial where Obama is still only an anonymous, but significant, factor.

"He who lives by the corruption of the Chicago Democratic Machine and the corrupt Illinois 'Combine' (hint: Barack Obama) dies by the Chicago Democratic Machine and corrupt Illinois 'Combine,' Martin will state. "One cut at a time.

"Rezko was indicted months ago; what took Obama so long to 'check his records?' Obama's own admission is that disclosures in the Chicago Sun-Times forced him to conduct these new reviews on Saturday, in January, 2008? Of the 2004 election? In the midst of a presidential election?

"Obama has been in the U.S. Senate for three years. And he is still giving back 2004 campaign cash? Whoa.

"Maybe Hilary Clinton was right when she said this man had not been properly 'vetted.' How many more skeletons is Obama going to disclose and disgorge in response to newspaper headlines and my news conferences, and what happens when the Rezko trial begins and Obama is sucked into the vortex?" Martin will demand at his Sunday news conference.

"Obama has been playing a game of 'fast and loose' with the nation's media for years, and I have been disclosing his shenanigans piece by piece. Last week I disclosed Obama's links to the Rezko trial; this week the Sun-Times followed up on my disclosures. Then I scheduled another news conference for the 19th. And Obama coughed up another $40,000 in tainted cash. Sounds suspicious, doesn't it?

"After almost forty years in Chicago's courts I can state unequivocally what it means: Obama is 'feelin' the heat' of the Rezko criminal trial.

"Obama's rise to prominence has been fueled by and riddled with Chicago corruption for years. Yet local media keep trying to suppress this evidence of impropriety because in a spasm of misguided boosterism and Babbitry they want to promote a 'Chicago' candidate for president. On the Contrary, Chicago's media are disgracing the people of this City and state by putting forward a paper maché candidate for president. Obama is a slick talker, but the only walking he has done is with his palms open to Chicago's legendary influence peddling elite," Martin will state.

"America's Third City is looking incredibly Third World in its media coverage of a local candidate. A city with a legendary inferiority complex is looking decidedly inferior in the way it presents the truth about a local politico to the world.

"Sunday I will disclose yet another piece of the Obama-Rezko puzzle. And, one is constrained to ask, who has a better batting average of accuracy and telling the truth about Obama? Chicago's mainstream media, or ContrarianCommentary.com and my own campaign? The answer is embarrassingly obvious.

"And in that spirit, Sunday we'll keep embarrassing our colleagues and competitors in the so-called mainstream. 'Mainstream' should not be a synonym for stupid. But in covering up and in failing to discover and disclose the truth abut Obama in a timely manner, Chicago's mainstream media have been just plain stupid."

Andy Martin on the Rezko Trial:
The Whole World is Watching

Martin's prediction on the outcome: Tony Rezko could walk

Chicago's resident expert on federal courts, Andy Martin, provides new insights as part of his two years of continuing coverage of the Rezko-Obama connection

Martin slaps Chicago's media for selling America a "pig-in-a-poke" presidential candidate

(CHICAGO)(March 7, 2008) We had scheduled a pure "Obama" column for today, but it will have to wait a day. People want to know where I stand on the Rezko trial. Rezko, of course, was Senator Barack Obama's long-time friend, promoter and financier.

Obama may have to invoke Shakespeare's Macbeth as the Rezko parade proceeds, "Out damned spot! Out I say." But the Rezko spot is not going away. Tony Rezko was an integral part of Barack Obama's rise to power over the past two decades in Chicago politics.

Obama may want to pretend Rezko was a nothingburger, with a "who me?" shrug. The only answer, "Yah, you."

First, a couple of "caveats," or legalese for "warnings." I have *not* been in court during the Rezko proceedings, and I have never met any of the participants. I don't believe I have ever spoken to anyone involved in the trial.

Second, you must forgive me the temptation to say "I told you so." I have been screaming about the extent and depth of the Obama-Rezko connection since November, **2006**. A long time. No one cared. No one believed. No one outside the case knew the true extent and expanse of the relationship, except me.

Now, slowly, the truth is coming to the surface. And truth is often not a pretty sight in Chicago politics. Over the past couple of months we have been providing special insight into the progress of Rezko's federal case and, again, no one was noticing. But it's all there on my net postings to see.

I have been involved in the federal court at 219 S. Dearborn for thirty-nine years (no, I'm not *that* old, but Jack Benny would approve, at least in my 39th year). I know how federal courts and federal prosecutors and federal judges operate. They want to win, and they will do virtually anything to win. Some judges let prosecutors get away with it.

With those caveats, here are my observations. I must also stress that these are my conclusions after the first day of trial. As the case unfolds my views could, obviously, change.

First, I think the federal government has a weak case against Antoin "Tony" Rezko.

Governor Rod Blagojevich is the obvious target of the proceedings, the invisible Great White Whale in the courtroom. But I sense something happened. For some reason, the case broke too soon.

I was stunned by the tepid way the prosecutors opened. In any solid prosecution, a prosecutor wants to wake up the jury and sound the alarm. THIS IS A BAD, BAD, MAN! The government's opening witnesses in Rezko's case were pedestrian, almost subdued. The FBI agent's testimony was peripheral.

Some of my columns on the pre-trial prosecutorial corruption and abuse fall can now be understood in context. I wrote that Rezko was thrown in jail before trial on trumped up allegations. Borrowing money to pay your lawyers is not, after all, a crime. It is hardly evidence of an intent to cut and run (earlier columns have addressed these shenanigans, see links below).

And so the federal government, facing a weak case and uncertain evidence, as well as a highly unstable key witness, decided to torture Tony Rezko to soften him up for trial. They asked the judge to jail him before trial, and locked him in a dungeon, 23 hours a day, and degraded him in every way possible, to the point of even denying him a belt for his pants in court, all "for his own protection."

Hey, it's the American way. Wherever we go in the world, we take our torture and our prisons with us. It sad, but true. Abu Ghraib was not an aberration. The people committing the abuses were as American as apple pie. Guantanamo? You don't need to go there. Just look at Tony Rezko, on trial in Chicago and jailed 23 hours day to prevent him from preparing his defense. We will have to see if the prosecutors' dirty trick works. The whole idea of jailing Rezko was to smear and demean him, not because the government had a strong case but because prosecutors came to the realization they had a weak case, and wanted to punish Rezko before he was convicted of anything.

How did the defense open on Thursday? Just the way I predicted weeks ago. By playing the Obama card. The Obama card was played softly, but it was there in counsel's opening statement. Rezko's attorney linked Tony to Republicans and Democrats and, among them, to Mr. Obama himself. Obama promptly issued a press release saying "this case is not about me."

Indeed the case is very much about Mr. Obama.

The Chicago media have sold the nation the biggest pig-in-a-poke in recent political history. They have sold Obama as the great savior, the Teflon "hope," when Obama is merely just another glib Sammy Glick, who challenged the Chicago Democratic Machine until he got his own slice of the pie, and then quietly slept with Emil Jones and the other slimy machine hacks in The Party.

If there was such a tort (legal wrong) as journalistic malpractice, all of Chicago's media should be put on trial and charged with defrauding the American people about Barack Obama. They wanted him to win, because he was a good story, and a great local story, and they engineered his ascent while fully aware of the cancer behind the curtain.

And so while Obama might claim the Rezko trial is not about him, and he is not actually a part of the scheme in which Rezko and Levine are charged, Rezko was linked to Obama in ways far deeper than Obama has yet admitted.

And that leads me to my second conclusion:

Obama's links to Rezko will cut both ways. They may persuade some jurors that Rezko was merely a "politician," and vote not to convict him. Or they may decide Rezko's sleaze tainted Obama, and convict anyway. Both prosecutors and defense counsel have to careful how they use and defend against the Obama connection. Prosecutors don't want to appear to be smearing Obama in the midst of an election, even if that is what they end up having to do to win their case.

Because I know that prosecutors holding a weak hand will invariably try to bolster their case with irrelevant smears, I read the judge's Rule 404 (b) order carefully. Nine single-spaced pages of rope-a-dope. The 404 (b) motion was an admission that prosecutors knew they had a case with big holes. Federal Rule of Evidence 404 (b) allows the admission of what is essentially "smear" evidence, because the evidence is irrelevant to the real charges on trial. So 404 (b) allows parties to introduce evidence, with court approval, that "links" the "other acts" to the defendant in a criminal case.

It was clear from the prosecutors' 404 (b) claims that they need extraneous and extrinsic evidence to bolster their presentation. A 404 (b) motion is not a sign of prosecutorial confidence; it is evidence of prosecutorial concern.

When you combine the government's desperate plea to the judge to admit smear evidence, together with the very tepid opening day of the trial, the Department of Justice has only one way to go: down.

Stuart Levine, the government's key witness, is a prosecutor's nightmare. Levin has apparently overdosed on drugs for decades. Some drugs I have never even heard of. Special K? Got me. I never heard of it before the Levine case.

In a drug prosecution you do expect druggies and dealers and lowlifes to testify against a defendant. Absolutely. Common sense leads a jury to accept the reality that lowlifes testify against lowlifes in drug prosecutions.

In a white collar case, a prosecutor wants squeaky clean witnesses, not drug addicts who arrived at the office each morning and starting "using." The jury is going to have a difficult time accepting Levine's testimony as a basis to convict Rezko, never mind what Assistant U. S. Attorneys say.

At the end of the day, when jurors went home Thursday (I don't believe they are sequestered even though there is secrecy about their identities) many of them must have asked, "Is this all there is?" Clearly, the government did not put on a strong opening against Rezko.

Rezko could still be convicted. Innocent people are convicted of trumped up charges every day.

But Rezko has one ace to play against the government's jokers. The State of Illinois itself. One of the ironies of the case is that Republicans are as dirty as Democrats. The evidence in Rezko's case does not reflect a Democrat-thing or a Republican-thing. Both parties are all mired in the same thievery, corruption and conflicts of interest. Here in Illinois we call these bipartisan pirates "the Combine." Rezko's defense will be he was engaging in routine Illinois politics, not criminal activity.

And although I am still somewhat confused by what money went where, and why, at the end of the day Rezko is going to appear to be acting as the agent of "Public Official A," i.e. Governor Blagojevich. Juries develop a collective sense of fairness. In a case where the government's witnesses are sleazy and bargained for leniency, and where the "big enchilada" is not a defendant sitting in the dock alongside his minions, juries have a harder time convicting the underlings. Which is why I feel Rezko could very well walk.

All of which brings me full-circle to where I started. Something tells me this case was "brought before it's time." The case is not fully formed; the evidence is not as strong as it should be. Rezko is a big fish, but he is not *the* big fish.

Finally, if I may be indulged to repeat some comments I have previously made, the worst blow for Obama is that whichever way the numbers are crunched in the Rezko trial or outside the Rezko courtroom, it is now clear that Barack and Michelle Obama bought their "dream home" in Kenwood with money indirectly provided by an Iraqi wheeler-dealer.

The ultimate twist of fate: Obama brags about opposing the war, then has his own home partially financed by someone who was, depending on whom you believe, a Saddam Hussein stooge or a Saddam victim. Either way, an Iraqi appears to have helped finance the purchase of the Obama "compound" in Chicago. Yekkkh.

Obama's defense will be (here it is!) "I didn't know." But people are finally waking up to the fact that there are a lot of things Barack Obama "doesn't know" these days.

My colleague John Kass calls all of this corruption "the Chicago Way." Indeed it is. For myself, I am much more sympathetic to the victims of the national press who are finally beginning to see Obama's puss ooze to the surface. To them I say, "Welcome to Chicago. Welcome to the real Obama." And, sadly, "Welcome to Illinois."

Public officials here still do things the old fashioned way. They steal. They lie. They take favors and give favors. They don't ask no stinkin' questions about where the money is coming from in a complicated real estate transaction. And when they get caught, they say "I don't know." Welcome to Barack Obama's Chicago.

Chicago's Mayor Richard Daley is the true master of the Chicago Way. Given how gullible the media are, maybe Daley, not Obama, should be running for president. At least people would be under no illusions about what they were getting in a candidate.

Welcome to Chicago. And, oh, "Book'em Danno."

CHAPTER SIX

Barack Obama and the Ticking Time Bomb:
The Illinois Legislature and the Blackwell Tax Fraud

I.

THE ILLINOIS LEGISLATURE: A CESSPOOL OF CORRUPTION

This author first went to observe the Illinois legislature in 1965, 43 years ago. The Illinois General Assembly was a cesspool of bipartisan corruption. Little has changed in nearly half a century. Today, Chicago Tribune columnist John Kass talks of a bipartisan "Combine" and bipartisan corruption and influence peddling as "the Chicago Way." (www.chicagotribune.com/news/columnists/chi-kass_bd11may11, 0,4134722.column; http://time-blog.com/real_clear_politics/2008/03/the_chicago_way.html, www.chicagotribune.com/news/opinion/chi-kass-06jun05,0,6175303.column)

Ironically, the 1965 session of the General Assembly was perhaps the most reforming session before or since. The 1964 "bed sheet ballot" in which the entire General Assembly ran at-large (statewide without any individual member districts) had brought in a handful of genuine reformers.

Among the leaders of the small reform block in the legislature, sometimes affectionately known as the "Kosher Nostra" because of its multi-ethic composition, was the very talented and very principled Abner J. Mikva. During our years in Springfield and in his early congressional career I got to know Mikva well.

Mikva was a reformer. He stood up and bravely fought against the overwhelming power of the First Daley Machine. Mikva paid dearly and often for his bravery and independence; the Machine was constantly undermining him and trying to destroy him politically.

It was only when the Machine slated Adlai Stevenson, III for the statewide bed sheet ballot in 1964, and Adlai arrived in Springfield in 1965, fresh and new as the offspring of a Democratic Party icon, that the reform forces had any publicity ammunition with which to fight the Mayor (Daley I) of Chicago.

II.
OBAMA: THE ILLINOIS STATE SENATE "REFORMER"

Why is Abner Mikva critical to understanding Barack Obama? Two reasons. First, Mikva was a genuine reformer. Mikva knew that there was a price to be paid for political corruption and fighting corruption.

Barack Obama, on the other hand, has never been a reformer and has never paid any price whatsoever for fighting the Chicago Democratic Machine. Obama may have occasionally taken on a "reform" project, such as taping police interrogations, but his "reforms" had more to do with confronting mossback Republicans than riling up Chicago Democrats. Obama's "reforms" never challenged the cathedral of corruption in Chicago, the Mayor's office. Quite the contrary, Obama has always been clear that, unlike Mikva two generations earlier, Obama enjoys cordial relations with the mayor, his staff and the rest of the Machine in Chicago and Springfield.

And so we must face the inevitable: Obama's imaginary career as a reformer exists in his imagination. He never fought the endemic corruption in the Illinois legislature. While trying to appear as a sleek and modern version of an "independent," Obama's public paper-maché persona was crafted for the Chicago media. He took on "reform" issues that were non-controversial either in the Democratic Party or the local media. Obama was very comfortable operating in the political sewers of Chicago and Springfield.

Obama was no Abner J. Mikva.

The second reason Mikva is important is that today Mikva is prominently identified as a lifelong sponsor and current supporter of Barack Obama. The reform movement in Chicago and the Illinois legislature is dead. There are no Abner J. Mikvas in Springfield today. And even while Ab Mikva is still alive, his political legacy is dead. He is backing the Daley Machine candidate for president—Obama.

III.
EMIL JONES, JR. AND OBAMA

The Democratic Party's leader in the Illinois State Senate during Obama's eight years there was Emil Jones, Jr., a man who moves comfortably in the cesspools of Illinois corruption. (www.ilga.gov/senate/Senator.asp?MemberID=990)

When he is not acting as an errand boy in Springfield for Chicago's Richard Daley II, Jones spends his waking hours trying to find public employment for his friends and relatives. Mulcting the taxpayers is the reason for Jones' existence.

As he has done constantly throughout his life, seeking powerful mentors and sponsors, Obama sought out Jones as a political father and attached himself to the senate leader as an acolyte.

Jones in turn assigned Obama to handle legislation that may have had a tint of reform but that was considered non-controversial by the Chicago Machine and City Hall.

In sum and substance, Obama never challenged the mayor, never challenged the senate leader, never challenged the Machine, never challenged anyone or anything of critical importance to his political future.

As Obama is still doing in 2008, during his Springfield years he spoke about "reform" in lofty rhetorical tones in public, while swimming in the mundane sewers of Illinois' political process. A reformer, he wasn't and ain't. As always Barry Obama was out for Barry Obama and no one else. He was perfectly happy to make a pact with the devils of Illinois politics. He has shown the same willingness on the national scene.

IV.
THE TICKING TIME BOMB OF ROBERT BLACKWELL, JR.

The Robert Blackwell, Jr. issue originally exploded during the firestorm about Obama's preacher, Reverend Jeremiah Wright. Unfortunately, Wright completely overshadowed the Blackwell corruption caper. The national media appear to have ignored the Blackwell scandal, and moved on.

The Chicago Sun-Times does not appear to have mentioned this conflict of interest. The Chicago Tribune relied on a story originated by a reporter who was formerly of Chicago but now writes for the Los Angeles Times, another Tribune Company paper: www.latimes.com/news/nationworld/nation/la-na-killer-spin27apr27,0,6789688.story.

The Tribune has the L. A. Times story on the Tribune's web site (ChicagoTribune.com) but Chuck Neubauer's disclosures never made their way into the printed version of the Chicago paper.

If everyone is ignoring the Blackwell scandal, why do I think the matter is a "smoking gun" or "ticking time bomb?" Why do I view the matter differently? Perhaps it is because the media that have discussed the Obama-Blackwell connection have looked at the issue as a question of whether providing "ping pong" funds from state taxpayers to an Obama contributor was a potential conflict of interest, not as a money laundering scheme involving Obama and Blackwell.

I see the internal machinations of Blackwell's payments to Obama as an intentional act of corruption and criminality.

The Robert Blackwell, Jr. affair personally links Obama to a form of political money laundering, and appears to link him directly and personally to political or personal payola and tax fraud.

Here is what Chuck Neubauer of the Los Angeles Times wrote:

1. Obama faced "serious financial pressure: numerous debts, limited cash and a law practice he had neglected…"
2. In "'The Audacity of Hope,' Obama tells how his finances had deteriorated…(a neglect that had left me more or less broke)."
3. "Six months later, Blackwell hired Obama to serve as general counsel for his tech company, EKI, …"

4. "Blackwell said 'Barack worked extensive hours advising the company on compliance and human resource issues,' negotiated contracts, reviewed confidentiality agreements and provided reports on topics requested by the company's senior management."

5. "The monthly retainer paid by EKI was sent to the law firm that Obama was affiliated with at the time..."

6. "On [Illinois state financial] disclosure forms for 2001 and 2002, Obama did not specify that EKI provided him with the bulk of his private-sector compensation..." He attached "a multiple-page list...of hundreds of other firm clients."

What does this entire legerdemain mean? Why do I believe the transactions are suspicious, and probably criminal:

1. EKI never announced that it had hired a prominent state senator to serve as general counsel, normally a full-time role, and there is no public record of Obama ever having had any role at EKI.

2. Until Neubauer's article appeared, no one had heard of Obama acting as a virtually full-time employee and "general counsel" for Blackwell and EKI. Both by the nature of the role itself, and by Blackwell's explanations of what Obama did, a general counsel's slot was a full-time job.

3. Obama's law firm had no role in any of EKI's legal business. The use of the laundry list of the firm's clients was an attempt to conceal and deceive. Although Neubauer says that "Illinois law does not require more specific disclosure," that turns the state statute on its head. The law requires **disclosure,** not concealment.

Obama was not disclosing. He was concealing. He had an intent to conceal and deceive, which amounts to a federal crime. Illinois law did not say a legislator can provide a list of hundreds of names of irrelevant "clients" with whom the legislator has absolutely no connection, merely to insert one name with which the legislator had a surreptitious relationship.

4. While the fleeting online and media reports focused on the ping-pong potential conflict, no one addressed or apparently recognized the issues of fraudulent concealment.

5. More critically, Blackwell appears to have used Obama's law license to pay a political contribution that he then deducted for tax purposes on Blackwell's firm's finances. If, as appears to be the case, Blackwell knew that Obama was not providing actual legal services, and yet paid him a "retainer" which he then deducted, both Obama and Blackwell were involved in federal criminal tax fraud and conspiracy.

6. Until the Blackwell deal surfaced in April, 2008, Obama had apparently never listed his role as "general counsel" to EKI on any political résumés or databases. Is it believable that he served as a full-time legal counsel to a start-up corporation and never mentioned that fact in his 2004 U.S. Senate campaign? Would Obama, who Al Gore-style often takes credit for things he has not done, have passed up an opportunity to take credit for something he had done, serving as a general counsel of a corporation? Who could believe that he didn't? After The L.A. Times story ran, Blackwell was removed from Obama's list of bundlers. www.buyingofthepresident.org/index.php/stories/obamas_rainmakers

Blackwell remains a major democratic contributor. (www.campaignmoney.com/political/contributions/rober t-blackwell.asp?cycle=08)

7. The element of criminal **scienter**, or knowledge and intent, is furnished by the admitted evidence of Obama's intent to conceal and deceive, the use of a laundry list of hundreds of irrelevant "clients" to disguise the reality of only one client that was paying him a large sum of money for nonexistent legal services. In short, State Senator Barack Obama was a crook—and he knew it.

And this man wants to be president?

Barack Obama Caught in
Crooked Money Laundering Scheme

Andy Martin says "retainer" by Robert Blackwell, Jr. was classic Illinois "pay to play" and may have been criminal behavior

In Illinois, even the good guys [Cynthia Canary] can be corrupted

What "legal work" did Obama do to earn over $100,000 from a minority contractor?

"Smoking gun" prompts Andy Martin to say Obama should withdraw as presidential candidate

(NEW YORK)(April 27, 2008) The disclosure today in the Los Angeles Times that Barack Obama laundered money through a law firm to conceal the source of his income while an Illinois state senator is the "smoking gun" that is going to doom his candidacy. (http://www.latimes.com/news/nationworld/nation /la-na-killerspin27apr27,0,6789688.story)

Barack Obama should withdraw as a presidential candidate. Immediately. The latest evidence of his professional corruption is going to doom the Democratic Party.

Although the L. A. Times' reporters have tried to present Obama's crooked deal in a fair and balanced way, there is no way you can avoid the conclusion that the substance of the transaction was intended to conceal that Obama was engaging in political money laundering to disguise the source of his income. Obama is exposed as just another corrupt African-

American legislator in Illinois cutting deals for other African-Americans. Is it any wonder he became the protégé of sleazy Senator Emil Jones in the Illinois senate?

Why was Obama's Blackwell deal "money laundering?" The L. A. Times story is not clear on that point. Laundering was involved because Obama used "disclosure" to conceal the source of his income while a public official. Obama's game also exposes that in Illinois even good government types, such as Cynthia Canary, can be corrupted. Canary tries to whitewash something that she would strongly condemn if the practice had been engaged in by any other legislator. In other words, Obama has even managed to corrupt Canary and the integrity of her organization. It's disgusting.

Obama's "client," Robert Blackwell, Jr. was also an operative in the machinations of crooked Illinois governor Rod Blagojevich. (http://www.eki-consulting.com/APPS/EKIHP1 .nsf/Content/BE14CC6D3CE4025586256D030075A471?OpenD ocument)

The Times details how Obama was still "of counsel" to his former law firm, but that he was not providing any services to that entity. Then Obama made a deal with Blackwell, and wanted to conceal that Blackwell was supporting him. So Obama "laundered" the "legal fees" by running them through the law firm and then issuing a list of the law firm's clients-none of which had anything to do with Obama—to disguise the Blackwell money in a laundry list of hundreds of unrelated "clients." This was a classic case of money laundering and business fraud. Obama wanted to conceal the large sum he was receiving from Blackwell, so he concealed that Blackwell was the source of his income by pretending he was providing services to the law firm's other clients. Utter fraud. "Barry O" ain't stupid, he's slicky and tricky, and he's a ticking time bomb for the Democratic Party.

Since the law firm had nothing to do with Blackwell, and was merely acting as a conduit for legal fees for Obama, this example shows that Obama was nothing but just another crooked Illinois politician.

Obama's "law firm" was also guilty of professional misconduct, because the lawyers knew that Obama had not provided services through the law firm, and was merely using the firm to obscure the fact that the major source of his personal income was one client on whose behalf Obama was later to advocate (there may have been earlier informal advocacy than the senate letter which has surfaced).

Time and time again, Obama's law firm stands guilty of being exposed for sleazy professional tactics and gross conflicts of interest. Obama's law firm was nothing more than a college of corruption for money laundering, conflicts of interests and other inappropriate professional behavior; and a collection of crooked lawyers that were stealing and concealing at every opportunity. Is it any wonder that honest lawyers get a bad name when crooked operatives such as Obama play games and use the law to conceal the source of their income?

Since the law firm had no relationship with Blackwell, running Obama's fees through the firm was false and fraudulent. Since Obama had nothing to do with the law firm's other clients, using a list of hundreds of unrelated clients to obscure that only one of those "clients" was paying him money was federal criminal mail fraud as well as a corruption of the ethics rules in Illinois. That Cynthia Canary tries to whitewash such blatant corruption shows that she has lost all sense of ethics and legitimacy when Obama is the one stealing the money. What's her link?

Finally, the L. A. Times article leaves unanswered the big question: **what legal work did Obama do to earn $112,000?** He has never disclosed that he was working half-time for Blackwell, and there is no paper trail or track record of Obama having ever done any legal services to earn such a substantial sum. Before today, no one knew of the massive Blackwell-Obama connection. So where is the evidence of providing legal services to earn the money? I am going to be asking for an FBI investigation later this week.

Barry "Barack" Obama: just one more crooked Illinois politician. He's a disgrace to the good, honest hard working people of Illinois.

Four years ago I disclosed that Obama was a fraud artist. I didn't know at the time just how true my conclusions were, or how expansive and extensive Obama's corruption really was. A big thanks to the L. A. Times for providing the "smoking gun" to document just how utterly sleazy Barack Obama has been in his professional life.

Obama should immediately withdraw as a presidential candidate. The "honest graft" that Obama engineered with Robert Blackwell, Jr. is going to doom the Democratic Party in November. Any delegate, pledged, super or otherwise, who supports Obama for president after disclosure of the Barnhill/Blackwell caper, has a death wish for the Democrats in November.

[Note: this column has focused on the crass political corruption Obama engineered to conceal the source of his income, and the way "good government" types such as Cynthia Canary are providing "cover" for Obama's corruption. The fact that Obama used his senate letterhead to gain money for his client is just one more angle of the same slimy story. Using his senate office for his client is self-evident; the use of a professional firm to launder and conceal that his major source of income was only one person, Blackwell, is not so obvious, which is why this column has concentrated on that aspect of the L. A. Times' revelations. The "senate letterhead" aspects, however, are no less important for what they reveal about Obama's "play to play" operations in Illinois politics.] Obama was just an African-American Tony Rezko. Is it any wonder the two were so close for decades?]

And is it any wonder that Barack Obama is now afraid to debate, given the latest sleaze cascading out of his past?

Chicago Tribune Downplays Obama Scandal over Money Laundering at Law Firm

Andy Martin says "smoking gun" nowhere to be found on front pages of Tribune's Web site, despite the fact story originated within the Tribune company

Media criticism from Chicago's #1 media analyst and critic

(NEW YORK)(April 27, 2008) Out of curiosity, I went looking for former Sun-Times and now L. A. Times reporter Chuck Neubauer's explosive story today exposing Barack Obama's money laundering when he was a state senator. (http://www.latimes.com/news/nationworld/nation/la-na-killerspin27apr27,0,6789688.story)

This afternoon I did my own extensive analysis of the significance of Neubauer's revelations. (http://www.contrariancommentary.blogspot.com/)

My emphasis was slightly different than Neubauer's, because I focused on the corruption aspects of Obama's behavior, rather than the suspected influence peddling that was the focus of the Times' report.

The story obviously originated within the Tribune Company and should have been front-page news in Chicago. It is a major piece of investigative writing in the midst of a campaign that has been hungry for some markers on Obama's political past.

Coming a week before the Indiana/North Carolina primaries, Neubauer's disclosures could/should stick a fork in Obama's campaign.

How could the Tribune ignore the story? I did find the report by using the search engine at ChicagoTribune.com, so the story is technically available. But because I am out of Chicago this weekend I can't check the hard copy of the newspaper. I doubt Neubauer's expose made it into the paper itself.

I have been critical of both Chicago dailies for forfeiting leadership in the exposure of Obama's sordid political past. As near as I can tell, Chuck is no longer based in Chicago. So someone appears to have tipped him on the Blackwell/Obama connection.

In the past my Lilliputian web site has repeatedly scooped all media in the city on the Obama/Rezko story. Why? Is Chicago such an ego-challenged city that major media feel a need to act as shameless boosters? And cover up the damaging truth about a hometown candidate for national office? The Obama cover-up has been embarrassing, disgusting, déclassé.

I'd love to hear your reactions.

And, who's going to scoop the Tribune and Sun-Times next? The New York Post? Or the Idaho Statesman?

When is Obama going to disclose what "services" he provided and performed to earn $112,000? There is no evidence or paper trail of him ever doing anything to earn such a massive amount of cash. Did "Black rage" make him hide the cash in plain sight? What's the excuse this time?

Are the Tribune and Sun-Times working on that aspect of the story? Or are they going to let me break the news for them?

Stay tuned. This one is big, big, big. And it is going to get bigger and bigger.

CHAPTER SEVEN

Obama in the United States Senate

This is a mercifully brief chapter. Obama has done very little but run for president since he entered the U. S. Senate.

During the 2008 primaries his opponents said that Obama was Chairman of a Senate Subcommittee with jurisdiction over Afghanistan. How is it then he had never convened a hearing of the subcommittee. (http://foreign.senate.gov/subcommittee.html)

Obama has accomplished nothing noteworthy in the U.S. Senate.

CHAPTER EIGHT

The Primary Election Campaign

I.
HE WON THE NOMINATION

I don't know if Barack Obama is one of the world's great managers, or if he attracted some of the world's best handlers, but history will record that he won the 2008 Democratic Party presidential nomination. Whatever happens in November 2008 his primary victory has changed American politics forever. He must be credited with that awesome upset victory.

Whether we dislike Obama or admire him as a person, the manner in which he defeated an overwhelming favorite in Senator Hillary Clinton will be studied by aspiring candidates and campaign managers for many years to come.

Hillary Clinton's collapse will also be remembered in the history books. Some may attribute her loss to sexual discrimination; but while she began as the favorite she failed to capitalize on her overwhelming lead.

Obama ambushed Clinton, and then held on to win the nomination by a narrow margin.

Calculating once again, Clinton decided not to take her campaign "to the convention" and withdrew in early June. No doubt she hopes to rise again. But whether her current support for Obama will ultimately help her long-term political prospects remains an open question.

It is difficult to believe that a candidate who raised tens of millions of dollars, and then hundreds of millions of dollars, as Clinton did, could be caught napping. But the Clinton "machine" failed to appreciate the appeal of Obama's promise to "change" America.

Clinton made one fatal mistake. She made many mistakes, of course, but one was fatal. She tried to run as a general election candidate before she had won the nomination.

It is a truism that activists and true believers dominate both parties and certainly dominate primaries and caucuses. The Republican Party's primary electorate is considerably more conservative than the general electorate, and the Democratic Party's primary participants are equally out of the American mainstream. Candidates are expected to win the nomination of their parties and then "move towards the center."

Clinton's fatal mistake was to move towards the center before she had won the nomination, leaving a glaring gap that Obama was able to exploit.

It was Clinton's flawed frame of reference that led to her defeat. She persisted in running as a front-runner long after she no longer held that position. Once she awakened to the threat posed by Obama she fought valiantly and successfully. By then it was too late.

Because of the undemocratic delegate selection procedures of the Democratic Party, which assign delegates on a complicated proportional allocation basis, Obama collected a lead in delegates during the early contests where Clinton's votes were diluted by a large cast of other candidates. Clinton was never able to recover from Obama's early lead.

Her failed strategy was also evident in the way she dealt with the Iraq War. Indeed it was in dealing with Iraq, and Clinton's defense of her vote for the Iraq war, that Obama proved his mastery of the primary battlefield.

Clinton had voted for the war. She was reluctant to apologize for her vote. She hemmed and hawed. She hedged. She rope-a-doped. She knew the war remained unpopular with many voters, including particularly the Democratic Party's "base," but she also recognized the war was popular with some voters who could be crucial in November. She watched as the "surge" in Iraq that Senator John McCain supported became increasingly more successful. And as the surge succeeded, Iraq receded as a campaign issue. Clinton held her fire. Until her "apology" was too little and too late.

Obama saw an opening in the weakness of Clinton's Iraq posturing; he played the opportunity which she provided with masterful direction and discipline.

First, although Obama was "against" the war in Iraq in 2002, he has always lied about the manner in which his opposition unfolded. He has pretended he was a "senate candidate" who courageously spoke against invading Iraq. This is a complete fantasy and sheer disinformation. In reality, he was still a state senator, and he was not yet a candidate for the United States Senate in 2002.

Second, Obama has sought to create the myth that he risked political retaliation when he spoke against invading Iraq. There was no risk for him in opposing an attack on Iraq. He represented an ultra-liberal state senatorial district, and opposition to the Bush administration's war policies was overwhelming in Hyde Park, Chicago. Thus, Obama was not, as he has falsely portrayed himself, a candidate for national office who was out ahead of other members of his party. He was a local pol running in a local race from a very liberal district that made a speech at no political cost to himself. On the contrary, he could have lost votes in his state senate district if he had supported the Iraq invasion.

Beginning in 2007, Obama flayed Hillary Clinton for her support and vote for attacking Iraq, despite the fact that he was an "opponent" who had never voted on the issue and who had only opposed the war from the safe perch of a local Illinois office. After entering the U. S. Senate in 2005 Obama voted in favor of appropriations for Iraq. It was not until the 2008 primaries loomed that Obama began to toughen his stand against a continued presence in Iraq.

Nevertheless, Obama played the Iraq card skillfully, and it served to confuse and disrupt and ultimately delay Clinton's defensive strategy. The critical "lost step" that Clinton forfeited through her "triangulation" on Iraq in 2002 by supporting an invasion, cost her precious momentum that she never recovered in 2007-2008.

II.
OBAMA BRINGS A NEW CAST OF CHARACTERS TO THE PRESIDENTIAL STAGE

Obama's victory over Clinton was not an easy one. Initially, Clinton fumbled. Obama gained momentum. He was glib, she was flustering.

Clinton also suffered because the large field of Democratic presidential candidates diluted her strength and her overwhelming resources in the early (2007) debates and in the first caucuses and primaries of 2008. Clinton could not play to her strengths in a cast of eight "presidential candidates."

During the early debates, the leading Democrats were put under pressure to buy votes with more and more extreme and unrealistic promises, competing with opponents who had no prospect of wining the nomination. Clinton sought to avoid buying support with proposals that she knew could bite back to hurt her during the fall election.

Once the Democrats' presidential choices narrowed to Clinton and Obama, she began to win, and win big. But it was too late. The passage of time and the Democrats' rigged delegate selection procedures handicapped her campaign to the day of her withdrawal.

Clinton never learned to go negative, and to challenge and confront Obama's strange association and affiliations in Chicago.

The Reverend Jeremiah Wright was the first to appear on the stage. Credit must be given to Sean Hannity of Fox News for constantly hammering away at Reverend Wright.

Obama initially defended Wright, and then jettisoned him. Wright has faded from the headlines, but he saddled Obama with a heavy burden going into the general election. Obama sat in the pews of Trinity United Church of Christ for twenty years, while anti-White rhetoric was routine, while anti-Americanism was virtually part of the liturgy, and where an Afro-centric theology spoke more of rage than reconciliation.

During the spring of 2008 Obama's close ties and flirtation with the Nation of Islam gained prominence. Obama's church had praised NOI leader Louis Farrakhan. Once again, the links between Obama, Farrakhan and Wright surfaced slowly. The connections only came to public attention grudgingly, with the mainstream media reluctant to provide any information.

As the controversy over Wright and Farrakhan began to recede, Catholic Priest Father Michael Pfleger surfaced with an incredibly bizarre attack on Senator Clinton. Pfleger was a vociferous advocate of rebellion against the establishment and a well-known Chicago character. The priest gained immediate national prominence and equally immediate condemnation for his remarks.

Once again Obama was forced to jettison an old friend and confidante. After having sent Father Pfleger to Iowa to speak on Obama's behalf, Obama was forced to disassociate himself from Pfleger. Obama also used the opportunity of the Pfleger controversy to resign from Obama's own church where Pfleger had delivered his outrageous remarks as a visiting pastor.

In the midst of Obama's theological travails over Reverend Wright and Trinity Church, Obama was hit by a bomb, almost literally, when the man I call the "mad bomber," William Ayers, surfaced as an issue. Again Sean Hannity of Fox News was a catalyst. And once again the mainstream media began a campaign of disinformation and damage control on Obama's behalf.

The first damage control was to publicize Obama's absurd response to the Ayers connection by showing pictures of Obama on a tricycle when Ayers was bombing buildings in the 1960's. No one suggested that Obama had been a confederate of Ayers in the 60's and 70's. It was Ayers' current views in 2008 that were critical, as well as his longstanding ties to Obama. Yet Ayers' attitudes were quickly passed over by the national media. Obama has been a confidant of Ayers since the 1990's. That relationship has never been explored by the national media.

The media inquisitors who did inquire into Obama's peculiar cast of associates in a national debate, ABC News' George Stephanopoulos and Charles Gibson, were trashed by mainstream competitors. But the damage had been done to Obama.

The ABC News debate gathered more viewers than any prior confrontation between the candidates.

The national media tried to ignore and then minimize Obama's close connections to Ayers in the 1990's Annenberg Foundation funding relationship. Ayers had established Obama as his front man while Ayers orchestrated the Annenberg funding behind the scenes. Only ContrarianCommentary.com exposed the significance of that relationship. The Annenberg/Ayers/Obama linkage remains a time bomb waiting to explode during the general election campaign.

Clinton was able to capitalize on some of Obama's lapses later in the primary season. His remarks at a closed fund raising meeting in San Francisco, where he told listeners that rural voters were clinging to religion and guns as a form of suppressed racism and intolerance, helped to fuel her comeback. She tried to exploit the Ayers connection, but Obama parried her efforts.

Nevertheless, as Clinton fired away at Obama, and as he increasingly allowed himself to be portrayed as an out-of-touch liberal, the so-called "Chablis and brie" contingent of the Democratic Party, Obama kept losing primaries.

The close of the primary season in early June 2008 left Obama looking weak, out of touch and rejected by mainstream voters, especially working class white voters. Obama had created a money machine that raised over $200 million. He had defeated Clinton in early contests, and hung on by his finger tips to gain a narrow victory in June. But he was beginning to lose his image of invincibility and inevitability.

Obama himself expressed fears that the "Republican attack machine" would soon be attacking him. At least he won't be able to claim he was "surprised" when the attacks come.

Wright, Ayers, Farrakhan and Ayers may have stepped off the stage temporarily. But they are surely going to return. They may not come back to prime time. But on the Internet, where Obama is most vulnerable, his long time associates will no doubt be given one more starring role in the fall presidential campaign.

Barack Hussein Obama Plays the Race Card: Early and Often

African-American "Chauncey Gardner" runs for president

"Obamatics" spectacle continues to amuse and abuse

(CHICAGO)(December 12, 2006) Barack Hussein Obama went to New Hampshire last weekend. The media scrum followed. But I went back to my library, to retrieve a dusty copy of the classic novel Being There by Jerzy Kosinski.

Being There's protagonist, Chauncey Gardner, is a one of the great characters in modern fiction. He is a simpleton who utters banalities that are taken as profundities by the media. Gardner's meteoric rise tracks the same trail traveled by Obama.

Is Obama a simpleton, or just another shrewd con man, working the American people the same way he has worked the system in the past? Is "Obamatics" just the latest snake oil being sold by a racial huckster? Could be. Perhaps reading the Chicago Sun-Times can help us.

Lynn Sweet is a Washington reporter for the Sun-Times. She is a true believer in the Obama crusade. She is the founding mother and unofficial "soccer mom" of Obama's rise to media imperviousness. But sometimes true believers have a way of innocently betraying the truth about their charges. Sweet may have done so in New Hampshire.

I read the Chicago Tribune's account of Obama's trip to New Hampshire. Christi Parsons had no mention of Obama *agonistes* as a racial exploiter. Adam Nagourney of the New York Times similarly missed Obama saying "race is a factor."

But Lynn sweet did report Obama playing the race card. Sweet quoted B. Hussein as saying "minority candidates have 'a higher threshold in establishing themselves with voters.'" Well.

That is a laughable claim but a shrewd use of the race card to position Obama for future manipulation of the electoral process.

The truth is exactly the opposite. Obama is being "seriously" considered because he is a racial curiosity. No white man with his tepid professional accomplishments would be considered as a serious candidate for president or showered with the attention Obama receives.

Obama graduated from Harvard Law School and became a "community organizer." Why is it that minority communities are perpetually seen as being in need of "organizers?" Are they perpetually "disorganized?" What did Obama organize?

Obama is a lawyer who probably has never tried a serious lawsuit, and probably would have a hard time drafting an appellate brief. He rose to prominence by exploiting the fact of his abandonment by a father who was also a successful racial huckster. Barack and his wife are attractive ornaments in Chicago's vibrant multicultural society, where many qualified and experienced and competent African-Americans are ignored and obscured by Obama's shadow.

Obama can best be compared to another salesman of "hope," John F. Kennedy, who ran for president in 1960. By then, Kennedy had served 14 years in Congress, not two. He had served in a war and been grievously wounded, not been an "organizer" who never organized anything. Kennedy had experienced life, and near-death. What has Obama experienced? Very little, it seems.

For him to claim that the barriers are higher, that the bar is higher for him to succeed, is nonsense. It is crass racialism. Obama is a product of the very "24-hour…small-minded politics" that he decries. "Barry" Obama? Makes a great speech. Absent the cablemeisters, Obama would be an obscure state senator in Springfield. He is the ultimate product of shrewd marketing and a pliable public, not the opposite.

The New York Times quoted one breathless New Hampshire admirer as saying "I was very impressed with the fact that he wants to bring people together." Betsy Shultis was identified as a "former" state representative. Maybe that's why. She is easily impressed. Has anyone recently run on a platform of trying to separate people? Is the Republican "base" any different in concept than the Democratic "base?" Not really.

Chauncey Gardner is a blood brother to Obama. Platitudes, bunkum, snake oil; Gardner and Obama share a common parent.

Two years ago I pointed out that Obama came from a Muslim family and that he misrepresented the impoverished origins of his father. No one wanted to pay attention to the facts or the truth. Except me. On December 5th Sweet wrote that Obama was not hiding his middle name, "Hussein," or his father's religion. Obama may not have hidden it, but the media did. They didn't want to bore voters with the facts about Mr. Obama.

Much has been made of Keith Ellison, the first Muslim elected to the U. S. House last month. Obama would be the first lapsed Muslim to run for president.

Of course Obama only plays the "dad" card when it serves him. No mention of dad's religion or the Hussein family name when the klieg lights are on. (Ellison, by the way, is a convert to Islam, just as Obama is a convert to Christianity. Or does Obama have his "white" relatives to thank for that?)

There was an orgy of media attention when Obama went to Kenya last summer. But, funny, I don't seem to remember a similar orgy when Obama made a visit to his mother's home town. He probably hasn't been there recently. Only Dorothy wants to return to Kansas.

When Obama visited New York last week, Cindy Adams wrote that his movements were as tightly controlled as those of a president. "Retail politics in New Hampshire?" Obama is the most closely scripted and controlled person in the media spotlight today. He is about as "retail" as the gold vault at Fort Knox.

Don't get me wrong. Americans are justifiably hungry to consider a qualified African-American candidate for president. Richard Parsons of Time-Warner comes to mind. Heard of him? Probably not. I thought so. Parson's qualified.

But Barack/Barry seems to have fooled New Hampshire. Don't let him fool you. Unless, of course, you want to be fooled. Personally, I would rather believe in Santa Claus or Rudolph the Red-Nosed Reindeer than Barack Hussein Obama.

In short, Obama is media construct who will disappoint a lot of people when the truth comes out. In 2004, Contrarian Commentary had it first. In 2006, we are still leading the pack, courtesy of truthful reporting by Lynn Sweet and the Chicago Sun-Times. Keep reading, and please don't be a true believer unless and until you know the truth about Obama.

Chauncey Gardner for president! Vote hope! And as we say in Chicago, "vote early and often!"

Barack Obama is "The Candidate"

Obama blasts the system that created him, bites the hand that feeds him

Hypocrite takes first steps towards presidential campaign

(CHICAGO)(January 16, 2007) In the 1960's I had a lady friend who loved Robert Redford. So, naturally, I got dragged to all of Redford's movies. I saw "The Candidate" several times.

In that film, Mr. McKay (Redford), a "community organizer" like Barack Obama, hatches a slogan, "McKay, The Better Way" to run for office. Ironically, Barack "Barry" Obama has now chosen "The Better Way" as his mantra through February 10th. Well. Obama's slogan has about as much substance as the celluloid version popularized by Robert Redford.

Obama is entirely a creation of wealthy contributors and powerful, liberal media interests. So what he does he do? He attacks the hands that created him, and bites the hands that feed him. So much for gratitude.

Obama says that he was once a "community organizer." What did he organize? I thought he was a "law professor." Or at least an adjunct professor such as myself. What cases did he win? Obama is entirely a creation of liberal media and fantasies. He has no experience; his entire career has been a complete mirage, advanced by affirmative action and a conscious avoidance by society of his lack of substantial professional accomplishments.

Other than traveling to Kenya to visit distant relatives related to the father who abandoned him, what does Obama know of the world? Is he the man best qualified to lead us into the uncertain waters of a war against terrorism and a restoration of American prestige in the wake of Iraq? Please.

Other than having a family that has become wealthy feeding off liberal pablum, and milking the "system" for every advantage that a guilt-ridden, affirmative action endorsing society has perpetuated decade after decade, what has he accomplished in any sphere of life? Not much, it seems.

Ironically, Obama has one of the most complex and conflicted psyches of any presidential candidate in recent history. Abandoned both by his mother and father, raised by his white grandparents, whom he keeps locked in the cellar, his personality is so unusual that it could form a basis for a course in psychology. We do not need another conflicted psyche in the White House. I'll know Obama is serious about life and leadership when he appears in public with his white grandmother and features her on the dais. Instead of hiding her in the cellar. Obama is clearly uncomfortable presenting his white relatives to the public. What a way to treat Grandma.

Obama attacks big money in politics. But who has been fueling his career for the past two years? Billionaires such as Warren Buffet. How can someone who is the product of "money and influence" run against the hands of "money and influence" that are fueling his own campaign? It makes no sense.

Talk about big money? What about Tony Rezko? Obama is linked to the sleaziest and most corrupt elements in Illinois politics. He says he made a "mistake" in dealing with Rezko. He didn't make any mistake. He new exactly what he was doing and he knew exactly who Tony Rezko was when they engaged in structured real estate deals together. It was "honest graft," very possibly a criminal offense.

Then Obama lied. He said he had not afforded Rezko any access. Subsequently, a Rezko-recommended intern popped up in Obama's office. Another "mistake?" Not really; the son of Joseph Armanda is the G. David Schine of 2008.

Of course, if you believe Obama's excuse and explanation about Rezko then Obama is an incompetent nincompoop. Obama says that while serving as a U. S. Senator he didn't really know who his partner was in a million-dollar-plus real estate transaction. He saw no appearance of impropriety. You want a jerk like that managing the U.S. economy?

Obama is no more grassroots at the national level than Hillary Clinton.

In the past few days Obama has been sashaying around the issue of cutting off funds for Iraq. The liberal left in the Democratic Party wants to turn off Bush's financial spigot. Obama is tap dancing around that one. He won't come out and say where he stands. He was hiding in the senate cellar last year when tough issues were being debated.

Frankly, he and Hillary make a nice pair. You can't get a straight answer out of either one. Which is why neither one is likely to end up in the White House. She thinks a whirlwind four-day trip to Iraq qualifies her as an expert. The last president we had who took a whirlwind trip to the Middle East before becoming a candidate was George Bush, and look where he landed us.

Still, I'm glad he's running. For decades now, in the wake of the civil rights revolution, we have had African-Americans belly-aching that they are held back, that government does not serve their needs, that taxpayers should do more. They want today's taxpayers to fund "reparations" for pre-Civil War slavery 150 years ago. Volunteers, anyone?

Where does Obama stand on reparations for slavery? That's a big issue in the Chicago City Council. Does he support or oppose reparations? Can he give us a straight answer?

Ironically, the same seniority system that minorities have castigated has now advanced several A-A's to committee chairmanships in the U. S. House. Let's see what they do.

A couple of weeks ago Obama played the race card and said barriers were higher for him. That's malarkey. No white man with his skimpy resume would be considered a serious candidate for president. It is precisely and only because Obama had a black father than he is even sitting in the senate. White guilt has propelled him into the senate. Let's see if white guilt can propel him out of the senate and into the White House.

Frankly, I wish Obama the best. I wish the best for anyone running for president. Or any public office (including myself). But, as for Obama, I have my doubts whether he has the "right stuff." I see no experience, no qualifications, and no strong inner core. He has shown he can talk the talk, yessiree. But he has never shown he can walk the walk. Barry, start walkin'.

Obama is right about one thing though. The system is "broken." A political system that would produce Obama as an instant candidate for high national office is broken. Seriously broken.

Is "Madrassagate" Really Over?
Maybe Not

Media try to bury legitimate questions about Barack Obama's past

(CHICAGO)(January 24, 2007) Chicago Sun-Times columnist Lynn Sweet politely attempted to end "Madrassagate" with a column yesterday entitled "Barack Attack Unfounded." Sweet's column can be combined with Sun-Times columnist Neil Steinberg's attacks on "crazies" who question Obama, a man who is "so appealing to Americans who are not nuts."

Well, is "Madrassagate" really over? No, not really.

First, the Roman Catholic Church used to have an expression, "Give us a boy until the age of 7 and we have him for life." Childhood impressions and experiences are really important, notwithstanding attempts to suggest Obama was "only 6 years old" when he lived in Jakarta. It was still a highly impressionable age in a very unusual environment.

Second, Obama's past is of particular interest because he has fantasized about and fabricated portions of the "facts" about his early years. It is entirely fair to say that if he distorted or concocted some parts of his autobiography in "Dreams From My Father," he may have concocted others.

Third, CNN is hardly an independent news source for many Americans. I know, CNN likes to bash Fox news, and Fox likes to bash CNN, but the reality is that supporters of each cable channel do not trust information from the other.

Howard Kurtz of the Washington Post appeared on CNN and sought to debunk the Madrassagate story as conservative nonsense. Kurtz complained about the lack of footnotes (attributions) in an article discussing Obama's madrassa experience.

CNN's report on Obama's alleged madrassa years sought to extrapolate backwards, from 2007 back to 1967. It is reasonable to ask what the school was like when Obama was there, not what it is like today. CNN, moreover, added another piece to the puzzle when it disclosed that Obama went to school in a ritzy neighborhood, down the street from the U. S. Ambassador's residence. Perhaps that is why ordinary African-Americans have never cottoned to Obama's pretenses of street smarts. They know he's not one of them, not genuine.

Obama, indeed, with his foreign background, is the John Kerry of the 2008 election. Both men were formed in the rarified environment of privilege and overseas influence.

Jakarta is a critical place for another reason: Obama was separated from his mother at age 10, and left Jakarta never to reside with her again. He was raised thereafter in a life of academic privilege and possibly emotional hunger, by his working class grandparents in Hawaii. Thus, Obama's years in Indonesia were extremely formative for him. It is impossible to comprehend the man today without understanding the feelings and experiences he had while living in Jakarta. Any psychologist could tell you that. Just ask.

Sweet/Steinberg attempt to suggest Obama is being "Swift Boated" by "right-wing" columnists. I have no idea what Hillary Clinton is doing with her campaign for president but I would be very surprised if her minions have not conducted some basic background research on Obama, and checked out the Jakarta years. I am also convinced that Jakarta is one of the keys to unlocking Obama's personality and psyche. As for myself, I hardly qualify as "right-wing" in the eyes of real right wingers; they call me pro-Muslim. But I just try to write accurate commentary.

"Swift boating" attempts to distort the facts. Legitimate research seeks to uncover the facts, and to connect them into a coherent pattern. Sometimes research leads somewhere, sometimes nowhere; that doesn't make it evil or mean-spirited. Since Obama is a modern-day Chauncey Gardner, in the vacuousness of his comments on current affairs, knowing more about his past is extremely helpful.

My guess is that we have not heard the last of Obama's "madrassa" years. Based on my own research, there is potentially more to come. People ignored my initial Obama disclosures in 2004; that research finally came to fruition in 2006. We are still looking. For facts. I am not a swift boat mariner.

Andy Martin Accused of Being
Obama Insight Webzine Exposé Author

Blogo blather for January 29, 2007

(CHICAGO)(January 29, 2007) Andy Martin has received numerous media inquiries concerning whether he is the author of the anonymous Insight magazine article accusing Barack Obama of receiving a Muslim education in Indonesia.

"I have issued a formal denial and I stand by that denial," Martin stated. "In an ethereal sense I am the author, because my research is used in virtually all Obama commentary. But because we rest upon our 'Just the facts, mam'm' standard of accuracy, we do not embellish even if we often focus attention on Obama's own embellishments of his resume.

"We did disclose Barry's Muslim family history and we hope to have more to say about that in the near future during our scheduled 'Obama Week.'

"I don't know why we have been flooded by all of these inquiries inquiring as to my authorship, but there must be someone out there pointing people in my direction."

Los Angeles Times Exposes
Barack Obama as a Fraud

*The man who brought down Obama,
Andy Martin, says "I told you so"*

*It's time for Barry Obama to be held to the standards of a white man;
the White House is no place for affirmative action*

(CHICAGO)(FEBRUARY 20, 2007) Later today we will issue a special analysis on Barack Obama's first week as a national candidate. It won't be a pretty sight. But before the big picture, we address a more focused picture, the larger deeper truth about Barry (Barack) Obama: the man is a complete fraud.

On **August 11, 2004**, while Obama was still a candidate, I held a news conference in which I stated, "The man is a complete fraud. The truth is going to surprise, and disappoint, and outrage many people who were drawn to him… In the meantime, Crown Books should stop selling Obama's novelization of his life." Well. (The news release can easily be located on the Internet, but here's one link: http://www.freerepublic.com/focus/f-news/1189687/posts.)

Earlier this month, during the period leading up to Obama's declaration for the presidency, we continued to question his qualifications for any office, let alone the presidency.

Monday's Los Angeles Times exploded one of the major myths in Obama's memoir, *Dreams From My Father*, that Obama had been the spearhead behind efforts to remove asbestos contamination at Altgeld Gardens on the South Side of Chicago: http://www.latimes.com/news/nationworld/washing-tondc/la-na-obama19feb19,1,7228837.story.

In reality, Obama stole the credit from real community activists and "organizers" and appropriated their efforts as his own. Obama covered the tracks to his burglary of the truth by using fictional characters to replace the "real" people in the Altgeld episode. It is no surprise that Sweet reports today Obama was "worried about a pending potentially negative...story."

Lynn Sweet of the Chicago Sun-Times, who is an unabashed Obama-lover, is also an honest journalist. She too, way back in 2004, questioned Obama's use of fiction as fact, and stated, "It is impossible to know who is real and who is not." (Sun-Times, 2/20/07, see http://www.suntimes.com/news/sweet/264478,CST-NWS-sweet20.article) Indeed, Ms. Sweet, it is not impossible at all. "Obama" is not real. Mr. Obama is a fictional cre-ation of a very talented and very intelligent bunkum artist, Barry (Barack) Obama. From end to end, from start to finish, Barack Obama is an imaginative self-invention.

In 2004, Sweet writes today, Obama could not remember the identity of one of the key characters in his book: "I don't remember what Smitty's real name was. I think it was Wally." He wrote a book about events that had taken place a few years ear-lier, and "forgot" the names of his key characters. So much for Obama's respect for fact checking.

Sweet also says that Obama's campaign staffers had to read his book over the past few days to decipher who the "real peo-ple" in his book were. They couldn't just ask the candidate. He couldn't tell them. And the man wants to be president? Be real.

Let's be brutally honest: If a white man, or a white candidate (Joe Biden, are you listening?) committed a fraud of this magnitude he would be driven out of the presidential race. But the national media ignores Obama's lies as they shamelessly pander to minority pressures. Biden's lies in 1988 (I was there in Iowa when the story broke) are piddling compared to Obama's prevarications. Biden was pilloried, and is still being criticized decades later, and Obama gets a free pass for his lies.

And Obama has the nerve to say he is being held to a "higher" standard as a minority candidate. Rubbish.

It is time for truth telling, as Barry O likes to say, and it is time for him to tell the truth to the American people and withdraw as a candidate. The Oval Office is no place for affirmative action. We need someone who is a real leader, not a self-imagined leader. Real experience, not imaginary experience, is essential. Joe Biden paid the price for a fictional resume in 1998. It is now long past the time when Obama should have been forced off the national political stage, and sent to Hollywood, where his brilliant fictional talents truly lie.

There is no "affirmative action" credit for the White House. There is only one standard, for Black or White. And Obama has embarrassingly fallen short of the minimum standards for our highest office.

As I wrote in 2004, long, long ago, "The truth is going to surprise, and disappoint, and outrage many people who were drawn to him."

Well, what about it Barry? I mean Barack.

[Is it any wonder ContrarianCommentary.com is the fastest growing and most authoritative news and information source for *intelligent* readers worldwide?]

I have previously identified myself in columns as the "man who brought down Obama." He's falling.

Obama Week, Part Two:
Mr. and Mrs. Barack Obama: Profiteering from Poverty

*"Health care" as a vehicle to improve the health of
the Obama family's bank account*

*"Obamacare" means more money for nothing except
Michelle Obama and other poverty parasites*

(CHICAGO)(FEBRUARY 8, 2007) The late Chicago columnist Mike Royko used to say that the motto of the City of Chicago should be "Ubi est mea?" ("Where's mine") to reflect the fact that Chicago was a city quintessentially built on greed, not public service.

Mike Royko, meet Barry and Michelle Obama.

Senator & Mrs. Barack Obama have become wealthy "playing the system" in Chicago, and playing up their own bank balances. Now Barack ("Barry O") wants to be president. In a "bid'em high" contest with Hillary Clinton and John Edwards, Obama proposes free health care for everyone: Obamacare.

It might behoove us to see how the Obama family has become wealthy at the expense of their "community."

Mrs. Michelle Obama is paid a third of a million dollars a year to serve as "Vice President of External Affairs" at the University of Chicago Hospital on the city's South (and poor) Side.

What is it exactly that Michelle Obama does to merit being paid a third of a million dollars every year? Like her erstwhile husband, who claims he came to Chicago to be a "community organizer," and never successfully organized anything but his own personal wealth, Michele Obama essentially does nothing for her cool third-of-a-million. She, too, is also an "organizer."

The reason health care in America is so expensive today is because we have allowed racial and political hucksters such as the Obamas to get rich exploiting poverty and the poor. The Obamas manage to use societal guilt to pyramid their own economic success and self-importance. They are quick to play the race card to improve the balances on their cash card.

Mrs. Obama has a law degree from Harvard. Why would she want to be engaged in superintending "community affairs" when she could practice law? Because "community affairs" is where the money's at, goofy.

Mrs. Obama's salary has gone from approximately $50,000 in 1999 to over $300,000 after her husband was elected senator. What does she do for that money? Well, according to the Chicago Tribune, Mrs. Obama is in charge of "women and minority vendor purchases, rejuvenation of [the hospital's] volunteer program" and a "collaborative effort" with South Side clinics to provide care for low income residents. Three hundred thousand dollars a year for that? Good work if you can get it. And good luck.

If you're sick, do you really need "outreach" to find the nearest hospital? Not really. People know where to do to find emergency treatment, a community clinic, a doctor.

So Mrs. Obama is not saving lives, working in an "ER" or contributing anything positive to the medical environment on the Southside of Chicago. Instead of being a part of the solution, she's part of the problem. If Senator Obama wants to find out why "health care" costs so much today, all he has to do is roll over in bed and talk to his wife. Barry, ask Michelle a few questions, painful as that may be to your bank balance.

Mrs. Obama used to work in a law firm. But at law firms actually have to work to get paid. Nonproductive people are weeded out. In "community service" organizations such as hospitals we have tolerated the creation of bureaucracies of highly paid people such as Mrs. Obama who produce nothing and contribute nothing to health care—except the improved health of their own bank balances.

Again according to the Tribune, the University of Chicago Hospital has approximately 17 "vice presidents" earning in the third-of-a-million-dollar range. What is Obamacare going to be about this kind of payroll padding that inflates health care costs? Add more people, more "community organizers," more Obamas.

Hospitals used to be charitable institutions. Doctors would treat the indigent as well as the wealthy. It was not a perfect system but then we don't live in a perfect world. But then the "poverty pimps" arrived. Or "poverticians" if you prefer. "Poverticians" became part of the medical landscape as part of the civil rights revolution.

Former New York Mayor Ed Koch described poverticians as people who got rich from poverty, people who made fat, easy livings profiteering from racial guilt and community fears of community rebellions. A little mau mau action (ah, those Kenyans again). A little Jesse Jackson give-my-family-and-friends a franchise to get wealthy or we'll shut you down on Thursday action. In short a "reverence" for personal profit instead of community progress. In short, Mayor Koch was describing Michelle Obama.

She contributes nothing to health care except increasing the cost. She collects a third of a million dollars—tripled since

Obama was elected to the U. S. Senate—to "reach out" to people who are desperate for medical attention and supposedly can't find treatment due to the "high cost of health care," due in large part to the fact that "health care" supports people like the Obamas. The health care system is "high cost" is because it supports lavish lifestyles of people such as the Obama family who consume mightily and contribute nothing to the healing process.

So if you are happy to have the Obamas become rich profiteering from poverty, meet Obamacare. Obamacare would deliver "free" health care to the masses. But such treatment is available today. Obamacare would substitute today's admittedly imperfect system for a perfect system of racial and community profiteering. We would have more people earning huge salaries to engage in "outreach" and "community development." Nothing would change in the operating room but everything would change in the operators' living rooms through the addition of more well-paid parasites that did nothing but get rich from doing nothing.

As I constantly like to remind people who are mesmerized by Barack Obama, what did he ever "organize" in Chicago? A strike? Heaven forefend. A successful community movement? Nope. He organized nothing except his own self-advancement. The poor that Obama claims to have organized are still poor and still there where he found them decades ago.

Now there is nothing wrong with wanting to be rich, and succeeding; but please don't tell me you were organizing the community when you were only organizing your own financial enrichment.

I want to be clear that that I am not saying that the Obamas are bad people. On the contrary, they are good people. They seem like a charming couple. But the "Godfather" would understand the financial reality of using race to get rich. The Obamas trained learned law school to use briefcases instead of legal briefs to advance themselves into the realm of the rich and famous.

We all want to achieve the American dream: a fancy home financed in part by someone such as Illinois' sleazy Tony Rezko at taxpayer expense. A job where you show up and collect a cool third-of-a-million for doing nothing and contributing nothing except serving as an ornament to our societal stupidity and guilt. Today, "wealth" is being created by public agencies that bemoan "high costs" while they support 17 " vice presidents" doing nothing.

Obama organized his resume as a "community" worker to catapult himself into Harvard Law School, then "public service' in Chicago. First he padded his resume; then he padded his bank balance. Then his wife padded hers. Ubi est mea. And they say marriage is passé?

Or, as Pogo would say to Barack and Michelle, "We have met reason for high cost health care; and it's the Obama Family."

But don't say, "Physician, health thyself," because the Obamas are lawyers, not doctors. Indeed. The last thing we need in hospitals is more lawyers. But that's what "Obamacare" would provide. And Obamacare has already provided well for the Obama family.

Mr. Royko, "Ubi Est Mea" it is. And Mr. Obama and Mrs. Obama have found their "mea" getting rich off the poor. Nice work if you can get it. Code Blue anyone?

Obama Week, Part One:
Why Obama is Winning and America is Losing

America's new pied piper of politics
The man from hype, not hope

(CHICAGO)(FEBRUARY 7, 2007) U. S. Senator Barack ("Barry O") Obama wants to be President of the United States. Well, why not? Or as the TV pitchman used to say, "Whyyyyyy not!"

I don't Bear Mr. Obama any ill will. As a slightly demented friend in New York used to say, "everyone has to have a scam." And Obama's scam is the presence of nothing at all except himself. Nothingness. He is the Camus candidate.

Cindy Richards, a columnist for the Chicago Sun-Times, today provided a distillation of why Obama is succeeding. And why Barry O is bad for America. Cindy *agonistes* wrote "Why Obama won my internal battle." She was fighting with herself over Barry O? Well, yes. And apparently she lost. Or at least America is losing.

I don't mean to pick on Richards. After all, unlike Mrs. Obama, Ms. Richards is a vice president of nothing. She writes for a living. We can list her as "entertainer." So why am I focusing on Richards? Because in her brief column she catalogs all of the ways that Barry has fooled us, and is fooling America.

It won't be pretty when the bubble bursts.

When we see the man behind the curtain. When someday we realize it was all Hype, not Hope. Barry Obama is America's latest pied piper of politics. With perfect pitch.

We usually count on people in a local community to know someone best. But now that the Chicago Bears have lost the Super Bowl and newspapers need to sell, sell, sell we can look forward to Obamamania. A media feeding frenzy over Kenyan-American Barack Obama. Only Chicago's media, and Ms. Richards in particular, don't know Barack Obama very well at all. Not well at all.

Richards lists ten (10) reasons why Obama should be president.

One: he is good at fund raising. Money talks, and the rest of us walk. OK. If you like to walk. But where is all of this money coming form? Rich people. Hollywood people. Business people. True to his huckster's stance as an "outsider," Obama is so far outside the system he's inside out.

Two: he has a blank resume (see below for Obama's lack of any professional accomplishments.) We used to elect distinguished Americans with identifiable achievements to the presidency, e.g. Dwight Eisenhower. It wasn't a perfect process, but no one dared suggest that having done nothing was a basis to allow someone to ascend to an aeropagus where they could do something, namely damage.

Three: Obama is a "constitutional law *scholar*." Well, presumably that can be verified. Has he written any authoritative law review articles? Tried any cases? Argued any appeals. Nope. Obama has done nothing but promote himself to the gullible as a "legal scholar." He has fooled a lot of people, not he least of which includes the media.

Obama is a lawyer. Yes. If every "lawyer" is a scholar, then Obama is a scholar. But if merely being a lawyer does not make you a scholar then Barry Is just a mediocre lawyer with no legal accomplishments and a nonexistent legal resume. Absent his sweet talk and confused psyche he would be indistinguishable from the many other minority lawyers out there. A "scholar," he isn't. But he's fooled Cindy. And triggered her "internal battle."

Indeed, because Chicago has evolved into a community of very progressive racial relations, there is a plethora of highly competent, highly successful minority lawyers in Chicago. Men and women with real accomplishments in the law. None of them are named Obama. My own law school has produced some. And none of them is named Obama. When we allow Obama's vacuous claims to legal "scholarship" to be accepted as truth we insult the very process of public debate over the qualifications of the person who will lead our nation in the future.

To be sure, years ago they used to write stories claiming Hillary Clinton was one of "America's best lawyers." And she wasn't. Hillary, meet Barry.

Four: Obama has the "audacity to hope." When hope is merely hype, and serves as a substitute for thought, hope is dangerous, not a reason to catapult someone into the White House. We need someone with the heft to lead, not the "hope" to accomplish something in the future that he has so far failed to accomplish in his entire adult life.

Five: Obama is "comfortable is a room full of steelworkers." He won't be comfortable with real workers when people realize what a classic and world class con artist he is. Obama "talks labor" but he has never accomplished anything significant for workers. He says he is for the poor folk, but only if he enriches himself in the process. He says he is against Wal-Mart, but then again few millionaires such as himself shop there.

Six: Obama's not "tainted" by the Iraq War. In the sense that Obama did not vote for the Iraq fiasco, she's right. But in the reality that Obama's recent statements are worthy Kerryisms ("I voted for before I voted against) Obama has been in a vicious bidding war with John Edwards and Hillary Clinton to see who can seem more inflated with their anti-Iraq flatulence. In 2009 hype/hope will have to confront reality/substance. In Iraq. But by then Barry O will probably be onto some new and nebulous cause. As the Chicago Tribune quotes his wife, Obama's a dreamer, not a detail man. Everyone has to have a scam.

Seven: His heart is in the right place. Puhlllze.

Eight: "He's got religion." Obama is a worthy successor to Chicago's late religious huckster "Billy Sunday." Only in the atheistic Democratic party of 2007 could Obama be deemed "religious." But oh he can sell. Truly, he deserves a revival tent, not a white house.

Nine: Obama doesn't want to impose "his religion" on "us." That's because there is no religion. Hype vs. hope.

Ten: He can win. He can't. Or, as Abraham Lincoln once said, (he of the venue where Obama will announce his candidacy this Saturday) "You can fool some of the people all of the time, and all of the people some of the time, but you can not fool all of the people all of the time."

And there you have it. Someone who has been entrusted with a column in a major metropolitan daily says she has struggled with herself over Barry O, only to be confused, confounded and ultimately convinced by one of the great hucksters in American political history that he is "right" to be president.

There is an expression for wasted wealth, "shirtsleeves to shirtsleeves in three generations." I don't know what the comparable expression for nations is, maybe "Empire to emptiness" in three generations." But whatever the term is, we are headed there. Good luck with your "internal struggles," Cindy. If indeed Obama wins, we will all be struggling. To survive.

First the Democrats produced "the Man From Hope." We all know how he ended up. With a cigar in his hand. Now they are offering us the "Man With Hope." "Close. But no cigar."

Announcement of Blockbuster Chicago News Conference Disclosing that under Kenyan Constitutional Law, Barack Obama is a Kenyan Citizen

(CHICAGO)(February 8, 2007) Chicago-based Internet jour-nalist, broadcaster and critic Andy Martin will hold a news con-ference Friday, February 9th at 11:00 A.M. to announce that U. S. Senator Barack Obama is a citizen of Kenya and became a citi-zen of Kenya under the Independence Constitution of Kenya in 1963. Obama has never renounced his Kenyan citizenship. He is also a U. S. Citizen.

"For our 'Obama Week' leading up to Barry O's announce-ment on Saturday that he feels qualified to lead the free world, ContrarianCommentary.com unleashed a worldwide team of constitutional law experts to delve into Kenyan law and the question of Obama's citizenship. They were also participating in our CIA-style psychological profile of Obama that will be released Saturday in Chicago. And what we discovered was amazing, a political blockbuster," says Executive Editor Andy Martin.

"Under the Independence Constitution of Kenya, Obama became a Kenyan citizen on December 12, 1963. He has never renounced his Kenyan citizenship. On his senate web site,

Obama tap dances around his own dual nationality when discussing his father. Obama obviously knows, because his father told him, that he also held/holds Kenyan nationality.

"Once again, we find Barry O concealing fascinating information about his identity. There is nothing unusual about dual nationality. Indeed, ancient Roman Law doctrines of *jus sanguini* and *jus soli* come into play, because both Kenya and the U. S. recognize dual nationality. Once again, the issue is not 'legality.' The issue is the cover-up; Obama's concealment of his own identity. From us, and most of all from himself.

"I find it amusing that Channel 2 in Chicago is (Thursday night) running a series on 'Do we know the real Barack Obama?' when they don't really know, because 2's news is produced by the same old hacks that take spoon-feeding from Obama & Co.

"Friday we will blow Obama out of the water with disclosure of his lifelong deceit and concealment. Obama's attempts to portray his father as an ignorant 'goat herd,' moreover, were part of his attempts at 'identity theft' against his own father, designed to create an imaginary picture of Barack Sr. It is inconceivable that Obama's father was ignorant of Kenyan law, since he served as a government official and held a Ph.D. from Harvard. And it is inconceivable that Obama Sr. never told his son that he was a Kenyan national. Why has 'junior' hidden this information for decades?" Martin will demand Friday.

"The American people, when deciding who to support for president, have a right to know if their 'president' is also a citizen of Kenya and owes dual loyalty to Kenya because he has never renounced his Kenyan citizenship.

"Further, I defy Obama or any of his flacks to defeat or deny the historical constitutional facts on which our blockbuster disclosures are based. We have nailed Barry O with his own hidden truths once again."

CHAPTER - CONSTITUTION OF KENYA | HOME

87. Persons who become citizens on 12th December, 1963.

Interpretation and savings. Persons entitled to be registered as citizens by virtue of connexion with Kenya before 12th December, 1963

Persons who become citizens on 12th December, 1963. **87*.** (1) Every person who, having been born in Kenya, is on 11th December, 1963 a citizen of the United Kingdom and Colonies or a British protected person shall become a citizen of Kenya on 12th December, 1963;

Provided that a person shall not become a citizen of Kenya by virtue of this subsection if neither of his parents was born in Kenya.

(2) Every person who, having been born outside Kenya, is on 11th December, 1963 a citizen of the United Kingdom and Colonies or a British protected person shall, if his father becomes, or would but for his death have become, a citizen of Kenya by virtue of subsection (1), become a citizen of Kenya on 12th December, 1963.

Obama Week, Part Three:
Is Barack (Barry) Obama a Christian?

(CHICAGO)(FEBRUARY 9, 2007) I am probably the only polit-ical writer or activist who attended a church service last week where part of the liturgy was read in Barack Obama's native trib-al langue from Kenya: Luo. I also spoke with some of our Luo guests after the service.

And, given that I have been engaged as part of a worldwide project to investigate and analyze Mr. Obama, I reacted with some sense of internal amusement when part of our service was read in Luo last week.

As an Episcopalian, I come from a particularly liberal denomination that is being challenged by issues of religious doctrine. And in the 1980's I studied to be a priest.

While the Episcopal Church was obviously not free from his-toric racism and slavery, it was the only religious denomination that was not torn apart by the Civil War. After being separated during hostilities, and after the fleeting existence of competing denominations, Episcopalians reunited shortly after the end of the war, unlike Baptists and others who continued segregation well into the last century. The ties between the Black church and the mainline Episcopal Church are seamless. At my own worker-priest seminary, minorities made up perhaps half of the students, maybe more than half. I wasn't counting.

Thus, I approached the question of Barack Obama's religious beliefs with both skepticism and understanding. I posed the question "Is Barack Obama a Christian?" to try and answer it.

The term "Christian" moreover, can be an extremely rubbery concept. For decades I have served as an usher, helping people who come to church, welcoming them, attending to their needs. At Easter and Christmas we are usually overwhelmed with people who show up then. Hordes of them. They only appear, as if miraculously, twice a year. Mr. Obama notes in the Audacity of Hope that his mother was apparently one of those Easter/Christmas Christians, while she denied any religious significance to her visits. The Christian church welcomes these twice-a-year-Christians and works to make them feel welcome.

As part of my church work I am also sensitive to generational conflicts over religion. Sometimes conservative parents generate agnostic children; those children later seek religion in adulthood and find it on their own, or their children do. In the Episcopal Church we also receive a fair number of converts from the Roman Catholic Church. So I am sensitive to the fact that religion is certainly an area where generational rebellion and denominational change can play out, as it apparently did in the Dunham household.

I am convinced by Obama's claims that his post-collegiate years working in Chicago introduced him to the Black church and lit the spiritual candle that resulted in his baptism. I am also pretty certain, though I can't point to any support in the literature, that Michelle Obama came from a churched home and that her own family habits were easily grafted on to her new groom.

The bottom line: yes, Obama is a Christian. I believe he is a sincere one although I don't know if he attends church regularly (that Dunham thing again). And, as a gifted public speaker, Obama is also skilled at sincerely playing the church card. The *political* church card. To which I can only say, as a Republican, good for him. Maybe he can convert some of his heathen Democrats.

There has been a great deal of confusion, largely fed by our own original research in 2004, concerning Obama's Muslim background and his father's family's religion in Kenya. Obama's family in Kenya was clearly a Muslim family, a devout one. I am not an expert in the Muslim faith but I would not be surprised if they also have the equivalent of Easter/Christmas Christians. The same pattern is also evident among Jews, where some parishioners appear at High Holy days, and then disappear for another year.

Obama himself did attend a Muslim school in Indonesia. His stepfather was also a Muslim, an unusual coincidence forty years ago on a Hawaiian college campus. Obama makes a lot of the fact that his father was "not a practicing Muslim," but in Dreams From My Father he also notes that when Barack Sr. died, members of his family wanted to give him a *Muslim* funeral.

Since Barack admits he had little-to-no contact with his father, it is entirely possible that his father kept his religious beliefs at a distance in Kenya, but nevertheless remained attached to his Muslim heritage. Otherwise, why would his family want to give him a Muslim burial?

Thus, it is my conclusion that Barack Sr.'s Muslim affiliation was not as remote and removed as Barack Jr. has strenuously sought to suggest, in conjunction with his apologists in the media.

Christianity, of course, welcomes voluntary conversions and so the issue of any familial religious beliefs is a non-issue for Christians. Barack professed his faith through Holy Baptism and that is enough for almost any Christian. He would be welcomed as an Episcopalian.

Finally, there has been some concern over the "Blackness" of Obama's church. I view that as a non-issue. Obama's Chicago church appears to be built on the views that Blacks have to do for themselves. It's hard to quibble with such practical, applied theology. As long as they preach the gospel of Christ crucified, that's enough for me. No one has suggested they don't.

On balance, and after exhaustive research spanning over three years and several continents, I think Obama has clearly been hyper-sensitive to his father's religious background, but that for himself Barack Jr. is a sincere and committed Christian. There is nothing to criticize.

(We welcome reactions, interpretations and comments to these conclusions, of course.)

Notice of Consumer Fraud and Corporate Fraud under New York Law

CONTRARIANCOMMENTARY.COM
Independent Worldwide News and Opinion
New York-London-Washington-Chicago-San Francisco-
Palm Beach

Headquarters mail:
Post Office Box 1851
New York, NY 10150-1851
Tel. (866) 706-2639
Fax (866) 707-2639
Web: ContrarianCommentary.com
E-mail: AndyMart20@aol.com

Anthony R. Martin, J. D.
Professor of Law (Adj.)
Executive Editor

February 21, 2007

LEGAL DEPARTMENT
Random House, Inc.
1745 Broadway
New York, NY 10019
Via fax (212) 572-6066

LEGAL DEPARTMENT
Crown Publishing Group
1745 Broadway
New York, NY 10019
Via fax (212) 940-7868

NOTICE OF CONSUMER FRAUD AND CORPORATE FRAUD UNDER NEW YORK LAW

Dear Counsel:

Approximately 2-1/2 years ago I notified Crown Books that Barack Obama (and Crown Books) were involved in a consumer fraud—by selling a fraudulent book on his life. He was selling a document that was being mischaracterized as an "autobiography" when it was a novelized version of his life.

Obama and Random/Crown have fooled others. I learned from my research, for example, that the free encyclopedia "Wikipedia" refers to your book as an "autobiography."

The issue of the novelization of Mr. Obama's life, as depicted in your publishing list, came to life again this week with stories in the Los Angeles Times and Chicago Sun-Times. I am also enclosing 2004 stories.

Mr. Obama admits he created composite characters and other fictitious elements to move along his narrative. By no stretch of the imagination does his work qualify as "biography" or "autobiography" as it is identified on your publishing list (see attached).

I have no objection to your selling Mr. Obama's book so long as you label it with a clear disclosure that it is a fictionalized version of his life, and do not represent on either your web site or in any other sales matter or manner that the book is "autobiography" or "biography."

Biographies are expected to provide scrupulous accuracy, not novelization. For example, you just don't say "I don't remember" a major character in a brief (then 35-year) life such as his; you go and find out that person's name and include it accurately.

Obama's "biography" is a fraud. The Sun Times reported yesterday that in trying to find out whom the "real" people in the book were, his own staff was forced to start from scratch, without any help from the senator who obviously can't remember his own fabrications.

If you refuse you take what I believe to be reasonable action I will choose a legal forum where the book is being sold, including the United Kingdom, and file a legal action under both general and consumer fraud laws to restrict the marketing/advertising of Obama's book by both Random House/Crown Publishing and any booksellers.

Please feel free to contact me to discuss this matter further. If you wish to rely on any legal authority to publish as "biography" what is clearly now fiction, then by all means provide it to me so I may review your legal research and respond to you appropriately.

Respectfully submitted,

ANDY MARTIN
EXECUTIVE EDITOR, CONTRARIANCOMMENTARY.COM

Obama Enters the Real World, and So Do His Supporters

Obambi gets to drink AIPAC's Kool-Aid

(CHICAGO)(March 2, 2007) Hosting a talk show and writing a column that is heard and read around the world creates a personal contact with many of my listeners and readers. You develop a sense of feel about people's expectations, and how they will react to developments in the political arena.

My views and columns are especially controversial because they advocate a balanced Middle East policy, and call for engagement and American leadership to end the endless Israel/Palestinian conflict. Yes, it could be done. If only here was the will in Washington. The Andy Martin Peace Plan is still the last best hope for a solution to the conflict. Ironically, after years of ignoring the AMPP, even our State Department is now coming around to supporting my views. But only ever so slowly and ever so quietly.

So I was not surprised when many of my pro-Palestinian readers expressed great discomfort at my columns criticizing Kool-Aid salesman Barack Obama, the current Lion King of American politics. I knew they would soon be disappointed, but

I didn't know when. Despite the occasional nasty e-mail about my attacks on Obama I knew I would be vindicated.

Today's the day.

All along I have known that our ultimate Kool-Aid salesman would eventually have to drink AIPAC's own brand of Kool-Aid, and genuflect to the masters of pro-Israel machinations in Washington. AIPAC stands for American Israel Public Affairs Committee. A couple of AIPAC's employees were recently charged with espionage against the United States. I was shocked, shocked to know there was Israeli gambling, I mean spying, going on. Round up the usual suspects, including Barry Obama.

Today is the first day of the rest of Barry O's political life: he enters the AIPAC den and he kneels at the altar. He will pledge to support Israel and to spend American treasure and blood to attack Israel's enemies. He will drink the AIPAC moonshine.

Surprised? I'm not. I knew all along that Obama would surrender to AIPAC. What's to be surprised about? And so my pro-Palestinian friends will have to go through an "agonizing reappraisal" of their support for the O-Man, and have to face the same reality that Obambi has: in the Democratic Party AIPAC calls the shots. Or you get shot.

Does this mean all Jews support war on Israel's behalf? Not by a county mile. Most American Jews favor moderate Middle East policies, and many of them want a sensible peace solution. They condemn the occupation. Especially young Americans. A majority is probably against the policies of the military junta in Tel Aviv. But in Washington moderate Jews are drowned out by the din of drum beating for the militant approach of AIPAC's pro-Israel Middle East policy.

At AIPAC, you drink the Kool-Aid first and ask questions later. In fact, you ask no questions, never, ever, no how. You do what you are told. That is why AIPAC's congressional parrots routinely adopt "pro-Israel" resolutions. No matter how contrary to American interests a law or resolution may be. When AIPAC talks, politicians listen. They are afraid of being branded anti-Semitic.

And woe to those who are labeled anti-Semitic. In the 1980's Illinois Senator Charles Percy was crucified for advocating a balanced Middle East policy. Likewise downstate Illinois congressman Paul Findley was similarly drawn and quartered. When southern Democrats make statements critical of Israel they suddenly find themselves smothered in AIPAC gold. Opponents materialize, campaigns are directed, the critics are silenced.

AIPAC is already sharpening its spears to lunge into my campaign when I file for the U. S. Senate. I am not pro-Israel enough. And I am equally pro-Arab. Horrors. I face a lonely battle.

These public executions send a message, and the message is "hooahed" right down the line to candidates of every party and persuasion: march to the tune of AIPAC or AIPAC will do its best to march you out of congress.

Obama may try to use a few of his famous weasel words and call for "audacity" for peace to appear "balanced" on Israel issues but the message will be clear: AIPAC orders, I march.

Ironically, Israel's friends have done that country no good, and continue to do extreme harm to Israel's long-term interests. By suppressing American debate on our interests and the long-term interests of Israel, policy is frozen, and made in whispers instead of out in the open by the people's representatives. It is not a healthy situation.

And so now the candidate of "hope," "boldness" and "audacity" will belly up to the AIPAC bar and drink the Kool-Aid waiting on the counter. End of debate. For Obama and for America.

The Democrats are now against the War In Iraq, even though they were for it before they were against it. Now where have I heard that before? And now they are for the attacks on Iran. But only "surgical" air strikes; no ground troops, no failed occupations. And so it goes. A long as someone else's kids are dying. Wasted? No, sacrificed.

Real tasty Kool-Aid.

But there's a very bitter after taste.

Just ask President Bush. He ended up having to deny he had gone to war for Israel. Only God knows, and maybe Bush, what AIPAC's policies hold in store for Iran. But whatever they are, Barry O will be marching in the AIPAC band.

Bottoms up, everyone.

And as for my disappointed pro-Palestinian readers and listeners? Well, I told you so.

This is only the first of many disappointments Obama is going to deliver to his followers.

"Massa" Obama "Not Surprised" His Family Owned Slaves

From Bill Clinton's "I share your pain" to Barack Obama's "You share my shame"

From the Democrats' "March to Montgomery" (1965) to the Democrats' "March to Hypocrisy" (2007)

Clinton won't apologize for her Iraq vote; Obama won't apologize for his family's ownership of slaves

And – more lies from the O-Man as the "myth of Daddy" persists

Obama continues to "spin" a fictitious and farcical family history

(CHICAGO)(March 4, 2007) Barack Obama, whose white Confederate Army ancestors owned slaves, will not apologize for that family history. "That's no surprise," Obama said, suggesting he knew he came from a slave-owning past. Instead of saying it was a tragic burden for *him*, he sought to swaddle himself in collective guilt by saying "That's part of *our* tortured tangled, history." Wrong.

Mr. Obama, my family did not own slaves. Yours did. Most Americans' have no family links to slavery. Yours does. Yours, not ours.

Bill Clinton wanted to "share our pain." You want us to "share your shame." No thanks. Speak for yourself, Barry. That's part of your incredibly tortured family history, and *your* own tortured psyche, not "*ours*."

Amazingly, it took the exposure of his slave-owning family history for Obama to even acknowledge that half of his family history came from white racists who waged war against the United States.

And Obama wants "African-Americans" to support his candidacy? His ancestors sought to continue enslaving legitimate African-Americans. Massa Obama. You are the living embodiment of *chutzpah*. Just ask your friends at AIPAC what that means.

Truly, what part of Obama is "African-American?" His Kenyan father's part, coming from the drunken polygamist that he continues to romanticize, or his white relatives' slave ownership? It's enough to make Hillary's mouth water. And most people vomit.

Obama's imagination and prevarication was in overdrive Sunday in Selma, where he now credits the civil rights movement for his sleazy father's arrival in the United States and bigamous seduction of an innocent and very gullible 18 year-old woman. Obama was quoted as saying his father left "goat-herding" in Kenya—with a wife and child—to come to America where he impregnated his "Kansan" "wife" in Hawaii. It is truly sad the way Obama romanticizes the rascal and racial predator who was his father.

If only Barry would read his own book he would find out that he is lying about his "goat-herding father." Barry senior came from a prosperous and educated family; he came to America to get out of Kenya during the war of independence after his links to the murderous Mau Mau led to his arrest. He left behind a wife and child in Kenya, and then took Obama's mother as a "wife" in Hawaii before abandoning mother and child and running off to Harvard, where he met his eventual third wife and sired the third of his four "families." Whew.

Because of racism, most Americans know little of the African-American community in our midst. African-Americans as a group are socially conservative, church-going people. They are family people. Why would they want someone who covers-up a family history of polygamy and alcoholism, and who can't deal with the reality of his slave-owning family history, to be their leader? Beats me.

Especially when Hillary Clinton was hoopin' and hollerin' like a holy roller on Sunday. All she was missing was a snake and maybe a little talking in tongues. Come to think of it...

Maybe Obama really needs Clinton after all. Bill could share his pain. It must be painful to run away from the truth, and try to confuse and ultimately lie to the American people and hope to get away with it.

Barry Obama is a decent human being. He was victimized by his mother, who created a completely false fantasyland portrait of the father who abandoned him, and he was victimized by his own family history when he discovered he had been sired by a womanizing, alcoholic polygamist and racial huckster. And he was victimized when he learned the people who really raised him, his grandparents, came from a slave-owning clan in the south. That's a trifecta of shame. Yours, not ours.

The Democrats took the March to Montgomery of 1965 and converted the event into a March to Hypocrisy in 2007. Walking alongside Bill Clinton in Selma was Al Sharpton. Is Sharpton really that essential to the Clinton effort to retain Black political support? Apparently so. I for one would not be comfortable with Al Sharpton in the White House. Of course maybe the Clintons should remember what happened to the last prominent political figure that had Sharpton at his side: Ned Lamont lost a "can't lose" race for U. S. Senate after Sharpton appeared at his primary election victory celebration.

Recently I was attacked by a pro-Obama, tax-exempt left-wing smear machine that has been set up by the Democrats to attack conservatives (more on that later in the week). Yes, Democrats too use taxpayer-supported smear organizations to attack Republicans. They must be afraid of Andy Martin if they have been digging up dirt to throw at me. They can't face the truth. But they have a problem. My facts about Obama will stand up, and their smears against me won't.

The reality is that Barack Obama is all surface and no substance. He has lived his entire life in a fantasy world. He can't accept who he is and where he comes from, so he keeps running away from the truth. I'm not against him because his Black father was a polygamist or because his White relatives were slave holders. Obviously, we don't pick our relatives. It would be unfair to attack him on that basis.

I am critical of Obama because he continues to lie about his relatives and, when confronted with the truth, unleashes his left-wing smear machine to defend him by making personal attacks on legitimate conservative journalism. If Obama would only admit who is father was, and apologize for lying and living in a delusional world for 46 years, I would respect him more. If he would just admit that his white relatives were slave owners, and he is embarrassed by the fact, I would respect him more. I can't respect him for lying. That's the basis of my opposition.

I do not see how we can seriously consider placing someone in the oval office that lives in a dream world and who cannot even deal with the reality of his family history. And, no, I do not believe the American people want to "share his shame" any more than they believed Bill Clinton was "sharing our pain." Most of us did not have relatives who owned slaves and we have no reason to apologize. I can't see how African-Americans would vote for a man for president whose ancestors had enslaved them. But then wonders never cease.

Finally, Obama is the obvious beneficiary of "affirmative action" by the news media. They have not reported the truth about his family history. There has been a conscious cover-up to keep Obama "viable" as a candidate. Obama is the creature of a media cover-up. He is being "enabled" to keep living a lie and selling a lie to the American people. What would have happened if a newspaper discovered slave ownership in Hillary Clinton's family history? You got it.

Hillary, apologize for your Iraq vote; Barry, tell the truth about your ancestors. Instead of saying "let the conversation begin," why not say, both of you, "Let the truth-telling begin? We have been living a lie. Let's start telling the truth."

London Newspaper Confirms Andy Martin's Original Obama Exposé

Martin lawsuit against Obama and book publisher imminent

(CHICAGO)(March 4, 2007) Later today we will witness the extraordinary shootout in Selma, Alabama where supporters of Barry Obama and Hillary Rodham meet in a political shootout over the Black vote. But before the big picture in Selma, we should revisit the larger, deeper truth about Barry (Barack) Obama: the man is a complete fraud.

A few days ago a major newspaper in London confirmed all of my accusations about Barry-O. It took the world two and a half years to catch up with our cutting-edge reporting.

On **August 11, 2004**, while Obama was still a candidate, I held a news conference in which I stated, "The man is a complete fraud. The truth is going to surprise, and disappoint, and outrage many people who were drawn to him... In the meantime, Crown Books should stop selling Obama's novelization of his life." Well. (The news release can easily be located on the Internet, but here's one link: http://www.freerepublic.com /focus/f-news/1189687/posts.)

As the media hysteria has continued to expand I have constantly questioned Obama's qualifications for any office, let alone the presidency. And I have previously identified myself in columns as the "man who brought down Obama." He's falling.

What we have seen is a "vast left-wing conspiracy" to whitewash Barry Obama's lies. No so in the Daily Mail in London (the article is part of this e-mail, below). http://www.dailymail.co.uk/pages/live/articles/news/news.html?in_article_id=431908&in_page_id=1770. The Daily Mail confirmed all of my accusations 2-1/2 years ago. The sad fact is that a London newspaper following my pioneering research dug out the truth about Obama. Not one mainline newspaper in the United states has done so. It is a massive cover-up.

We will be going to court soon to block Obama from continuing to peddle his pack of lies.

[Is it any wonder ContrarianCommentary.com is the fastest growing and most authoritative news and information source for *intelligent* readers worldwide?]

Barack Obama:
Joshua Generation – Or, Just Joshin'?

Obama goes into overdrive lying about his family history to African-Americans in Selma

(CHICAGO)(March 6, 2007) Barack Obama went to Selma, Alabama last week to honor the heroes of the civil rights era. He called them the "Moses generation." That was all true. Few people have demonstrated more bravery than the civil rights workers of the 50's and 60's who put their lives on the line to free America from the oppressive yoke of segregation.

But Obama went further, and placed himself in a "Joshua Generation," who are the heirs of the Moses contingent.

Unfortunately, Obama was no Joshua; he was just joshin'.

Obama demonstrated that he holds African-Americans in contempt, that he holds the media in contempt and, ultimately, that he holds the American people in contempt.

[I am indebted for the source text in this column to a copy of Obama's speech posted by Lynn Sweet on the Chicago Sun-Times web site. Although I often disagree with Ms. Sweet on Obama, she has occasionally reflected genuine integrity in the way she has addressed his flaws.]

To put it bluntly, Obama is a congenital liar. Obama grew up lying to himself. When he went to Kenya and discovered that his mother had painted a fantasy world concerning his father Obama paused, and then just resumed and kept on lying. He is still lying.

I recently reread "Dreams From My Father," Obama's "biography" of his early years. Afterwards, I notified Random House, the current publishers (Obama dumped his original publishers when he became famous) that Obama's book is not biography or autobiography. Much of it is complete fiction and fabrication.

In "Dreams," when Obama visits Africa he discovers his grandfather, Hussein Onyango Obama.

Onyango is an incredibly powerful figure and an absolutely impressive human being. During the colonial era Onyango educated himself, ingratiated himself with the British, went on to adopt western ways, traveled with British officers across Europe and Mesopotamia during World War I and ended up making a fortune in farming and real estate. Decades after his death, Onyango's legacy endures. In 2004 the Kenyan Newspaper The Nation of Nairobi stated Onyango's descendents lived in a "vast well-kept compound with [Onyango's last wife's] brick house sitting imposingly at end far end."

Yet Saturday in Selma Obama defamed both his grandfather Onyango and his father Barack, Sr. He lied about his very impressive family history in order to pander to African-Americans in the audience and to appeal to their basest instincts and most unfortunate prejudices.

FACT: Grandfather Onyango was educated, wealthy and owned property. Yes, Onyango did begin working for the British, and he lived a British life. He adopted British ways. He insisted on scrupulous cleanliness in his home at a time when rural Africans were not aware of western standards of hygiene.

Onyango converted to Islam during this period. As The Nation story stated "The Obama family are among the few

Muslims in the locality." Onyango was a proud man, an imperious man and a "founding father" to a successful dynasty. He would be disgusted at the way Obama has tap danced to avoid admitting his Muslim family heritage.

LIE: Obama told Selmans that to his death Onyango was a "boy" for the British, who called him by his first name, not his last.

I grew up in a restaurant, worked in a restaurant and eat out several times a week. In places where I am known, I am called "Andy" and I respond by telling servers "Hello, George" or "Hello Angelo" or "hello" whomever is taking care of me. There is nothing sinister about referring to staff by their first names. We do it all the time.

I don't know anyone, anywhere who eats in a restaurant regularly who would walk in and refer to the maitre d'hotel as "Mr. so-and so." Obama degrades Onyango by telling his audience his grandfather was called by his first name. For shame. He took a man who was incredibly impressive and a giant for his time in Kenya, and ultimately deprecates and diminishes his grandfather.

Obama's disgrace of his grandfather is a telling insight into his unstable personality. He will lie about anything and everything to pander to his audience and to stimulate base and hostile instincts in his listeners.

FACT: Obama's father, Barack, Sr. came to American in 1958. He married Obama's mother in 1960 and Barry was worn in 1961. Onyango **opposed** Barack, Sr. going to America because his son had a wife and child in Kenya.

LIE: Seeking to hijack the civil rights movement and to attach the suffering of civil rights workers to his own personal aggrandizement, Obama told his audience in Selma "[M]y grandfather began to imagine something different...His son, who grew up herding goats...So the Kennedy's decided we're going to do an air lift..This young man Barack Obama **got one of those tickets...**"

Barack, Sr. arrived in Hawaii two years **before** Kennedy even ran for the presidency, three years before Kennedy took office. There was no Kennedy "air lift" and no Kennedy "ticket" which brought his father to America. Obama's speech was all a lie.

Obama also repeated the lie that his father was "herding goats." I am sure Onyango insisted that his son help care for the large amount of livestock on his wealthy farm, no doubt because Barack, Sr. was a bit of a wise guy and his dad wanted to make him toe the line. But Barack, Sr. was a bright student, indeed a brilliant one, who initially went into commercial work and had no part of any career "herding goats." The "goat herd" lie is one which Obama has constantly repeated over the past three years.

FACT: Obama was born in 1961. The riot in Selma, Alabama took place in 1965. By 1965, Barack, Sr. had abandoned his second wife (Obama's mother) and moved back to Kenya after going to Harvard University, where he cavorted with the woman who would become his third wife and bear his third family. Barack's father and mother had no relationship at the time of Selma.

In "Dreams" Obama never mentions at any time any connection between his parents and civil rights, or any support that his grandfather had for his son Barack, Sr. going to college in America. All of these lies have arisen recently, as Obama has expanded his pandering and false family history.

LIE: Obama told the audience in Selma, "There was something stirring across the country because of what happened in Selma,...so [my parents] got together and Barack Obama, Jr. was born." Among the nation's media, only the Chicago Tribune, to its credit, even bothered to inquire about this bald-faced lie. Obama's spokesman said Obama was "speaking metaphorically" about his birth date. (Chicago Tribune, March 5, 2007). How can someone speak "metaphorically" when stating the facts about one's conception?

Over and over again Obama lied to the Selma audience. By 1965, Obama, Sr. had returned to Kenya and joined the Kenya government. The civil rights movement and Selma had absolutely no impact on him and his "wife" in Hawaii in 1960. None.

There was nothing "metaphorical" in Obama's lies Sunday about his grandfather and father. Nothing metaphorical about the lies concerning the date when Obama's father came to America. Nothing "metaphorical" about misrepresenting the relationship of his parents in 1965. How can someone lie about basic, objective facts about himself and then, when challenged, claim that he was being "metaphorical?" Still, only the Chicago Tribune even bothered to challenge this torrent of lies.

Syndicated columnist Linda Chavez recently wrote of Obama that his pain comes not from the racism Obama claims as its source but rather from his parental abandonment. It is absolutely true that children who are abandoned bear those scars into adulthood. Obama was abandoned and in flashes of candor he returns to the lingering pain of that abandonment. Abandoned children usually create fantasy worlds, in which the absent parent is a fantasy figure. These fantasies can linger into adulthood.

In Obama's case he went to Kenya and got the shock of his life as a young adult when he confronted the reality of who his father was and what he had done. Obama, Sr. was having children simultaneously with different wives. He had four wives and was a polygamist. But instead of accepting the pain and trying to deal with it, Obama retreated back into his "fantasy family" world.

How can Obama lie this way, over and over, year after year?

In childhood, compensation for an absent parent begins as fantasy and "pretend" to comfort the child. Gradually, as a child becomes an adult the fantasies and pretenses morph into self-deception and then outright lies. A disconnect persists and grows between the real world and the inner child-life fantasy refuge that offers comfort and solace.

In "High Risk: Children Without a Conscience," the authors described children who suffer from incomplete bonding. Obama is such a person. He can lie about the facts because reality is meaningless to him. His fantasy world is what controls. And because of the hope, and guilt, that have surrounded his political climb his supporters and his audiences have failed to confront Obama over his confusion of fantasy and reality. Obama's supporters have been his enablers. The more he lies; the more he gets away with. The bigger the lie, the less he is called on it.

I want to emphasize that this column is not concerned with family history *per se*. This column is focused on an adult individual who can't keep himself from lying about facts, who fabricates a fantasy family history and who spends his public life in a pretend world. This column is about Barack Obama's personality disorder. On February 10th as Obama was announcing his candidacy we issued a psychological profile of Obama. It should be read and reread by anyone concerned about Obama's unstable personality.

A few weeks ago, when the Los Angeles Times was reporting on Obama's fabrications involving his role in the Altgeld Gardens asbestos removal program, Obama's staff members had to go to outside sources because Barry himself had no recollection of the lies he had told in his book, and the fabricated characters he had inserted in his "autobiography." That is why I think I have a fair chance of wining a lawsuit against Random House if that company continues to enable Obama's fabrications.

After the controversy over Altgeld Gardens exploded, Lynn Sweet of the Sun-Times reposted her August, 2004 article in which she expressed frustration and exasperation at Obama's deceptions in "Dreams."

The media do not want to admit that Obama is disordered, because that would prick the balloon they have created around him. They have a vested interest in his survival. If there is a Democratic Party slugfest for the presidential nomination due to Obama, the media will make hundreds of millions of dollars in extra advertising as Edwards, Clinton and Obama raise huge amounts of money and spend it on ads. If Obama implodes, media stand to lose hundreds of millions of dollars in advertising. I am not suggesting that reporters covering the election are controlled by management. But reporters can't be oblivious to the fact that newspapers and television organizations are shrinking, and hundreds of millions of dollars in political advertising will extend the life of these organizations into 2009. You be the judge if there is a subconscious conflict of interest.

THE BOTTOM LINE: Someone who lies habitually about objective facts, someone who fabricates a family history, someone who trashes his ancestors and diminishes them with false claims, is not someone that most of us would trust to be in the Oval office.

The truth about Obama is there in plain view. It is there for all of us, and especially the media, to see. But there are "none so blind as those who will not see, none so deaf as those who will not hear." And none so stupid as those who consciously avoid the truth because they want to keep on reporting Obama's lies.

Both Mr. Obama and the mainstream media owe the American people an explanation and an apology. But don't hold your breath. Obama's too busy making up new lies to even know what the truth is any more.

Obama is not part of any "Joshua Generation." He has been "joshin'" us all along, and we keep taking it. He may be a Kool-Aid salesman. But we keep buying and keep drinking.

Two and a half years ago I held a news conference in Chicago to denounce Obama as a fraud. Events since then have all corroborated my facts and confirmed my conclusions. I told you so. In 2004.

Obama in the Bunker – Again
"Ethics Joshua" Caught, Just Joshin' – Again

"Boneheaded" Barry caught – again

Obambi caught in the headlights of national scrutiny – again

Bill Burton must be circulating his resume

Tony Rezko must be smiling

(CHICAGO)(March 7, 2007) Today's Barack Obama scandal *du jour* appeared on the front page of the New York Times with the disclosure that Obama was making parallel investments in risky stocks recommended by a campaign advisor. Shades of Whitewater.

Obama is a masterful Kool-Aid salesman of "hope" and "audacity" but he has yet to brew up some "competence" for his audience.

Last year Obama was caught in another sleazy financial deal with a campaign supporter, when indicted wheeler-dealer and alleged extortionist Tony Rezko helped Barry O finance some "privacy" for his $1.6 million dollar home. And maybe a future garage for his Rolls Royse-to come.

Today the "Joshua" presidential candidate was "just joshin'" again. Or maybe Barry Obama is just not very competent.

Recently I endorsed Rudy Giuliani for president. On balance, I would probably rather have Obama as a neighbor, not Giuliani. But I would want Giuliani in the White House.

The scandals this week at Walter Reed Army Medical Center in Washington have shown what happens when bad management infects an institution: embarrassing things happen. Giuliani may not win a personality contest, but he has a proven record as a good manager.

Obama was embarrassed when the Obama-Rezko real estate transaction was disclosed. He called his actions "boneheaded." Now Obama is linked to a contributor, again. Boneheaded, again? Tony Rezko must be laughing.

It is not enough to display good intentions in Washington. In order to sit in the oval office a candidate must demonstrate a history of management ability sufficient to grab control of the federal government. Rudy Giuliani tamed something much more savage than Washington—City Hall in New York. It was not a pretty sight but he subdued many of the special interests during his eight years.

Obambi, on the other hand, has never managed anything, and has demonstrated over and over again "boneheaded" attitudes towards power and control. There is no way anyone could seriously consider him a candidate to manage the federal government. He likes to preach, but he lacks any evidence he knows how to practice. Today's mini-scandal over Obama's ill-advised investment program is just one more example why he should not be president.

Left-wing blogorrheans went into a panic over the latest disclosures. Indeed. In their mind every fact about Obama that doesn't fit their predetermined matrix of Obama's neutered superiority is part of a conspiracy to destroy him. The truth cannot be allowed to get in the way of the O-Man's myths.

But even if we take Obama at his own word (Chicago Tribune, March 7, 2007 8:25 P.M.) that he made a dimwitted investment, what kind of man would say words to the effect that "I've got $100,000 burning a hole in my pocket; find me some hot stocks." ("George, I've got $100,000 that I'm interested in doing more...") Obama's demand for "more action" was a subliminal suggestion for hot stocks and fast profits. And, Obama learned, pursuing hot stocks you often get burned.

Obama spent years in the Illinois legislature pushing "ethics" legislation. He didn't come to Washington as a neophyte. He knew there were lines, some clear, some blurry. He chose to approach the blurry lines and take his chances. Obama wasn't trying to break the Bank at Monte Carlo. But he showed he could be stupid and innocent. Is this the man the left wants in the White House. Heaven forefend.

As for his News Secretary Bill Burton, start circulating your resume. Obama's joshin' is bad joss.

The Bravery of Barack Obama: Obama Gets Swiftboated and Thinks He Joined a Yacht Club

(CHICAGO)(March 9, 2007) Barack Obama is a brave man. He's not afraid—to cut and run when he sees conflict ahead.

When Hillary "Catwoman" Clinton and her bubonic mice went looking for him a few days ago, Obama said he safely ducked into one of his favorite locations, a barber shop. I hope he remembers the name of that barber shop better than the shop he wrote about in his book; that barber was fictitious.

Obama is perhaps the most effete, fey candidate to seek the White House since—I don't know when. Dennis Kucinich?

Teddy Roosevelt called the presidency the "bully pulpit." Obama seems to think it is a pulpit to hide from bullies.

Obama invited his pastor of twenty years longstanding to give the invocation at his announcement in Springfield on February 10th. But on the night before, Obama was not afraid to dump the preacher—to "avoid controversy." Obama "bravely" raises religious themes when it serves his purpose; and then boldly dumps his pastor when it doesn't. He of little faith.

Loyalty is important to me. A friend of mind steered me to my first web service nearly a decade ago. I'm still there with the same provider. In the meantime my buddy has changed Internet providers constantly. When I ran for governor, the company that printed my petitions had first done work for me almost forty years before. I believe loyalty says something to me, and I hope it says something about me. I value loyalty.

And Obama's loyalties say something about him.

A small book publisher took a chance on a rather sophomoric book of fiction styled as Barry Obama's life story. "Dreams From My Father" was published to modest success. But as soon as Obama became famous he was not afraid to dump the small publisher that had invested in him, and walk across the street to the mega publishing firm that paid him millions. Now that's loyalty for you. He's not afraid to dump those who helped him up the ladder.

I wonder if they will be there on the way down.

Barry Obama says he represents "new" politics. Today Lynn Sweet reported in the Sun-Times that Obama is afraid to release his campaign schedule: http://blogs.suntimes.com/sweet/2007/03/sweet_column_obamas_stealth_fu.html.

How very "old politics." He's not afraid to look foolish by concealing his whereabouts. Not at all. And he's not afraid to ask for big bucks from big donors and make a mockery of his "new politics" supporters. I hope Obama is using smoke-free rooms instead of smoke-filled rooms for his secret sessions. But then he's a smoker, isn't he?

Barry, stop blowing smoke in my face.

Obama wants to run a "stealth" campaign? Richard Nixon, where are you when we need you? How pretty. A public campaign for his post-pubescent parade of believers. And a secret campaign for those in the know, and the dough. How cute.

Barry wants the media, as well as the rest of us, to play his "pretend" game and not "mix it up" over the obvious mendacity of his campaign strategy.

Obama is bravest where he claims to be the boldest: in the legislative arena. Just don't get in his way when he is running for the cellar.

I wrote about Obama during the debate over congressional intervention in the tragic case of Terri Schiavo. Where was Barack? Hiding in the basement. He wasn't afraid to cut and run, again.

Obama has never been afraid to run and hide. When he served in the Illinois legislature Obama was always willing to be "present" when controversial legislation was on the floor. See http://www.realclearpolitics.com/articles/2007/02/the_everpresent_obama.html.

Obama told my muse at the New York Times Maureen Dowd that he "came up through politics in Chicago." Tough? No way. He came up through politics in Hyde Park, a liberal bastion surrounding the University of Chicago. His base was the brainiacs, not the Bridgeport (Chicago) brawlers. The only "tough" race he ever had, against incumbent Congressman Bobby Rush, he lost. Obama is no more a "Chicago" politician than Chablis and brie are the bestselling foods of the city.

Obama told Dowd he would not "mix it up" until he could discuss "health care" or "Iraq." With Chablis and brie. He has the real world upside down. Tough guys tackle tough issues. Barry wants to be a tough guy—in a TV studio with rehearsed answers to manufactured questions. He probably thinks the Friday Night Fights on TV were shadow boxing.

Yes, Obama has been against the war in Iraq. Or rather, Obama was against the war. Before it started, and before he reached Washington. Once safely ensconced in the Senate

Obama was not afraid to do a tap dance on Iraq that would do Fred Astaire proud. Where does he stand? Good question. He wants to get out, but not too soon. Obama's "St. Augustine" solution for withdrawal; do it, but not yet.

Obama told Dowd that his essence revolves around "overcoming a father's absence and reconciling the strands of my background and coming out whole." But he didn't come out whole. That's the problem. He thinks he's whole. And he's not.

Obama has sold and resold and oversold the myth of his "absent father," the bigamist from Kenya who dumped wife number two and family number two (Obama) on the way to wife number three and family number three. All, apparently, simultaneously. Just because your dad was a cad and you survived the shame of learning the truth does not make you a tough guy.

Obama wants an end to "tit for tat" politics. Of course he does. He can't handle the combat of the arena. The Clintons are ruthless operators. They swiftboated Barry O over David Geffen and Obama doesn't even realize it yet. He bravely abandoned Geffen and said he would not fight to defend one of his most important supporters.

Geffen raised over a million dollars for Obama. But when Catwoman Clinton sent her mice to attack Barry he did the brave thing—yup—back in the barber shop for a "cut." I wonder if the "Cut and Run" is the only style in Obama's barber shop. Cut and run. And, oh, yes, it was "Take your daughter to school day." His cell phone was off all day. Another dead zone.

The mainstream media missed the Clintons' clear message: Obama won't stand by you even if you stand by him.

Obama has lived life in a protected bubble. Only he does not realize that fact. First, his forgotten mother's parents got him into an exclusive school in Hawaii. Then he went Ivy League at Columbia and later Harvard. Then he "organized" something in Chicago. But all along the way Obama has never been a real fighter.

He is a "lawyer" that apparently has never tried a case. He has never made an argument to a jury. He has never faced an adversary in the courtroom. Too much "tit for tat" behavior for him.

One of these days I am going to give in. And belly up to the bar at Obama's Kool-Aid stand. I want some of that "Jesus-but-not-controversial" juice so I can see why it is that sane people really think Obama is anything but a crass opportunist who has parlayed a placid and pleasant and intelligent personality into a pyramid of cash and public success, all because he was **not** a fighter. Not because he was a fighter.

This week Vladimir Putin killed another journalist. The Iranian mullahs are plotting something. After all, Iranian oil wells are running dry and the future is bleak. Something has to give. The world is a very tough place. Who knows what is going on in Korea, the Middle East and elsewhere? In South America we face the challenge of, can you believe it? Socialism. And Venezuela's Chavez.

Instead of "tit for tat" Barry will have to go "mano a mano" with the gang of thugs than runs the world. It will not be a pretty sight if he stumbles into the White House. Today New York Post columnist John Podhoretz predicted a "Jimmy Carter"-style administration. Chaotic, defeatist, disastrous.

Just look at the road kill Obama has bravely "Obamaed" on the way to the White House:

The publisher of "Dreams From My Father."

The pastor of his church, Reverend Jeremiah Wright.

Votes in the Illinois Senate and U. S. Senate.

And a strong defense and endorsement of David Geffen when he was mercilessly attacked by the Catwoman and her bubonic mice.

And I am sure there are more.

Who's next? Who will Obama "bravely" abandon next?

Barack the Brave. He's not afraid to dump friends, associates, pastors, anyone and everyone as long as it is in Barry's best interest to do so. When the battle is raging, Barry can be found: in the barber shop or the basement. Brave. Brave. Brave.

The Catwoman is already gassing up her swift boats. She won the first naval engagement. Barry got seasick when he saw her swift boats on the water, and decided he needed a haircut. On shore. Lord Obama of Hawaii was beached before he launched.

Barry (Barack) Obama: no rational person could believe Obama is even remotely capable of sitting in the Oval Office. Help. Our "long national nightmare" is just beginning. All over again.

New York Times Joins Contrarian Commentary's Obama Parade – and Stumbles

Barry Obama's strange family continues to fascinate with its bizarre ways

(CHICAGO)(March 19, 2007) On the day that Barack Obama announced his campaign for president, Contrarian Commentary.com ("CCC") published the first psychological profile of the candidate. "The Mask of Barack Obama: A Psychological Profile" remains the most analytical study of Obama's strange persona. (http://www.contrarian commentary.com/community/Home/tabid/36/mid/363/newsid363/79/Default.aspx)

We received the usual pro-Obama attacks on our motives. The Democratic National Committee has a deranged woman who writes a blog largely directed at trashing our coverage of Obama and pillorying me as a "racist." The poor ignorant DNC creature doesn't know I have been a civil rights activist for over forty years. My opposition to Obama has nothing to do with "civil rights."

We have continued to be especially energized because CNN sent a "correspondent" to Jakarta to "put an end" to questions about Obama's "Madrassa" madness. Notably, CCC has never used the term "madrassa" in any of its Jakarta coverage of

Obama. Obama's media manipulators demanded that CNN's cover-up be the last word. It was not and it will not be.

Recently the Los Angeles Times sent an excellent reporter to Jakarta to plow the same Jakarta furrows in Obama's life. (http://www.latimes.com/news/nationworld/la-na-obama15mar15,1,26632.story)

The L. A. Times essentially corroborated what we had started reporting 2-1/2 years ago, namely that Obama's Muslim history was far more extensive than he had ever admitted. The L. A. Times prompted Obama to change his stock denial from "never having been a Muslim" to the more nuanced "never having been a *practicing* Muslim." As I have pointed out repeatedly, Obama's childhood would be of little interest if he did not work so hard to suppress the facts and to paint a false picture of his family's religious history.

Saturday, the New York Times felt constrained to join the Obama's-family-history parade, and sent Jennifer Steinhauer to Hawaii to speak with Barry's sister. (http://www.nytimes.com/2007/03/17/us/politics/17hawaii.html)

Steinhauer got one of the key points in her story wrong. She wrote "When he was 10, the family returned to Oahu.." My understanding of the facts is quite different. Obama's mother and half-sister Maya remained in Jakarta; at the age of 10 Barry/Barack was separated from his mother and sent to live with his grandparents.

Steinhauer thus missed one of the key psychological elements in what we called the "Mask of Barack Obama," his constant familial loss. First he lost his father, and had to invent a father in his "Dreams." Then his mother sent him away and he was forced to join a "new" family, living full-time with his grandparents who were white. All of these episodes of loss are critical to understanding Obama's psyche. Unfortunately, Steinhauer confused the facts and misreported the reality of Obama's life-long feelings of alienation.

Nevertheless, the fact that Ms. Steinhauer tries to relate Obama's fictional account of his early life in his book "Dreams" to the reality of what he endured at a prestigious private school in Honolulu shows that we were absolutely right when we first focused attention on Obama's early life many months ago. The Times' return to that topic with a front-page story validates out own continuing news judgment.

Although we have been urged to "drop Obama" we won't do so. His candidacy says a lot of about the vacuousness of American politics, and the vulnerability of this nation to yet another bunkum artist in the White House.

What of the Dunham/Obama/Soetoro family? Obama continues to live in a fantasyland about "family," and he continues to shield the truth in order to perpetuate the myth of his "Africanness."

So what' so strange about Obama's family? Well, his sister refuses to be photographed. She has claimed in past that she is an "adviser." When has a presidential adviser or family member refused to be photographed? It's weird. Do Obama's presidential advisors/relatives walk around wearing grocery bags on their heads? What do they have to hide?

Likewise, Obama's white grandmother is apparently forced to maintain the fiction that she is "not well enough" to be photographed or interviewed. It would be politically embarrassing for Mr. Obama, trying to portray himself as the first "Black president" in the words of his sister Maya Soetoro-Ng, to produce a white grandmother. So granny stays locked in the closet. Obama perpetuates the myth of his "blackness" at the cost of his closest family. What kind of a person would do that? Not someone we would want to be president, for sure.

Indeed, the "granny locked-in-the-closet" figure of speech says it all about Obama's campaign and the way he is likely to ultimately damage the Democratic Party and disappoint his followers.

Sunday in the New York Post Leon Wieseltier of the New Republic published a column in which he admitted "skepticism is sedulously arriving" about Obama. Thus it is particularly unfortunate that the New York Times sent a reporter to Hawaii and missed both the forest and the trees about Obama's early years.

In the meantime, as the L. A. Times' and N. Y. Times' belated attempts to profile Obama reflect, our own psychological profile remains the gold standard by which all other media analysis will be compared. From 2004 to 2007, we have been the first, and the best and, unfortunately, often the only Obama media analysts willing to write the truth about this seriously confused candidate.

"It's Getting Crowded on the 'Obama Skeptics Bus,'"
Says Andy Martin

Obama's "cult" begins to deflate as
reality slowly sets in for nation's media

(CHICAGO)(March 26, 2007) Who'd a thunk it? Tickets on the "Obama Skeptics Bus" are selling like hotcakes.

Somehow Obama the glib Kenyan witch doctor is slowly falling to earth. And not in the White house.

Obama's cult may still have drawing power among the unwashed masses of the Democratic Party. But among the washed media, skepticism is rapidly setting in.

As if waking from deep winter hibernation, media types have suddenly started demanding the same high standards of candor and accuracy from Barack Obama that they impose on others in public life.

Obama's father, the Kenyan bigamist/predator who seduced an unsophisticated 18 year-old student, Obama's mother, stands exposed in today's Chicago Tribune (March 27) as someone who "never asked about his ex-wife or his son." Owww. So, as I have written so often in the past two and a half years, Barack Obama, Jr.'s "Dreams From my Father" are really dreams from himself. They are the bleeding wounds and cries of a young child abandoned by a callous and greedy psychopath from Kenya. That explains why Obama is the most fantasy and deception-prone candidate in a long, long time. His real life was utterly unbearable.

Indeed, Washington Post Columnist Richard Cohen performs the ultimate indignity on Barry O today: he compares Obama's fantasy "movie" to that of the Democrats' nemesis: President Ronald Reagan. I guess that makes Obama a "Reagan Democrat." Or at least Richard Cohen thinks so.

Cohen calls Obama a man seeking to "wrap raw ambition," as a "successful packager of himself" in the service of "manipulating facts" who is "starring in his own movie." And that from a favorable columnist.

Another newspaper waking from a deep sleep is the Chicago Tribune where today's "Swamp" catalogues the shift in coverage of Obama from positive to negative. The Obamacrats in the media are starting to abandon ship.

The Tribune goes so far as to expose a forgotten side of Obama's family life. His mother was "from Kansas," but her formative teen years were spent on Mercer Island, Washington outside Seattle. Those years are virtually missing from Obama's compendium. It's interesting that it has taken the Tribune three (3, count 'em) years to start looking at Obama critically.

Both Tribune reporter Frank James and Mr. Cohen focus on a "Dreams" story extensively examined by the Tribune, in which Obambi claims to have been seared by the sight of a Life Magazine cover. It turns out the entire episode was a fabrication and fantasy of Barry O. Never happened. More ammunition for my forthcoming lawsuit that Obama's book should be shelved under "Fiction" and not "Biography."

James notes that a recent forum Obama said among his qualifications for the White House was his work on "nuclear proliferation." The claim that Obama has any credentials in the area of nuclear proliferation is even more of a hoot that Al Gore's claim he invented the Internet. Still, reporters are stating to pick up on Obama's lies. Better late than never.

Obama was 34 years old when he wrote "Dreams." And the book is filled with fantasy, fabrication and imagination. Great fiction but not the kind of work that would commend itself to a young lawyer.

Lawyers like facts, precision, accuracy and, above all, "candor to the tribunal." Obama' propensity to lie may explain why he has never been before a tribunal in any meaningful way.

Maybe that's why both Obama and his wife have surrendered their licenses to practice law in Illinois. Too demanding, too detailed-oriented, too lawyerlike for them.

Jennifer Hunter, someone to whom I probably owe an apology for my initial thought she might be an Obama flack on the Sun-Times staff, produced a searing "book review" March 26th of Obama's second book, "The Audacity of Hope," calling the tome a "grind," "cod liver oil," and "hard to swallow." Whoa. Hunter says the book "bores me to tears." I do not think Ms. Hunter would have exhibited such devastating candor a month ago. She is now. Jennifer, if the book moved you to tears, there is more to the Obama fantasyland; keep crying.

Hunter looks like she has peeked at our own ContrarianCommentary.com psychological study of Obama— still the best analysis of his convoluted and conflicted psyche. Hunter says she wants "more answers" about the role Obama's 18 year-old mother's struggles played in his anger. Well.

It was only a month ago, during Contrarian Commentary.com's "Obama Week," that we were still a lonely voice focusing attention on Obama's psychological profile and disturbing family history. Aside from me, the "Obama Skeptics Bus" was empty.

Now the seats are filling rapidly.

I produce a newspaper called "Contrarian Commentary.com" precisely because most reporters often miss the real significance of news. They parrot what hucksters like Witch Doctor Obama want them to say. They do not act this way because reporters are necessarily evil; they do so because they are prisoners of the "news cycle."

CCC has time for a more analytical approach, and over the past 2-1/2 years our efforts have paid off in trend-setting investigative reporting on "The Real Obama."

Finally, the Internet is a great discipline. A great leveler. A "Great Equalizer," the Colt. 45 of Communications. You can see what we have written, and what others did not; and you can see what others are writing now, following in our footsteps.

Boys and Girls of the media, "All Aboard the Obama Bus." There's more to say, more to investigate, and more to reveal about Mr. Obama, someone who is probably a very decent person but nevertheless totally unfit to sit in the Oval Office.

Of course, if you had paid attention to my comments in 1999, you would have heard me say "George Bush wants to bomb Iraq." Now where did I get *that* idea? In 1999?

Barack Obama:
Is America Ready for Reparations?

Obama's supporters see reparations in their future
if Barry O is elected

Ready to pay? Obama's the way

(CHICAGO)(April 4, 2007) Is America ready to pay reparations for slavery? What is that you say, "Doesn't Senator Barack Obama oppose reparations for slavery?" Well, no. He doesn't.

In fact the reparations crowd in Washington and Chicago is salivating at the prospect Obama might stumble into the White House and put them on track for a reparations gravy train for slavery which took place centuries ago.

To tackle the topic, first, a simple question: is Obama opposed to reparations? Indeed, the question is not so simple. Nothing is ever simple and straightforward where Barry Obama and words come together. Obama's pirouettes on the question of reparations would enchant any balletomane; his position always depends on who is asking and who is listening. And who is watching.

Prior to his election to the U.S. Senate in 2004 Obama opposed reparations for slavery. After his election, Obama subtly changed his view, stating he was against "just signing over checks to African-Americans," leaving open the possibility of other forms of reparations would be acceptable to him (Chicago Tribune 11/14/2004).

Second, whom does Barry O "hang" with? Well, Obama hangs with the reparations crowd. Now guilt by association is certainly unfair. But if you hang with the reparations crowd, they must see something in you they like. Indeed they do. U. S. Representative John Conyers, Chairman of the House Judiciary Committee, is reportedly waiting for Obama to be elected so Conyers can rush a reparations law through Congress. (The Hill, 3/13/ 2007) Hmmm. Does Conyers know something we don't?

Finally, the most telling indication that Obama has a secret addiction to reparations is reflected in those who support him and those whom he supports: the most notorious race-baiter on the Chicago City Council, Alderwoman Dorothy Tillman.

Haven't heard of Dorothy Tillman? You better learn about Obama's #1 supporter. And fast. You really should know who she is. Tillman has almost single-handedly made a joke of the City of Chicago in the public finance industry over her preoccupation with slavery and reparations.

Tillman supports Obama and Obama supports Tillman.

Last week Obama endorsed Tillman for reelection. Tillman was forced into a runoff after her opponents failed to agree on a single candidate to oppose her. Tillman was an early supporter of Obama's in his rise to prominence over the past decade.

And Tillman is a disgrace. Her favorite pastime is abusing banks and financial institutions that want to do business with the City of Chicago. A regular feature of council proceedings is Tillman flaying banks for "owning slaves" at some remote point in history over 150 years ago.

Using a 2002 "Slavery Era Disclosure Ordinance" that she authored, Tillman has accused Bank of America of having a predecessor bank that made "leg irons for slaves." Wachovia, J.P.

Morgan Chase, LaSalle Bank, Lehman Brothers, American General and Nationwide Life Insurance were all brought before Tillman's mast and whipped for their ties to slavery, however remote, over 150 years ago.

Indeed, Tillman has been quoted as saying her goal is to "repair the damage of 400 years" of slavery. "America owes us," Tillman demands (Sun-Times 3/26/2007).

And yes, Obama has endorsed this carnival-style extortionist for reelection. So much for the audacity of Obama, so much for the "smallness" of politics in Chicago.

Tillman abuses and opposes anyone who thinks that slavery is not a major issue any more. When the City wanted to refinance $800 million in debt, Tillman was there claiming slavery should be an issue. Last fall, the City tried to lease parking garages for over a half billion dollars: the deal hit a "slavery speed bump." Tillman filed suit because her slavery ordinance was brushed aside (Sun-Times 12/1/2006). "The whole world is watching us just disregard this law for black people...We're totally disrespected as a people...," (Sun-Times 10/31/06). On and on it goes. Sounds like the race card to me.

Tillman accused Morgan Stanley of "getting rich from investments and profits in slavery" (Chicago Tribune, 10/30/2006). Morgan Stanley was formed in 1935.

[Full disclosure: My maternal ancestors arrived in the United States in the Twentieth Century. Unlike Obama's forebears, my grandparents had nothing to do with slavery. Why should I pay for the earlier sins of others? Why should anyone pay for events that took place in history?]

When Obama's critics attack him for the sermons of his pastor they are going too far, in my opinion. I am not responsible for what my minister says. Preachers get a lot of leeway in the pulpit.

But when a public official files a frivolous lawsuit against a half-billion dollar public finance deal, claiming that Blacks are being disrespected because of slavery, and Obama goes on to endorse that kind of nonsense, Obama should be charged with endorsing the antics of the reparations gang.

When confronted with the claims of some of his more controversial supporters President Reagan used to say, "They endorsed me; I didn't endorse them."

In the case of Barry Obama and Dorothy Tillman, he **has** endorsed her and her unseemly reparations crusade for slavery.

Only Obama doesn't want his national audience to know it. I seriously doubt that many of the tens of thousands of people who have succumbed to Obama's pleas for "hope" realize he "hopes" to force them to pay tax dollars to provide some form of compensation to people who weren't alive from people who weren't alive, all for the evils of slavery. They have no idea who Dorothy Tillman is, or what she stands for, or the damage she continues to do to taxpayers in Chicago. All in the name of slavery.

And yet ignorant suckers keep on giving, not knowing who Obama is and what he wants to accomplish if he should end up in the Oval office.

Psst. Ready to pay reparations for slavery? Obama's your man.

He just doesn't want you to know. Yet.

He's too busy working to reelect Dorothy Tillman in two weeks.

Pass it on.

Don Imus Becomes "Political Basketball" for Obama, Clinton

Hillary's fast break and sharp elbows steal the ball from "Basketball Barry"

(CHICAGO)(April 12, 2007) Don Imus has become a political basketball in the Democratic Party. And Hillary Clinton has sent Barack "Basketball Barry" Obama into overtime with her fast break and sharp elbows.

Senator Barack Obama fancies himself a basketball player. He was on his high school team. And he makes a point of playing basketball on vacation in Hawaii. Maybe elsewhere too.

But Hillary Clinton's fast break and sharp elbows have stolen the ball from Obama on the Don Imus Imbroglio, forcing Barack into overtime.

Even worse for Obama, his intemperate remarks to ABC News involving his "two young daughters" on the Imus Imbroglio may have opened the door to even greater embarrassment for Obama concerning his ties to and campaign contributions from Black music entrepreneurs who profit from violent and misogynistic lyrics. Wassup Barry? Jump ball?

I want the hot dog concession. This "game" may have "legs."

The Imus fracas began with the disgusting, disgraceful, deplorable remarks from radio shock jock Don Imus. No one can defend his comments; no one pretends to. But Imus's lines were brief and a one-off. Nevertheless, the "civil rights profiteers" and hypocrites have been pig piling on Imus big time.

Al Sharpton and Jesse Jackson got there first. Didn't Obama ever hear the old saw "If you lie down with dogs, you catch fleas? Obama may have caught some fleas from Al and Jesse.

In the meantime, you have to love Hillary Clinton. She is something.

Clinton is struggling for black support in the face of Obama's national media frenzy. Hillary is learning it is not easy running against an African-American star in the Black community. But the "You go girl" has snatched the ball from Barry O and now confronted him on his own turf, thanks to a little boost from ContrarianCommentary.com.

Due to our pungent criticism and analysis (and a little extrapolation) Obama may be facing major embarrassment for his ties to and contributions from Black music sextrepreneurs.

Here's what happened. Never one to miss an opportunity, Hillary jumped on the Rutgers/Imus scandal by putting the players' pictures—five young Black faces—on her campaign's home page [http://www.hillaryclinton.com/]. Bold move. I love it. Hillary, the battle is to the brave. You *are* good. You may wear pants suits on the basketball court but you move with the best.

You can click through to a second Hillary page to "send a message" to the Rutgers women. There Hillary talks about "coarse sexism" (sounds like Bill Clinton to me) and a "disregard for basic decency" (more Bill Clinton). She says Imus was "disrespectful and degrading." Hey, that's my Bill. Pure Bill Clinton. What was she thinking? Who wrote *those* lines?

But Hillary ultimately set a trap for Obama, and he fell in.

Hillary gave Barack agita with her bold move, forcing Obama to play catch-up ball. (I'll have catch-up on my hot dog;

this is getting interesting.) I imagine Obama's team said "captain, we have to do something."

So Obama brought his two daughters into the campaign confrontation. He is, after all, a family man and by all the evidence a warm and loving parent. But he made a big mistake. He fumbled. (Will you forgive my mixed metaphor?) Game rules should always be: keep the kids out of it.

Obama spoke to ABC News. The Chicago Tribune quotes Obama [http://newsblogs.chicagotribune.com/news_the swamp/2007/04/obama_fire_imus.html] as saying "[M]y two young daughters are having to deal with…It was a degrading comment," thus linking his daughters to Imus' gross stupidity and "coarse sexism." Trying to counter Hillary and top her web site's invitation, Obama demanded that Imus be fired. End of story. Not by a mile.

Who is the bigger threat to Obama's "two young daughters?" Don Imus or the relentless violence, filth and misogyny peddled over hundreds of "urban" hip-hop and rap radio stations?

But Obama has never launched sustained attacks on rap lyrics, or demanded that Black hip-hop/rap sextrepreneurs who use "coarse sexism," violent imagery and misogyny to excite young males, should be fired. Puff Daddy (P. Diddy or whatever) are you listening?

My guess: Obama has collected a part of his $25 million in campaign cash from precisely the hip-hop/rap smut merchants who are the greatest threat to his "two young daughters." And yet he attacks an old white man, seedy and goofy Don Imus, while allowing Black sextrepreneurs and misogynists to make billions with their violent lyrics on America's radio waves.

Is there a double standard here? Yes, there is.

The most intelligent commentary on the Imus Imbroglio came from a writer at the Chicago Sun-Times, Deborah Douglas, who stated "[Imus] is an idiot. What's our excuse?" [http://www.suntimes.com/news/otherviews/335859,CST-NWS-contro11.article]. To do Ms. Douglas one better: What is Obama's excuse for attacking Imus and not the Black sextrepreneurs who peddle filth, violence and misogyny much more devastating to his "you young daughters?" Well, what about it Barry?

To repeat: Who is the greater threat to Obama's "two young daughters?" Don Imus or the relentless rap/hip-hop filth broadcast over Chicago radio stations and in every major market? What about it Barry?

A Florida writer recently suggested that every time Obama slips, ContrarianCommentary.com will be there to comment. We are. I have never met Mrs. Clinton, and I have absolutely no contact with her or her campaign. None. But it is hard not to admire a woman who could have been an extraordinary leader in her own right if she was not liked to the "coarse sexism" and "disrespectful and degrading" behavior of her husband.

Hillary, baby (can I call her that?), you just stole the ball from "Basketball Barry." Game point to you.

P. S. The most amusing Midwestern response to the Imus scandal came from Phil Rosenthal in the Chicago Tribune. His take: no one here knows Imus. Imus? Who he? You just have to love the left coast and right coast, and everything in between.

Obama's Mojo Deserts Him in Chicago as Long-time Supporter is Defeated for Reelection

(CHICAGO)(April 18, 2007) Senator Barack Obama's long-time supporter in Chicago politics, race-baiting Alderwoman Dorothy Tillman, was defeated for reelection yesterday. The defeat was announced by ContrarianCommentary.com's Executive Editor Andy Martin.

Obama had endorsed Tillman for reelection. Tillman favored "reparations" for slavery, a position that Obama has also supported with a "wink and a nod."

"Well, Obama has no coattails in his own home town," Martin said in announcing the election results. "African-American voters know 'pie-in-the-sky' promises when they see them, and Obama-Tillman were offering pie-in-the-sky. If Obama can't carry a ward in his own home city with his very visible endorsement, what does that say about his 'coattails' nationally? Barry O has no mojo.

"Mr. Obama is a creation of liberal national pundits that want a 'horse race' between Obama and Hillary Clinton in 2008. But both of these candidates are deeply flawed, and they will be rejected by the American people. I am sure Dorothy Tillman is wondering how she lost when she had Obambi's support. Well, she's out. And Obama's mojo is exposed as skin deep.

"Our Obama coverage has been sidetracked by the press of developing news in other areas, but we will be back covering the 'Betrayals of Barry O' next week," Martin stated.

Andy Martin Demands Michelle Obama
Cut Link to Wal-Mart Supplier

(CHICAGO)(May 15, 2007) Chicago-based Internet journalist, broadcaster and media critic Andy Martin will hold a news conference Tuesday, May 15th at 3:00 P.M. to demand that Michelle Obama resign for the Board of Treehouse Foods. Treehouse Foods is a supplier to Wal-Mart.

"Everyone says that politics and politicians are two-faced," Martin will charge. "But the Obamas are in your face with their two faces. Barry Obama attacks Wal-Mart, and Michelle Obama serves the same Wal-Mart through Treehouse Foods. What a twosome. On both sides of the same issue and at the same time.

"I say it's time for the Obamas to 'End the Hypocrisy!'

"Let me state unequivocally that I am a supporter of Wal-Mart," Martin will state." I have found the political shenanigans involving Wal-Mart in Chicago disgraceful and self-destructive. Can Wal-Mart make improvements? Surely they can. Do they provide a valuable service to working America? You bet they do. Are they responsive? I think they are.

"Barack Obama and his wife work both sides of the street of the Wal-Mart controversy. Pretty soon we're going to have a new expression: "That's a real Obama," (meaning, you talk out of both sides of your mouth for political profit).

Since the 1960's Andy Martin has been Illinois' leading public interest advocate (see AndyMartin.com, AndyforUS Senator.com).

Andy Martin Demands Barack Obama Step Down as Presidential Candidate

"Ghost of Rezko" haunts Obama campaign

"Soft-core" corruption stains "Barry O," prompts his campaign staff to lie as Sun-Times furnishes new evidence of Rezko-Obama links

(CHICAGO)(June 14, 2007) Chicago-based Internet journalist, broadcaster and media critic Andy Martin will hold a news conference Thursday, June 14th at 1:00 P.M. to demand that Barack Obama step down as a presidential candidate "because Obama has brazenly lied to the American people" about his links to Illinois influence peddler and indicted alleged extortionist Tony Rezko.

Martin's demand on May 15th that Michelle Obama resign from Wal-Mart supplier Treehouse Foods prompted Barack Obama's wife to step down from Treehouse shortly thereafter.

"Last November 16th I asked to appear before the United States Grand Jury to testify about the extensive links between Barack Obama and indicted influence peddler Tony Rezko," Martin will charge. The Chicago Sun-Times' latest disclosures confirm more of the basis for my testimony.

"Wednesday, June 13th's Chicago Sun-Times exposed yet another layer of links between Obama and Rezko.

"Plainly put, Obama lied when he claimed his contacts with Rezko were innocent and that he was simply a 'boneheaded' naïf, the 'Obambi Defense.' He lied when he said he had no idea about Rezko's real estate activity.

"It is simply not credible that Obama and his senior law partner and Rezko were all holding hands without knowing what was going on, and that Obama was writing letters on behalf of his 'community' for Rezko. Obama's earlier story was that he 'knew nothing' about Rezko's real estate shenanigans. Now the Sun-Times has published a letter on Obama's senate stationary boosting Rezko. Will wonders never cease? Obama has what Illinois Republicans would call a 'Jack Ryan' problem, i.e. damaging disclosures to come after the primaries next year.

"We don't need an African-American Bill Clinton in the White House, who thinks that he has a 'license to lie' as he seeks the nation's highest office. Obama has cruelly lied to his supporters about his links to Tony Rezko. He is hoping that his ongoing 'modified limited hangout' through press agents will allow him to tough it out.

"Obama's response to the latest disclosures about his links to Rezko were more of the same: hiding behind campaign press assistants. Barry needs to come clean.

"The Democrats may be paying footsie in their presidential 'debates,' afraid to ask each other tough, penetrating questions, but the 'Ghost of Rezko' will not soon depart from Obama's presence. Not only has Obama lied to the American people, he has lied repeatedly and sought to misled flaccid journalists about his years as a practicing lawyer in Chicago, when he dealt in the same kind of soft-core influence peddling and corruption as countless other attorneys and state legislators.

"When Tony starts to sing, he'll be singing 'Barry Obama's Song,'" Martin says.

Andy Martin Will Ask Obama to Provide Dates for When Obama Claims His Mother was on Welfare

Andy expresses skepticism at latest revelation by senator, and notes lack of reference to food stamps in "Dreams From My Father"

(CHICAGO)(June 16, 2007) Chicago-based Internet journalist, broadcaster and media critic Andy Martin will hold a news conference Saturday, June 16th at 3:00 P.M. to ask that Barack Obama disclose the dates when his mother/family was on welfare (food stamps).

"The Chicago Tribune web site for June 16th (http://www.chicagotribune.com/news/politics/chi-070615oba-maspeech15jun15,1,7040230,print.story?coll=chi-news-hed) quotes Barack Obama as saying is mother was on welfare, and received food stamps," Martin will note, "although that comment is not in the Associated Press story of the same event.

"I have read 'Dreams From My Father' and I find no mention of food stamps or welfare. This latest claim is such a startling one I fail to see how he could have omitted it from his book. Perhaps I missed the comment. But I am concerned by this latest 'rabbit out of the hat,' when the claim that Obama grew up on food stamps has apparently not appeared before today.

"Given that Obama's grandparents were middle class, it is surprising that they would have allowed their daughter to apply for and receive welfare.

"Obama of course, in the past has offered imaginary claims for when he was conceived and other critical events in his life. I believe he owes the American people a detailed factual explanation of specific dates when his family was on welfare if he wants to become the first American president to rise from 'Welfare to the White House.'"

Martin will state he is considering Freedom of Information requests to the State of Hawaii, which appears to be the only state where Obama resided with his mother and where he could have received welfare payments.

Barack Obama: Welfare Thief
Obama's Mother, the Welfare Queen

(CHICAGO)(June 16, 2007) For young people today it is difficult to imagine the arrogance and corruption that characterized welfare recipients in the 1960's and 70's. Barack Obama wants to bring back the "good old days" of welfare fraud, when his mother was "ripping of the man."

Obama, of course, is a master pickpocket. But he doesn't pick our wallets, he picks at our emotions, speaking boldly with the use of emphatic but hollow phrases. And every so often he drops in a zinger, just to confirm that he knows everyone else wants to "rip off the man" too. A vote for Barack Obama is a vote to bring back the old days of welfare thievery. Exhibit A: The Obama Family.

Today's Chicago Tribune (June 16th) has a huge picture of Obama telling us to have "responsible" fathers. What about responsible mothers? Dropped into the Tribune story is this gem: "[Obama] noted that, without support from his father (who was in Kenya siring more children and drinking up good whiskey) he and his mother at times turned to food stamps to make ends meet."

I found this reference startling, because I did not remember any admission of welfare use by Obama and his mother. I checked my notes on "Dreams From My Father" (dreams after a night of whoring and whisky in Kenya?) and found no reference either. So I started digging.

It appears that the Barack-Obama-On-Welfare claim originated in Time magazine in a story by Joe Klein. (See: http://www.time.com/time/magazine/article/0,9171, 1546302,00.html.) Later, Larry King picked up the story and asked Obama about it on CNN. Then the issue faded. Until June 15th.

In Klein's story the line is slightly different, and more arrogant: "For example, I was going to a fancy prep school, and my mother was on food stamps while she was getting her Ph.D."

Well, the origins of the Obama-On-Welfare reflect a callous indifference to "ripping off the man."

First, we have been led to believe that while he was at prep school in Hawaii, Obama lived with his grandparents. His grandmother worked at a bank. How is it they were able to afford tuition for prep school and could not afford money to feed their grandson? Strange. Maybe that's why grandma is hidden and avoids the public. She knows the Obama family's dirty secrets.

It is possible that Obama might have lived with his mother at some point while she was a doctoral candidate in Hawaii, and voluntarily unemployed after competing two college degrees. Obama seems to think it was all right for his mother to collect welfare while she "invested in herself." Unfortunately, they had a name for such abuses, even in the 60's: criminal fraud.

Welfare was never intended as a public subsidy for people who wanted to become long-term college students. Mrs. Obama (if that is the name she should be given, given her former husband's frolicking in Kenya) seemed to think it was perfectly all right for her to claim welfare benefits at the taxpayer's expense while her son went to prep school, and someone paid thousands of dollars of private school tuition and she pursued endless academic studies. What about student loans? Well, those would have to be repaid, of course. No need to repay welfare. Just "rip off the man." Man.

While he served as mayor of New York, Rudy Giuliani tightened requirements for welfare and food stamps. Hundreds of thousands of cheats like the Obama family left the public trough. Now Democrats are trying to liberalize welfare and food stamps in New York again, and the parasites are salivating at the new opportunity to "rip off the man." Democrats want to bring back the "salad days" of welfare in Washington too. Or, rather, the private school tuition days of welfare.

By coincidence, my mom was studying her for Ph.D in the 1960's. She did not apply for welfare and supported her family on a teaching assistant's salary of $4,800 a year. She did not have money for private school tuition at exclusive academies of the type Obama's family enjoyed. There was a lot of white bread and baloney sandwiches. My mother would have sooner died than apply for welfare. But then that's the difference between an honest American family and Obama's Kenyan-American rip-off artists. For us, welfare was a form of shame. Obama, obviously, is shameless.

And the liberal morons keep sending him money and swooning. Instead of "Obamagirl.com," we need a "Barrysmomwasawelfarequeen.com" web site to alert Obama to the need to improve his standards of public morality.

There are few, if any, Americans who would deny a neighbor help in a time of genuine need. I have served at church soup kitchens, and many of us have contributed to programs for those in need. But few of us feel the need to subsidize people who want to get a doctorate degree, or who want to "save" their money for private school tuition or who are too lazy to apply for a student loan or work part-time, like Mrs. Obama. Many of us remember standing in supermarket lines and seeing people use food stamps to buy food, and then using their cash to buy alcohol and cigarettes. They called it "ripping off the man."

The fact that Obama refers to the fact that his mother was a welfare queen, and that she thought nothing of ripping off society for her own selfish benefit, tells a lot about the man. This is another example of why Obama has such a troubled psyche. Instead of shame, Obama is telling us he wants to bring back the good old days when his mom was ripping the man.

Is it any wonder people voted for Ronald Reagan for president in 1980? Obama's mother was one very obvious reason the thievery and arrogance and corruption had to stop. It did. Except in Obama's mind, where stealing from taxpayers is what he promises for his future presidency.

Maybe, as a matter of conscience, Obama should repay the money that his mom ripped off from the "man." The "man" was and is the American people that he now claims he wants to serve.

Barack Obama owes the American people an explanation. And an apology.

Really, Barry, you should get a life. And get a mom.

What is Wrong with Republican State Senator Kirk Dillard?

Mid-life crisis?
Angling for a job from Barry Obama?
Or just plain gullible?

(CHICAGO)(June 16, 2007)   Republican State Senator Kirk Dillard is a thoroughly decent, intelligent and normally sensible public official. But he gets all gooey where senate Barack Obama is concerned. And this time Dillard may have crossed the line between bipartisan friendship and sheer loopiness. (http://www.nytimes.com/aponline/us/AP-Obama-Big-Leap.html)

Public officials, of course, do develop respect and admiration, and friendships, on city councils, in legislatures and in government. That's normal and healthy. Unlike some people, we don't settle our differences with guns. We work hard to compromise, accommodate and reach consensus. Democracy requires compromise, even if some conservatives don't always want to admit it.

But Dillard's "bipartisanship" is lately rising to a screwy level. He is quoted today as stating "I would not lose a night's sleep worrying about my young children's future if Senator [Barack] Obama were my president...he would probably surround himself...with exceptionally experienced people."

Who has Obama surrounded himself with? The sultans of sleaze of the Democratic Party in Illinois. Mayor Richie Daley? State Senator Emil Jones, who thinks every government job should belong to one of his relatives? Alexi Giannoulias, the Chicago Crime Syndicate's representative in Springfield? Dorothy Tillman, the race-baiting White-hating former Alderperson? Tod Stroger, who is also shamelessly looting local government?

What was Dillard thinking?

And what about the current the clown prince of corruption in Chicago, indicted influence peddler Tony Rezko, concerning whom Obama refused to speak with reporters from the New York Times this week? Rezko helped financed the Obama family's estate in Chicago.

What was/is Dillard thinking? Or as Dillard's BFF Barry Obama might say, "Whassup?"

Dillard wants to put Obama in charge of nuclear defense? Middle East wars? The energy crisis? Welfare? Dillard is comfortable entrusting these crises to Obama? Entrusting *his children's future?* Is Dillard going completely nuts?

Kirk, we hardly knew ye.

Is Dillard thinking of switching parties? It sure seems like it.

Does anyone have an answer or explanation for Dillard's bizarre comments and behavior? He owes us one.

What is Wrong with Republican State Senator Kirk Dillard? Part Two

Is Dilly "crazy," or "crazy like a fox"?
An insult to the intelligence of – Senator John McCain
Illinois Republicans should also be offended

(CHICAGO)(June 27, 2007) State Senator Kirk Dillard of DuPage County did it again this week: he said he was not "endorsing" Senator Barack Obama for President, and then Dillard endorsed Obama in TV ads. What gives? Is Dilly crazy, or crazy like a fox?

After Kirk Dillard was quoted by the New York Times two weeks ago making pleasant comments about Barack Obama some Republicans told me that Dilly's remarks were from "old interviews." What are they going to say about Dillard's TV endorsement of Obama? Old TV ads?

Dilly insults our intelligence when he is quoted by the Chicago Tribune as saying he has "stopped short of an endorsement." Please, Kirk, do not insult us. When you appear in someone's TV ad, *you are an endorser*. Appearing in a TV ad is an endorsement.

If I were Senator John McCain I would quietly and politely ask Dillard to step down as a McCain backer. Politicians are known for working both sides of the street, just like streetwalkers. But even streetwalkers know enough not to be too obvious. Dillard obviously doesn't.

The DuPage senator apparently thinks he can be active in both parties, simultaneously. Dillard was quoted in the Daily Herald criticizing the Republican Party, stating "maybe if my party understood the issues of racial reconciliation, less partisanship and *hope*, they would be the majority party." I have news for Dilly: Republicans *are* the majority party.

"Racial reconciliation?" In a party that appointed two (Count 'em: 2!) African-American Secretaries of State? "Hope?" What is Dilly drinking? Or thinking?

Most Illinoisans know where I stand on "intraparty" battles and "party issues." As to intraparty battles, I stay on the sidelines. Being a candidate is enough of a challenge without thrashing away at internal politics.

As to party "issues," I have not hesitated to criticize the Iraq invasion and President Bush's Middle East policies. Bushie doesn't like me. I disagree with him. And I am right. Boom.

But I would no more blame the Republican Party for President Bush's mistakes than blame the Democratic Party for Bill Clinton's sexual escapades.

Where was Dillard when he claims the party was going to hell in a handbasket? Keeping his head down. And keeping quiet. He was not critical then. Now that Kirky-boy thinks the Republicans are mortally wounded he has his shank out. *Et tu Brute*?

There is nothing inherently wrong with switching parties. People are entitled to change their minds and even change their views. And they are certainly entitled to "make a statement" by jumping ship. But Dillard wants to represent the Republican Party in the Illinois Senate while he backs a Democrat for president from the U. S. Senate. It won't work.

Senator John McCain has sometimes been accused of having a temper. I would be surprised if McCain is not having a fit at Dillard's ongoing "support." Dillard has become *an embarrassment.*

After Dillard was quoted in the New York Times as praising Obama I made the obvious observation that legislative politics turns on legislators working together. We *expect* elected officials to cooperate.

But no one has ever suggested that someone can work both sides of the street as an elected Republican official and TV endorser of a Democratic presidential candidate during the same election. Maybe Dillard is auditioning for the role of Chairman of Republicans for Obama.

We also expect candidates and elected officials to demonstrate a certain amount of opportunism in their campaigns and public service. After all, no one ever got elected by working for #2.

But Dillard and another Illinois state rep who switched to the Democratic Party are demonstrating reprehensible opportunism. I predict their disloyalty will backfire on them. Dillard and his fellow traveler obviously expect the Democrats to win, and they want to jump aboard the winning float at the start of the parade. Wrong.

These hogs are going to get slapped, not slopped.

No one can predict the outcome of the 2008 election. I know, I know. Democrats are measuring for curtains in the executive branch. But they better not overdo décor dementia.

Right now Republican prospects look bleak. As bleak as the Democrats' electoral prospects in 1968? About the same. The "in" party during a botched war is not the favorite to repeat. But Hubert Humphrey came within a whisker of being elected in the midst of a horrible war. Some Republican could do likewise. And likely will.

But, if a Republican is elected, Dillard can look forward to being appointed a federal judge. To the U. S. District Court for the Moon.

People who switch parties because of philosophical differences can sometimes succeed. I also lived in Florida during the 1980's when the political structure went through a wholesale realignment, and people switched parties regularly. It was acceptable and accepted. But then the parties stabilized and the process came to an end.

People who switch parties for opportunism, however, often are rejected. My prediction? Dillard's days in the Illinois senate are over. And the switching state rep will be retired in the next primary. By Democrats. Thanks for nutt'in.

So will Dilly and Barry (Obama) ride off into the sunset together? Only if they are marching in their own parade. They may be holding hands; but don't hold your breath.

Andy Martin on "Obama the Conqueror" – Part One of a Two-Part Series: The Democrats' Delusions on Foreign Policy (and Maybe Some Republicans Too)

Andy's "Barry O" fires a slap shot at right-wing, left-wing in presidential politics

Campaigns must address a coming "sanctuary gap"

Obama touches the "third rail of foreign policy" with speech raising issue of Pakistan's Al Qaeda sanctuaries

(CHICAGO)(August 2, 2007) I don't often get to defend Barry Obama. My earlier columns this year have done a pioneering job of exposing his prevarications and evasions. But this one's for Barack. He has managed to fire a slap shot at both the Democrats and Republicans with his foreign policy speech yesterday.

First, the obvious background for those who do not wait breathlessly for Anderson Cooper and YouTube users to feed you foreign policy perspective. In the recent CNN/YouTube debate, Obama said he was prepared to meet with "bad" foreign leaders without any preconditions. Hillary Clinton called that "irresponsible and naïve." Obama's remarks were no more "irresponsible and naïve" than the eight years of the (Bill) Clinton White House.

Yesterday Obama said he would use "actionable intelligence" to take action against Al Qaeda in Pakistan's tribal areas if Pakistani authorities refuse to pursue terrorist sanctuaries. Well, what's controversial about that?

At ContrarianCommentary.com we prize our reputation for independence and integrity (and foreign policy insight and expertise). And so while we do not hesitate to trash Barry O for his personal nonsense, we will salute him for touching the third rail of foreign policy: What to do with Pakistan and the Al Qaeda sanctuaries? The New York Post is in a paroxysm today, [http://www.nypost.com/seven/08022007/news/national-news/obama__id_invade_ally_nationalnews_charles_hurt_____bureau_chief.htm] showing Obama in a Dukakis-like pose sticking his head out of a tank. "Barack the Conqueror" seems to be their subtext. A Post columnist calls Obama's speech a "blunder." The Post's editorial page calls Obama's remarks a "bomb." So surely the left is celebrating?

Not on your life. The extreme left of the Democratic Party has also gone into a feeding frenzy. What? Obama? Basketball Barry? Pop and grandpop Muslims? Invade Pakistan? The Democratic Party's also-ran presidential candidates have also attacked Obama for his remarks.

Muslims have not yet been heard from, but they will no doubt be squealing as loudly as Republicans and Democrats at Obama's suggestion.

Obama is to be congratulated for exposing the nonsense in both parties.

His remarks expose the utter failure of the tough talking Republicans to get Osama Bin Laden "dead or alive" six (6!) years after he bombed New York. Bush has failed to expand our military and has starved the Afghanistan mission to ramp up U. S. Forces in Iraq. Bush has allowed "Busharraf" to play games with tens of billions of U. S. aid dollars, promising action but mainly delivering low-level Al Qaeda operatives, the Pakistani version of "round up the usual suspects."

So, to be honest, President Bush has been a failure in coming up with an effective strategy to eliminate Al Qaeda. More critically, he lacks any policy to eliminate Al Qaeda's sanctuaries in the "tribal areas" of Pakistan.

The issue of what to do with Al Qaeda's sanctuaries will be the foreign policy issue in the presidential campaign. Obama has put that question on the table. Neither party has a meaningful response. Ladies and gentlemen: what are you going to do about the "Sanctuary Gap." Unlike the imaginary "Missile Gap" in 1960, the absence of any proposal to deal with "the Pakistani problem" is a real issue in 2008.

The Republicans' "see no evil" pretend policy will not work, because sooner or later Al Qaeda will strike again. And when it does the party-in-power will be condemned for allowing the sanctuaries to exist.

But the Democrats "play dough" policy of pretending the sanctuaries are not a problem also offers no solution.

Obviously stung, both parties are trying to misrepresent what Obama said yesterday.

Obama did not say he would invade Pakistan with an army. The attempt to portray Barry's suggestions as some sort of "Obama the Conqueror" plan is ridiculous. He made no such proposal. Generals make those types of decisions. Obama, ever the cautious-one, would allow generals to make tactical decisions. He said he would act on intelligence. In principle, that has been U. S. policy since Bill Clinton's days. Where Obama went further is to direct that "action" at Pakistan's tribal areas.

What is so sacred about an area of the world where no government exercises effective control, and where we have allowed sanctuaries to develop? Good question. How do we deal with Osama-in-the-mountains? Obama has asked the right question and given a respectable stock answer. Give chase to Osama, wherever he is found. With all due respect to my Republican colleagues, Bush & Co. have had six years to catch Osama and failed miserably at the task.

"We can't find him" is not going to be an acceptable response in 2008 when the CIA says Al Qaeda is a growing threat, all managed from a mountain retreat somewhere in an "ungovernable" and "ungoverned" area of the world.

Republicans as well as Democrats will need to address the sanctuary issue. I had already identified that question of the sanctuaries as the principle foreign policy issue in my own campaign and commentary. The American people are going to want answers: why can't we find him? Why can't we catch him? Why do we allow the sanctuaries to exist when the CIA states they are a growing threat to America and the world?

Obama, of course, was desperate to find some way of responding to Hillary Clinton's taunts. But desperate men sometimes tell the truth. There was Obama last night, cloyingly (same old Barry O) saying his speech had been in preparation "for a long time," and was not a response to Hillary's attack. But whatever his motives, Obama performed a useful service for the American people: he put the issue of Al Qaeda's sanctuaries on the table. Both parties will have to come up with answers. To date, Obama is the only candidate with an honest approach.

Game ball to Obama. ContrarianCommentary.com will not "take sanctuary" in opposition when Obama makes an intelligent attempt to challenge the presidential campaign process with *the* issue in 2008. Desperate or not, Obama has triggered a very, very sensitive issue and confronted both parties with a problem they would both prefer to avoid. The Sanctuary Gap.

Which is why the extreme elements in both parties are attacking him. Barry O has pricked their balloon.

We will now see the first true test of the man as a leader.

Andy Martin on "Bombardier Barack" Obama and "Hellfire Hillary" Clinton

Democrats begin to eclipse Republicans with threats to use nuclear weapons in Asia

"Bomb, bomb, bomb, bomb, bomb Iran" sounds pretty tame by comparison

(CHICAGO)(August 5, 2007) Almost exactly fifty years ago, in July 1957, Senator John F. Kennedy caused a foreign policy commotion by condemning America's inaction on Algerian independence. The reaction from Paris was fast in coming. "Who is this Senator Kennedy and how is he making foreign policy?"

This past week Barack Obama let the cat out of the bag, and raised the obvious issue that our policy against Al Qaeda is a failure. The terrorist organization has regrouped in Pakistan, and poses an increasing threat to the United States. Obama said he would not hesitate to attack terrorist sanctuaries in Pakistan's "tribal areas." He later fumbled over whether he would use nuclear weapons to do so.

Air Marshal "Bomber Harris," the British commander who bombed the Third Reich into ashes, must be smiling. General Curtis E. LeMay, my old commanding officer, who threatened to "bomb our enemies into the stone age," must be stunned.

Hillary Clinton, wife of draft dodger Bill, will not rule out the use of nuclear weapons in Pakistan. What!

Well, well, well.

The use of nuclear weapons has not been in such vogue since the 1950's.

The Republicans look like tame tabby cats in comparison to the suddenly muscular bombardiers in the Democratic Party. Except for Republican congressman Tom Tancredo, who wants to bomb the holy sites of Islam. Fortunately, Tancredo is no-big-deal-o.

A few months ago, Senator John McCain was excoriated for singing a ditty "Bomb, bomb, bomb, bomb, bomb Iran." There was no media criticism when Clinton put her finger on the nuclear trigger and said she would not rule out the use of those weapons. Was that Bill's advice? Nuclear pillow talk?

And, as Kennedy did in 1957, Obama is causing an overseas furor in 2007. The Pakistani government has condemned Obama's suggestions. George Bush apparently took notice. In a story with no major sourcing, the New York Post stated August 4th that Bush told Pakistani Dictator Musharraf that Bush condemned Obama's "unsavory" suggestions.

What is happening to the presidential campaign when the Democrats are suddenly falling over each other to appear tough guys, and the Republicans are sitting quietly on the sidelines?

Reality is setting in.

The "netroots" were in Chicago this weekend (more of them in a companion column). The Democratic Party's extreme lefties were singing songs of surrender in the Middle East, and dreaming of measuring their offices for carpet in a new Democratic administration. Well, well, well again.

Contrary to what mainstream pundits say, my instincts tell me that the American people are totally undecided. They are disgusted with the Republican incompetence and hubris in the Middle East. But they are equally skeptical of the Democrats. Forget what the polls say about Bush. The presidential race is wide open. For either Republicans or Democrats to win or lose.

Obama found that he could no longer namby pamby his way to the nomination. Hillary was stealing his bombs. And Clinton could not appear to be indecisive when Bombardier Barack was ready to launch into Waziristan.

The reality, of course, is vastly different from what Obama and Clinton suppose or propose. I know; I've been there. The "ungoverned" areas of Afghanistan and Pakistan are not a place to use nuclear weapons. So, Barry O doesn't have to worry. And, no, Hillary, you can release your trigger finger. Osama Bin Laden is not going to be brought down with nuclear weapons.

Rather, the United States and its allies will have to fight a counterinsurgency campaign in Pakistan using CIA troops and special operations units. The Democrats probably know that. Maybe they are just falling over themselves to honor the memory of General LeMay and Bomber Harris.

And poor, old Senator John McCain, who actually dropped bombs on Hanoi, is left behind as the Democrats zoom ahead with their nuclear weapons. Bomb, bomb, bomb, bomb, bomb McCain.

But certain inevitable truths are slowly oozing to the surface in the Democratic Party's pre-primary season:

First, Pakistan—Musharraf's defenses notwithstanding—has totally failed to eradicate the terrorist threat, and he is completely incapable and unwilling to do so. The Taliban and Al Qaeda are increasing in strength.

Second, an open invasion of Pakistan is not in the cards. It won't happen. Finding and killing Bin Laden & Co. is a classic special operations mission. That operation is already in progress from a control center at Baghram Air Base in Kabul.

Third, bravado sells. Obama got an honorable mention from the Wall Street Journal ("Barack Obama, Neocon") and from New York Post columnist John Podhoretz ("Thanks Barack").

Finally, the Democrats are coming to the realization that as tattered as the Republicans may appear to be, the American people are not going to turn the White House over to surrender junkies and screaming "netroots" sissies.

National security is still the first responsibility of the federal government. Neither party to date has convinced the American people. It remains to be seen whether the Democrats' current bellicosity will resonate with their primary voting base. I have my doubts. Most Democrats have come to conflate the failures in Iraq with the need to combat terror. They should be forgiven; George Bush made/makes the same mistake. But Iraq never was the terrorist hornet's nest. The terrorism threat is real. It will not go away. Not now. Not soon.

As for Obama and Clinton, Bombs Away. "Into the air junior birdmen…"

Barack Obama:
Missing in Action

Barry O is missing at a candidates' debate; missing in Jena, Louisiana; and missing on the floor of the U.S. Senate

"One, two, three strikes you're out" on the old campaign trail

(CHICAGO)(September 21, 2007) Barry Obama is hiding under his bed, again. Now that I am a candidate for U. S. Senator in Illinois I don't get to write about him as much as I used to. My job as an investigative editor in 2004-2007 was to be a pathfinder, to point out the truth when the "mainstream" media were hiding the truth about Obama from their readers and viewers. And I succeeded. Big time.

Now even the main street media have "discovered" that Obama is not all that he claims to be. Unfortunately for his supporters, they have not yet discovered that Obama is only out for #1 Barry O and for no one else.

This week Obama went missing in action three times. Maybe it's three strikes and he's out. Obama knows he is not going to be elected president. Don't sell Barry short. He's not stupid. He is using the "hopes" and fears of his supporters to build a national, even worldwide platform for a mega-millions killing after the campaign ends. Obama will be a valuable commodity. Business will pay big time. And when the time comes,

Obama will be selling. That's the only way to explain his curious behavior in the past few days.

Obama had his first Norma Desmond moment at a candidates debate in Iowa. Like the fictional Norma Desmond of Sunset Boulevard, Obama said that the debates had become too "small" for him. Obama issued a "statement" saying he was not going to waste his time debating his opponents. Obama was too big for that. Statement #1.

Then there were Jessie Jackson's comments, promptly denied, that Obama was acting "white" and not supporting African-Americans. I will have more to say about Jena, Louisiana and the racist justice there in another column. But Jena is a legitimate news story, made larger by the outstanding national coverage of the Chicago Tribune, and it has become a focal point of the "soft" racism that still infects the South and the Democratic Party. They don't lynch people any more; they just hang nooses to remind people who is in charge.

People went to protest in Jena, but Barry O was missing. Another issue that was "too small" for him. Instead, like a distant emperor Obama issued a mealy-mouthed "statement" supporting the marchers. Martin Luther King led the civil rights moment from the front of the parade, not by issuing statements from his office. Statement #2.

Obama does not want to be an African-American leader. Not enough money in that. No, Obama may not have been to the mountaintop; but he has been to the bank vault and the stock broker. He knows where the real money is. He wants to be what he has become: White America's African-American leader, the Democratic Party's African-American leader, their antidote to Al Sharpton and Jesse Jackson and the others.

Rightfully or wrongfully, Obama thinks he is too big and too good to waste on mere African-American issues, the same way he was blind to the slum housing being run by his white contributors in the backyard of his state senate district in Chicago. Obama' blindness is cold and calculating.

Finally, there was the senate vote to defend General Petraeus. Obama betrayed his friends and emboldened his enemies.

I happen to agree with President Bush and most Republicans—and most Americans—that the anti-Petraeus ad was despicable. People should be able to Bush-bash if they want. After all Bush makes the policies, not Petraeus.

But we have had over two hundred years of civilian, non-political military leadership in this country. Politicians make the decisions and take the blame; soldiers obey their superiors or resign. In turn, we don't attack our men and women in uniform for doing what we tell them to do. Elected officials are responsible. And the system works well.

Petraeus is an honorable officer. And whatever you may have thought of invading Iraq (I was against it when Barry O was against it) we have to deal with the reality that we made a mess and we have to clean up the mess and not run away from the mess we have made. Petraeus is an honorable officer and, more importantly, a good officer who has learned from the mistakes of the past and is trying to get us, well, OUT. It is worth remembering that the U. S. Army was ADAMANTLY AGAINST THE IRAQ INVASION. So moveon.org's ad was even more despicable and dishonorable than our politicians have claimed.

More importantly, Obama was a friend of moveon.org. He has spoken at their functions. Did he stand by his friends and vote against the resolution condemning moveon.org's anti-Petraeus ad? Nope. Obama betrayed moveon.org and stood silent.

Once again, Barry O was there with a "statement." Statement #3. Statements, statements, Barry issues more statements than a banker. Always from the rear echelon. Obama explained he did not vote on the moveon.org condemnation to "protest" against the dynamics of democracy, which is, after all, based on voting.

In plain simple English, let me make my statement: Barry Obama is a political coward who has no business running for a leadership role in our nation. If the people of Illinois are stupid enough to reelect him, well they were stupid enough to elect Obama in the first place. But he is only one of 100 votes. But whatever else Obama has proven this week, he has been missing in action on three (count 'em) battlefields. He betrays friend and foe alike. Barry Obama is not a leader. Never was. Never will be.

Obama is just a very glib, successful huckster and snake-oil salesman who is building himself up for an auction sale to the higher bidder. Take that from the "old pathfinder;" that's my statement on his "statements."

CLOSING NOTE: A word of congratulations and appreciation to Chicago Sun-Times reporter Lynn Sweet. Three years ago, in the early days of the Obama phenomenon, I felt Sweet took a sycophant's approach to reporting on Obama. But the Sun-Times has developed the most comprehensive and the most honest coverage of Obama. Sweet has grown into a genuine skeptic about the true dimensions of the Barry O scam. Congratulations Lynn. And welcome.

The Fall of the House of Obama
The Death of "Hope" on the Campaign Trail

Obama becomes a pinup for left-wing Democrats, a pinhead for the liberal media that advanced his career and pinned down under Hillary Clinton's fire. He has lost his underpinnings.

(CHICAGO)(October 6, 2007) On September 21st I wrote that Barack Obama is not really running for president. Yes he is a candidate and yes he goes through the motions. But no, he knows he is not going to win, and he is looking forward to early retirement and a fat paycheck from corporate America.

When the history of the 2008 campaign is written the week of October 1st will probably be the week when the Obama campaign unraveled.

Obama began the week with what his handlers called a "Judgment and Experience Tour" and ended up demolishing both his judgment and his experience. By the end of the week Obama had been stripped of any appearance of either judgment or experience. He was bleeding from every pore.

This column actually began before the now celebrated flag pin fracas. I could see the end coming. The emptiness of Obama's campaign, the hollow rhetoric was a sure tip off to me he was dying. But Obama's contempt for the American flag and for the values it represents finally did him in. Friday's (October 5th) Chicago Sun-Times implored Obama to "put the Stars and

Stripes back on his lapel." The Sun-Times could see that Obama had self-destructed even if Barry himself could not.

Earlier this year I assumed a Sun-Times columnist, Jennifer Hunter, had been put on the Obama campaign bus to act as a flack for a homeboy from Chicago. By this week even Hunter was intimating Obama was really a resume-inflating dissembler. Hunter wrote that Obama's much-ballyhooed opposition to the war in 2002 was really riskless, and that Obama had distorted the time line of his opposition speech. (http://www.sun-times.com/news/hunter/583542,CST-NWS-hunter02.article) There you go again Barry.

Whew. I, of course, was accusing Obama being a resume-inflating, time line distorting phony way back in 2004. Welcome, Jennifer (and please do something with your hands in that stock picture the Sun-Times uses!).

How and why did it all unravel? First, Obama claimed to be an "outsider," but he was an ersatz "insider's outsider." On September 30th the Chicago Tribune detailed how Obama had been hobnobbing with Pritzker money since the 1990's, long before he announced for the senate. (http://www.chicagotribune.com/services/newspaper/printedition/sunday/chi-pritzker_bdsep30,0,2168891.story)

Now there's nothing wrong with rich people, especially when they invite you to their "bonfire on the beach," but don't pretend you're from the 'hood while you swim in a billionaire's pool.

Second, Obama really has nothing to sell but his sales approach. The great literary critic Isaiah Berlin once said "T. S. Eliot writes marvelously but says nothing." The same could be said of Obama, who lives a life of bold rhetoric ("fundamentally change the game") but hasn't really changed anything since entering politics except his bank balance.

Barry's perfervid supporters still have not realized what a huckster Obama is; they probably never will. In just a few weeks they will be yelling that the Clintons "stole" the election from Obama. They didn't. Obama fumbled. Eight months after he announced he still has an animated but sliver-thin base of support. He raises money but he can't raise his standing in the polls. Ron Paul will get further with his newly found $5 million than Obama has gotten with his $75 million.

I was an early opponent of the war in Iraq. Still am. I marched against the war and I wrote about the war, and what a disaster it would be. And then I ended up in Baghdad and lived to experience all of the insanity and incompetence I had predicted. Barry Obama was safely at home. Obama has used the war to advance his political career; he has not been an opponent so much as a manipulator and exploiter of the war, for political profit and self-aggrandizement. All while voting 500 billion dollars to support the war. Yo!

But this week Obama was a sad figure when he tried to revive his 2002 speech in opposition to invading Iraq. Jennifer Hunter dumped on the "bravery" that Obama claimed and showed that Obama had even distorted the timing of his speech. Liar. Obama said he gave his antiwar speech in the "middle" of his senate race; she showed he gave the speech before he even announced!

Obama doesn't realize that he is a complete wuss. Wusses seldom do. Especially when they have highly-paid sycophants and retainers to tell them they are making history. Obama was elected to the senate, and started voting to support the war, until Hillary changed course this year and he was forced to follow her tail.

Ultimately, Obama, who fancies himself a basketball player, is a very poor strategist and field general. You can't beat the top dog by being a lap dog. And that's a fact. Obama has been afraid to take on Hillary, and he has tap danced around her with the finesse of a Fred Astaire, all while Hillary ignored him and used Bill as her counterattack dog. When Hillary wanted to attack Obama, she used Bill to suggest Barry O was "inexperienced." What a pair. But love or hate the Clintons, they are ruthless, ferocious predators. You can't beat Team Clinton by being Mr. Newbie.

And so Obama has fallen back on his fund raising as a mark of his manliness. It hasn't work. Now Hillary has surpassed Barry in the fund raising department as well and stripped him of his manliness.

In the middle of the fund raising deflation Obama decided to dump on the American flag. That was too much even for the Sun-Times, a paper that has been remarkably sympathetic to Obama for a long time. I remember when wearing the flag last became an issue, way, way back in 1969-1970. Democrats just pinned on their flags and walloped the Republicans in the 1970 election. Now Republicans and Democrats are both walloping Obama.

Who was the genius that told Obama to make an issue out of the "phony patriotism" of wearing the flag? Probably the same guy who told Rush Limbaugh to use the phrase "phony soldiers" (Limbaugh says he was quoted out of context). Maybe Obama should try Limbaugh's strategy, and say that he really meant true patriots wear the flag, to show what's in their heart. I studied semiotics under Joseph T. Tykociner at the University of Illinois. Barry should talk to me before he decides to diss the flag. And, by the way, I have a flag on my lapel.

Don't expect the Obama balloon to deflate overnight. But right now he looks like a pinhead who's pinned down and has become a pinup for the radical left in America. He has lost his underpinnings, and probably his underpants as well. Hillary and Bill must be smiling. And no, he is not going to be vice president. Hillary is smarter than that.

Rather, Obama will spend his $75 million or $100 million or whatever he raises sashaying across the political spectrum until he senses the timing is right to sell out and join corporate America. That's what I said on September 21st. That's still my story and I'm sticking to it.

"Bye, bye Barry. Too bad you had to go" (to the tune of By By Birdie)(suggested lyrics welcomed).

The House of Obama has fallen. It only took eight months for the great dissembler and resume inflater to fall from grace.

Now about Jennifer's hands and arms in her Sun-Times picture. Lighten up lass.

The Last Days of Obama

(CHICAGO)(October 25, 2007) On October 4, 2007 I wrote about the "Fall of the House of Obama." (http://www.contrariancommentary.com/community/Home/tabid/36/mid/363/newsid363/141/Default.aspx)

Today, Senator Barack Obama's eventual demise became all but official when David Broder, the dean of America's political columnists, published a funereal piece on Barry O. (http://www.washingtonpost.com/wp-dyn/content/article/2007/10/24/AR2007102402336.html?hpid=opinionsbox1)

Over three years ago, in August, 2003 I began exposing the Obama scam. (http://www.freerepublic.com/focus/f-news/1189687/posts; see also http://www.dailykos.com/story/2007/1/21/14036/4115)

When Barack began to run for president in February, we published a series of columns including a psychological profile that presaged his eventual collapse as a candidate.

ContrarianCommentary.com has been far, far ahead of the curve, as the national media and Chicago-based press continued to gulp down Obama's campaign Kool-Aid. Why were we right and they wrong?

First, the national media failed to evaluate Obama's phony track record in Illinois politics. Apart from his first campaign for the state senate, when he used truly nasty tactics, Obama had never been one to fight for victory. He was always the candidate offering himself for coronation.

On the Illinois football team where I played as a freshman, we used to talk about "dummy scrimmage All-Americans." They were players who would hit the dummies hard, during the week, and then tremble when they saw the behemoths on the other team on Saturdays. Obama was a dummy scrimmage All-American. He could hit the dummies. He could not hit a real opposing team.

As long as Barry O was facing the dummies in Illinois politics, he was an All-American. The moment he came up against real competition, Team Clinton, he wilted. I saw this coming; the media pretended it wasn't happening. I took the heat, and the abuse, from the Obama troupe and their media troopers, but I was right and they were. Well, what were they?

I have had a column in preparation for most of October about the pathetic way Obama has returned, time and time again, to his 2002 speech against the war in Iraq. It was Barry's security blanket. His sense of entitlement because of that speech was overwhelming. Broder alludes to the panic in Obama's campaign when Hillary Clinton upstaged him on October 2nd and obliterated Obama's grandiose celebration of a four year-old speech.

What has Obama done since then? Precious little. He never really moved beyond 2002. He thought being right on the war in 2002 was a ticket to the White House. What conceit. What incompetence. What self-absorption. I was also "right" on the war in Iraq, but I don't for a moment believe that as a result I am entitled to a seat in the U.S. Senate (for which I am a candidate). I am working to win. The old fashioned way.

Obama was a fundamentally immature man who had been spoon fed by the white establishment that anointed him as their African-American champion. Obama had no credible professional record. He was slavish in prostrating himself to the sleaziest elements of Chicago and Illinois politics. His sole claim to fame was his glibness and his invented ethnic heritage.

What made Barry's rise to national prominence ludicrous is that Chicago is something of a Mecca for African-American advancement and accomplishment. There are outstanding lawyers, business persons and others who have accomplished much—on their own. People who have not sold out to politically-connected law firms and crooked politicians. Who have not been advanced by sleazy public officials. Or manqué billionaires. And yet out of this cornucopia of African-American achievement and merit, it was Obama that the establishment chose to promote to the national platform. But he was hollow. And weak.

Obama had no ideas, no firmly held convictions, nada. He never had to. Like Chauncey Gardner in Being There, Obama was worshipped for the profundity of his platitudes. This is not to say Team Clinton has morals or ideals; indeed, they have only one idea, and it serves them well: "Me." Their self-advancement, self-promotion, self-aggrandizement and selfishness and hunger for power are all-consuming. The Clintons are totally concentrated on themselves—and it works. For them. For now.

Obama pretended he was in it for the people. But that was never saleable. For "change." "For hope." For s—t. He never used the platform he was given to build a strong personal presence. Obama never attacked or exposed the Clintons. He never became a real leader. A man that men would follow into battle. Months after he became a candidate, he was still pussyfooting around Team Clinton. A few days ago, he promised a "tough, new Obama." "No more Mr. Nice Guy!" with Team Clinton. But it was more of the same sashaying around Hillary. He never laid a hand on her. All the while, he was being emasculated by Team Clinton.

It was left to me to begin the odyssey of Obama's exposure three years ago. There were no believers them. The believers began to arrive earlier this year. I even began to get "credit" for stories I had not written. (Everything that we send out has our name on it. We do not do "anonymous.") Now I am left to write his political obituary. "No," his true believes declaimed to Broder. "Z." Obama lives. But the answer really was "No." Gertrude Stein understood Obama. There was no Obama there. No, really.

Barry may have tens of million of dollars in the bank. But he is bankrupt as a serious candidate for president. Like Cubs fans in Chicago, Obama's sycophants will have to wait until "next year" for him to "arrive." Don't hold your breath. And, "no," I don't mean January, 2008. Maybe 2012. Maybe never. By, by Barry O.

"Mr. Broder, welcome to the 'Last Days of Obama.'"

U.S. Senate Candidate Andy Martin Charges Obama Campaign with Trying to Scapegoat Martin for Obama's Campaign Collapse

Martin retorts, "I accept full responsibility for the collapse of the Obama campaign"

(CHICAGO)(November 1, 2007) Republican U. S. Senate candidate Andy Martin will hold a Chicago news conference Tuesday, October 30th at 1:00 P.M. to accuse the Senator Barack Obama's campaign of trying to scapegoat Martin for Obama's campaign collapse. Martin will plead guilty to torpedoing Obama's prospects for the White House.

Martin filed nominating petitions for the U. S. Senate in Springfield, Illinois on October 29th.

Beginning in August, 2004 Martin, one of the Internet's most influential independent opinion journalists, began exposing Obama's secret life and hidden childhood as well as his invented family history, http://www.freerepublic.com/focus/f-news/1189687/posts; see also http://www.dailykos.com/story/2007/1/21/14036/4115.

During 2007 Martin has chronicled Obama's unfitness to serve as president, see ContrarianCommentary.com. Now Martin's criticism of Obama is being confirmed, as Obama raises more and more money and seems handcuffed by his fear of political combat with Team Clinton. "The tougher he talks the wussier he gets," Martin says.

"Not surprisingly, Obama's staff is looking for a scapegoat for his poor performance. And, not surprisingly, the Obama staff is now trying to scapegoat my writing as the reason for Obama's downfall. Obama's staff, sobbing about the unfairness of my criticisms, was an admitted source for *The Nation* article.

"*The Nation,* America's oldest left-wing journal, suggested I am the mastermind of a 'New Right-Wing Smear Machine' that may have inflicted a fatal blow on Obama's chances for the presidency. I have never written anything but factually correct articles, as well as prescient opinions on Obama's unfitness as a national candidate.

"In the warped lexicon of the left, 'truth telling' is now a 'smear.' Nonsense. Finger pointing at me will not salvage Obama's desiccated campaign.

"On the other hand, if Obama wants to blame me for the collapse of his campaign, I know what Rush Limbaugh would be telling me to do: *take full responsibility, Andy.* OK, Rush, I am proud to do so. After all, I was the first and most persistent observer to document Obama's evasions and evasiveness.

"I plead guilty to puncturing Obama's balloon. And because I am pleading guilty to *The Nation's* conclusions, though not to their factual insinuations, I can't sue them for defamation. Truth is their defense. Andy took down Obama. Yup.

"My own senate campaign has been subjected to bombardment from The Nation and other liberal media, for telling the truth about Obama. This week, when I was scheduled to file in Springfield, they unloaded with their latest 'smear machine' attack on me. The timing was not a coincidence.

"But in reality there is no 'right-wing smear machine.'

There is only me, a plain-talking, truth-telling writer commenting on a senator who is not even remotely fit to be president and who has been refracted into a dazzling aurora by liberal news media and left-wing campaign contributors.

"*The Nation* engages in its own left-wing smear when it admits it has no evidence linking me to anonymous e-mails attacking the senator, and then slyly suggests I really am the source. As a journalist, I do not believe in anonymous attacks, and I have never made any against Obama. Period.

"What is surprising is the powerful impact my research and writing has had on the national psyche. *The Nation* admits my commentary has been devastating for Obama. Indeed, I just might be responsible for his downfall. People keep reading what I have to say, and they keep falling away from Barry O. He started the year closing the gap with Team Clinton, and he has been widening the gap since he announced. He is running a 'campaign in reverse.' His balloon is deflating. Hisssss.

ContrarianCommentary.com is very proud to be credited as the 'giant killer' of Obama's flatulent campaign for the presidency. We take full responsibility. Obama just doesn't have the 'right stuff' to be president. Period.

"The left may scapegoat me, but ultimately they are fooling themselves if they blame ContrarianCommentary.com for Obama's collapse. To paraphrase Shakespeare, 'The fault, dear Obama, likes not in my columns, but in yourself,'" Martin will state.

Obama Talks Tough,
and Wusses Out Again

Can the New York Times put
Humpty Dumpty Obama together again?

(CHICAGO)(November 3, 2007) Last Sunday Barack Obama gave the New York Times a front-page interview. The story said a new, "tough" Obama would tackle Hillary Clinton in the upcoming debate. At the actual debate, moderator Tim Russert asked the obvious question. You said in the New York Times you were going after Hillary, so "Where's the beef?"

Obama wilted, and backed off. How could he hype his new aggressiveness on Sunday, and then deny he was being aggressive on Tuesday? He's an embarrassment to his supporters. He is a "champion" who is not a champ. If they had cast Obama in the movie "300," he would have to stay home with the women. Or as we say down home in Southern Illinois, "That dog won't hunt." Barry O said he was a predator on Sunday, and ended up being a pussycat on Tuesday.

Friday (November 2nd) Obama was back on the front page of the New York Times. It is painfully obvious that even as people in Chicago have come to the realization Obama is not presidential material, the New York Times persists in giving him front-page coverage to salvage his sinking campaign. Obama's views are no longer "exclusive" front-page news in Chicago's newspapers, not even in the Sun-Times. But in the New York Times, Barry O is still the Sulzburger Family's last, best hope to derail Hillary Clinton. So the front-page coverage continues in New York even as we in Illinois now know better. More's the pity.

Yesterday Obama sent out an e-mail with an extract from the debate. It was his "moment" of confrontation when he told Hillary to release her secret Bill Clinton-era presidential files. Bill Clinton has demanded in writing that Hillary's files be kept from the public until 2012. I wonder how he picked that year. What are they hiding?

Hillary tried to dodge the question over the files. Obama promptly put his hand up to comment and Russert recognized him. Obama should have gone in for the kill, and said "Hillary, stop dodging. It's time for some pillow talk with Bill. Ask him 'Bill, please revoke and reverse your secrecy letter.' Stop stalling and stop pretending the National Archives are to blame, when your husband is the one who imposed the secrecy demand." Boom. He could have blown Hillary away.

Instead, Obama went into a rambling, convoluted discourse that eventually got around to the issue of the secret files. But in the mumbo jumbo about everything else, Barry O fumbled the point that Mrs. Clinton should simply talk to her husband, and ask him to revoke his secrecy letter.

Cross-examination is a talent that is partly learned and partly innate. I was taught "Federal Courts" in law school by a brilliant trial lawyer who went on to become a federal judge, Judge Prentice Marshall. Professor Marshal taught me the rudiments and significance of cross-examination. I had a natural talent for combat in the courtroom. I have cross-examined lying witnesses who collapsed on the witness stand, and cross-examined evasive witnesses that reveled hidden truths in Perry Mason moments. I am comfortable in the courtroom, and the arena, as those who have seen me debate on TV will agree.

As for Obama? He screwed up a golden opportunity. The man is not a warrior; he is not even a competent lawyer. I would not want Obama representing me anywhere near a courtroom. He can't take the pressure. He has no presence as a debater. He has no presence as a cross-examiner. He has no ability to go for the jugular. And he wants to run against Team Clinton? Obama compared himself to Rocky Balboa? Come on. Casper Milquetoast is more like it. He had a classic opening to skewer Hillary, and he botched it.

What does all this mean for the Democrats?

1. Obama is doing exactly what I said in my column last week, deflating.
2. John Edwards is a lawyer. He knows how to go in for the kill. That poor boy didn't get rich by backing off a battle in the courtroom. As Hillary stalls because of the utter mendacity of her botoxed presentation, Edwards is going to pass Obama and become #2. Once Edwards realizes that he really has to do what he really has to do, take on Hillary or see his campaign die, he will be up for the task. Obama is not. Obama's deflation opens the way for Edward's reflation.
3. There is an Obama who could sit in the Oval Office, but she's not running. Michelle is the "real Obama." Michelle vs. Hillary, now that would be a fair fight. She must have been sitting on the sidelines cringing as her husband fumbled a great campaign opportunity to tackle Hillary.

Barack vs. Hillary? It's enough to make me scream, "Barry O, you just can't cut it in presidential campaign combat. You may be the $75 million dollar fundraiser, but you're still a cowardly lion. Money can't buy bravery.

"Over to you, Michelle."

Barry and the Witch:
From Obama to Army Brats

(CHICAGO)(November 21, 2007) Regular readers of this column know Senator Barack Obama does not catch a lot of slack from me. In fact a recent diatribe in *The Nation* Magazine accused me of leading as "right-wing smear machine" that had devastated Obama's campaign. (http://www.thenation.com/docprint.mhtml?i=20071112&s=hayes)

But, as regular readers also know, I "call 'em as I see 'em," and when Barry's right I back him. Especially against The Witch.

Obama actually said something truthful this week about his childhood. Usually Obama is feeding us his gauzy myths about "Dreams from My Father," and similar disinformation.

Obama said "I spent four years living overseas when I was a child." See e.g.: http://blog.washingtonpost.com/the-trail/2007/11/20/the_passport_primary.html#more.

The Witch promptly pounced with the sarcastic reply that "Now voters will judge whether living in a foreign country at age 10 prepares one to face the BIG..."

Actually, Obama was right; he was telling the truth. And The Witch was wrong. But then how would she know. She grew up in Park Ridge (Illinois).

And, I can speak in Obama's defense from personal experience.

First, the obvious: children crave conformity, uniformity, continuity, stability and predictability. All of us know that, because all of were children at some point in our lives. Some of us still are. If anyone doubts my sociological observations, you can peek at Eboo Patel's memories of childhood in today's Washington Post, http://newsweek.washingtonpost.com/onfaith/eboo_patel/2007/11/american_thanksgivings.html. "Mom, I want a baloney sandwich in my lunchbox. PERIOD." Now that's conformity.

I grew up on the campus of Wesleyan University in Middletown Connecticut. That was our park. I delivered papers there, and happily accepted slices of pie, cake and other baked goods from the fraternity houses where I delivered newspapers. It was in some respects an idyllic existence. What could be more predictable than having a job, and making deliveries seven days a week? At age 11. And growing up with the same kids from first grade until seventh grade.

Then my family moved to Oxford, England where I lead a double life for the next two years, Adolescent by day. Oxford student by night. It was a mind bender. I was thrown into two alien worlds, one with other adolescents and one with mostly young adults. Learning and living in that strange environment made me more flexible, and more comfortable in all sorts of ways. We traveled to the World's Fair and stayed in youth hostels. We were on the continent, visiting new friends.

I came home, alone (yea!), a young man on an ocean liner, and landed in New York as someone who had left as a child and returned as an adult. I would never be the same.

Had I stayed in Middletown, well, who knows. But I was never the same. I had seen the world. Had met Vietnamese kids (before anyone knew where Viet-Nam was) and had seen my best friend cry his heart out the day the King of Iraq was assassinated.

Anyone who has lived in different worlds, in different stages of life, knows that these experiences change us forever. Even "study abroad" during college can be transformational. Which is why college kids love going to Europe, love backpacking summers, and sometimes stay on during college or after graduation.

Clinton seeks to equate traveling in her Air Force jet as the president's wife with the transformational childhood experiences Obama had in Indonesia. She's dead wrong. You gotta love The Witch. The wronger she is, the nastier she gets. (You can hiss here.)

Traveling in an American presidential bubble is no way to see the world, or to transform your character, personality and views on life. On Air Force 1-1/2? Meeting "the people?" Come on Witchie. Well, Hillary did kiss Suha Arafat. (Hissing allowed.)

Kids playing, that's transformational. Obama is 100% correct.

The best proof has nothing to do with me, Obama or The Witch. Just look at Army Brats.

Why have the children of our military families, who have to move every several years, at home and around the world, been so successful as a group? Because travel, exposure to different people, sometimes even different cultures, all help to make someone flexible, and provide coping skills in adult life. Just ask Senator John McCain.

Again drawing on my own adult experiences in Asia and the Middle East, it was the skills I learned dealing with international kids in prep school and at Oxford that allowed me to travel through some of the most dangerous conflicts in recent history, often exposed to great risk, and always be protected by local people who took a liking to me. I'm alive to prove it. (You can hiss here if you support my opponent in the primary.)

Indeed, one of my selling points as the "most qualified" Republican to face Senator Dick Durbin is that I have lived a full life all around the world, while he has been totally immersed in politics and political chicanery all of his adult life. Not much exposure there. Unless you think that backstabbing prepares you for foreign adventures. I know the world. Durbin doesn't.

And so, this week The Witch betrayed her provincialism. She attacked Barry Obama where he is actually strongest. Obama had real problems as a child. But he saw the world and survived.

While I don't come from a multi-racial family and so my experiences are much more limited than Obama's, I grew up in a partially immigrant family. I was bilingual from birth. I had a hard time, as I am sure Obama did at some point, understanding why some people would discriminate against my wonderful Greek relatives. Indeed, I am almost unique among Republicans in that I experienced familial discrimination firsthand. Which is why I am so committed to civil rights and civil liberties. Back to childhood. Again.

And so, Hillary, you leave my Barry alone. If Barry needs beating, I am the man to do it. Just ask *The Nation*. Obama knows I will thrash him when he inflates his resume. Or dreams dreams that never materialized in reality.

As for You, my Dear Witch, you are the poorer for never having experienced what Obama and I did: a disruptive and transformational childhood. On the other hand, you have lived with Bubba and all of his mistresses. Now that was transformational. But look what it transformed you into.

Is Obama a Doper, or Just a Dope?
Or Are we Dopes for Believing His Flip-flops and Lies?

What can you believe about Barry?

Democrats "puff" and "snort" to the finish line in Iowa

(CHICAGO)(December 17, 2007) A reporter from the Miami Herald interviewed me last week. She asked me what I had against Barack (Barry) Obama. I said nothing. I find Obama's tap dancing and prevarication endlessly entertaining. Obambi gets away with stuff that would never pass if another candidate were involved. And, as usual, ContrarianCommentary.com focuses on the ignored story. Feast on.

The "big" news this week, of course, was whether Republicans next year could smear Obama because he used marijuana and cocaine up to some still-uncertain date (Teens? Twenties?). What Obama should have said to counter Hillary Clinton's claim that Obama was planning to run for president while still in kindergarten was, "Would anyone planning a run for the White House write a book and admit to using cocaine?" Not on your life. Well, Barry has not offered me a job as a speech-writer, yet, so he will have to take this long distance advice. (Obama's staff has offered to promote me for a job as "fiction writer.")

But to the point, will Republicans raise the issue of Obama's cocaine use? They could. But I doubt they will have to. Bill

Shaheen, one of Clinton's leading supporters in New Hampshire, provided a preliminary list of questions that could be asked: did you sell? When did you last use? Did you give it to anyone else? You get the idea.

On the contrary, I think that rather than Republicans raising the cocaine issue, the media will. Absolutely the issue of cocaine use will be a question asked in any nationally televised presidential debate. How could it not be? The media loves salacious little tidbits. Bill Clinton "did not inhale" and we are still talking about his lack-of-inhalation 15 years later. What if he had inhaled?

Since Obama admitted to using the stuff, he is in a difficult position. People are curious, and the media wants to ask what is on peoples' minds. So puffing and snorting have to be on the agenda of questions to be asked in any fall debate.

I am a complete nerd when it comes to drug use. Never have, never will. But even I could come up with a few questions. Who was your supplier, Barry? What was the good stuff? (Hint: "Maui Wowie?" comes to mind.) I have been in opium dens in Asia, and on military reservations where bags of hash were sold for a buck, and even an occasional party where marijuana was used, but I stayed away. Far away. Can't stand the taste; can't stand the smell. Just a whiff was enough to cure me for life. So, no, I did not inhale, either.

Clearly, Obama does have some "exposure" on the drug issue. It would be fanciful to deny that fact. Why do Democrats deny the obvious? Here's a possible explanation.

Democrats have now entered the real kindergarten phase of the campaign. This past week Hillary promised not to run negative ads if her opponents do not run negative ads. Obama has threatened to fire staffers who engage in negativity. Are they all running "positive" campaigns? I am waiting for one of them to cite Adlai Stevenson, who once said "I offer my opponents a bargain: if they will stop telling lies about us, I will stop telling the truth about them." But the reality is that no one can displace an entrenched front-runner without aggressive tactics. And that's a fact.

Now on to ContrarianCommentary.com's take on Barry Obama's latest "lie." Once again, although the following comments originally appeared in the Chicago Sun-Times, under the byline of the increasingly skeptical Obama observer Lynn Sweet, they were totally ignored by national and mainstream media. (http://www.suntimes.com/news/sweet/692594,CST-NWS-sweet12.article)

Sweet says that "someone" started passing out Obama's responses to a 1996 IVI questionnaire when Obama was first running for the Illinois state senate, and Obama's answers popped up on Politico.com. I have run for the state senate, and the U. S. Senate, and I can tell you that candidates for state senate have small districts and very little to do. Moreover, Obama was a Democrat in an overwhelmingly Democratic district, so his election chances in 1996 were 100%.

So how did Barry O lie, again? Well, he tries to claim that in running for a nothingburger office, Illinois state Senator, he was too busy to fill out answers to the IVI questionnaire, which he "never saw," and that his campaign manager "unintentionally mischaracterized" Obama's views. Yah, sure.

Caught in a flip-flop, Obama says, "The woman did it!" Isn't it just like Barry O to blame a woman for his flip—flop? If any other male candidate said he "never saw" a questionnaire and some "woman" filed it out for them, can you imagine the uproar? But not in Obama's case. The story was buried. The double standard for Obama carried the day, again.

Obama's latest lie dovetails with the way Obama was two-faced in attacking Hillary Clinton for concealing her presidential files, while claiming he had destroyed the files of his own state senate office.

Politicians are world-class pack rats. At the time he claims he destroyed his own state files, Obama had just been elected to the U.S. Senate and was planning a presidential campaign, in 2005. He had lots of money to rent a storage space. Can you really believe he wanted to destroy the history of his first office? Or was he destroying incriminating evidence of his links to crooked Chicago politicians like Tony Rezko, and to a former name partner of Obama's own law firm, to which Obama had previously passed out a cool $1 million in "honest graft" as part of a charitable contribution? (http://www.suntimes.com/news/watchdogs/672314,CST-NWS-watchdog29.article)

Most likely, Obama destroyed his state senate files because they contained unflattering and even incriminating evidence of his extensive links to the sleazy world of Chicago Democratic Party politics and politicians. Barry's record in the Illinois state senate was taken to a laundry and disappeared. The way Obama plays these games with opponents, and the way the media always put him in the light of the innocent target, is a scandalous double standard.

And so on and on it goes, the media cover up of Obama's flip-flops, blaming women for his mistakes, and still-uncertain history of using illegal substances as part of his coming-of-age.

Bottom line: the only reason Obama is doing well in Iowa and elsewhere is because Hillary Clinton is running an incompetent campaign and has Bubba popping up to sling mud, when she should be the one confronting Barry O and ripping his credibility to shreds. A good lawyer could, and would, do precisely that. But, contrary to 1992 Clinton disinformation machine propaganda, Hillary was never a good lawyer, and as a result she has very poor forensic skills as a candidate. So what goes around comes around.

Maybe Hillary should hire me and dump Bill.

As I said, we are now in the kindergarten phase of the Democratic presidential campaign. Dennis Kucinich, anyone? (Just kidding.)

Internet Editor/Columnist Andy Martin "Terrorizes" Obama Campaign with Facts about Obama's Muslim "Roots"

Andy Martin becomes the most influential internet journalist in the world, and the driving force behind news coverage of Obama's presidential campaign

"Takedown" of Senator Dick Durbin is next, says Martin

(CHICAGO)(December 18, 2007) Senator Barack Obama sees a face; in Oprah-speak, "Is it him?" Yes it is. Andy Martin, the crusading Chicago journalist that has driven the Obama campaign to the point of distraction, forced Obama to make his current religion an issue, and eclipsed Internet stars from earlier campaigns.

Martin is preparing to focus on a new target on February 6th: Illinois Senator Dick Durbin. Martin is a Republican candidate for Durbin's seat.

Monday's national coverage (December 17th) of Obama's campaign was all driven by Martin's original research and commentary on Obama's religious roots in Islam. In the New York Times, Katherine Q. Seelye wrote that Obama's campaign "worked to dispel false rumors spread on the internet that he was a Muslim and had ulterior motives for running." (http://www.nytimes.com/2007/12/17/us/politics/17campaign-1.html?_r=1&ref=politics&oref=slogin)

Both the Chicago Tribune and New York Post carried extensive stories on former Senator Bob Kerrey's "endorsement" of Hillary Clinton while stating he likes "the fact that his name is Barack Hussein Obama, and that his father was a Muslim..." (http://www.nypost.com/seven/12172007/news/national-news/kerreys_praise_of_barack_a_big_o_bombo_445748.htm; http://www.chicagotribune.com/services/newspaper/printedition/monday/chi-obama_17dec17,0,2144595.story)

Obama's campaign has been driven to distraction by Martin's columns and original research, which began in 2004 and have been continually updated. In the process, Martin's impact on the presidential race has eclipsed that of former Internet stars from earlier presidential races such as Matt Drudge.

In order to dilute and dispel the impact of Martin's continuing reporting Obama has been forced to make his church attendance a public event, with TV cameras and reporters in attendance, all because of Martin's seminal research on Obama's religious roots and Obama's attempts to evade accurate reporting on that Muslim history. The Nation magazine recently credited Martin with devastating Obama's campaign and orchestrating a "Right-Wing Smear Machine." Martin denies the accusation.

"While the national media always use the term 'rumors' to describe confusion about his religious roots, the 'rumors' largely flow from Obama's evasive responses and his refusal to engage in a Mitt Romney moment of full disclosure," says Martin. "Most of my columns are on the Internet. I have never dealt in rumors, false facts or innuendoes. I have generated hard facts for hard news. And I am no more responsible for the misuse of my information than if someone exaggerates based on a New York Times editorial. Both my reporting and my opinions have been and continue to be rock solid.

"I kept the story alive on the Internet when earlier this year the mainstream media tried to cover up Obama's own cover-up. Now the N. Y. Times and others are having to play catch-up ball with my editorial writing. Obama is having to play catch-up ball with my reporting. And from the looks of the national coverage, I'm winning and Barack is losing. I have pursued what we call the 'Joe Friday approach,' 'just the facts, ma'am.' That's how we will continue to play the story."

Martin is planning to target Illinois' Senator Dick Durbin on February 6th, says a senate campaign volunteer. "His high-impact journalism is going to be devastating when Durbin is the target. Andy has become the most influential Internet journalist in the world though his reporting on Obama. Mainstream reporters may dislike his commentary but they respect Andy's impact on national coverage and, more importantly, on the actions and reactions of voters across America.

"We like to pass around an old Chicago Tribune editorial which called Andy 'an absolutely brilliant campaigner' whose 'public relations skills are masterly.' That sounds like a description of what he has done to Obama, and what he plans to do to Durbin once he wins the Republican nomination. When Andy is the nominee against Durbin we expect the Martin/Durbin race to be the most exciting senate campaign in the nation, here in Illinois.

"It's an improbable story, but right now Andy's reporting out of Chicago is driving the national political agenda in the 2008 election cycle. The nation is hungry for a tough opponent to confront Durbin. Andy has shown he can do the job on Obama, and he will do the job on Durbin. And, as he says, it will be a 'just the facts, ma'am' campaign. Honest. And tough."

Where's Barack Obama?
Kenya is on Fire; 275 are Dead

In yet another unexpected incident in this presidential campaign, Obama abandons his "brothers" and "sisters" in Kenya as that country burns, because it is politically expedient for him to do so

What about Granny? Why won't millionaire Obama, who lives in a Chicago mansion, pay to install running water and plumbing for someone he calls "Granny"?

Is Obama staying at the same Holiday Inn Express as Huckabee?

(CHICAGO)(January 2, 2008) Senator Barack Obama is missing in action. Nothing so reveals the character of a man as how he acts during a crisis. Last week all of the presidential candidates were evaluated on their responses to the murder of Benazir Butto. Earlier, Governor Mike Huckabee made light of a foreign policy question by attesting he stayed at a "Holiday Inn Express last night." Tuesday it was Obama's turn to roast and revel his mendacious character and hollow principles.

In 2006 Obama went to Kenya and cried out "All of you are my brothers; all of you are my sisters." (http://www.usatoday.com/news/world/2006-08-27-obama-trip_x.htm)

It seems Barry O has forgotten his brothers and sisters now that Kenya is on fire.

Obama's Luo tribe, of which he is so proud in presidential debates, trotting out his "international" relatives as evidence of his expansive and experienced world view, are at risk of losing their lives and their "big man" in Washington is ignoring the situation.

And while we are at it, why does Obama brag about his "granny's" lifestyle with no running water and no plumbing or flush toilets? He has made millions; can't he send his step-grandmother a thousand bucks to install a well and faucet? Or does he prefer that his relatives live in squalor so he can make political capital of their deprivation? What a creep.

Obama, the more you know, the more disgusted you became.

I would not be writing this and blaming Obama if he had ignored his Kenyan relatives. But when he constantly tries to exploit the existence of his foreign relatives and makes political hay out of both their poverty and loyalty, as Obama has done, doesn't he owe them something more than nothing when they are in danger?

Kenya has just gone through a national election that was relatively peaceful. Until this weekend when tribal loyalties trumped democracy and unleashed mass murder. When the ballots were counted in a suspicious manner, riots broke out. Over 275 people are dead. Over 50 people died in a church that was torched. People are literally being hacked to death with machetes.

And Obama is silent. Not a peep out of him about either the violent situation or concern for his Kenyan relatives. He's "doing a Huckabee" about current events in Kenya. Who? Me?

Well, any fool in Iowa, and there appear to be a lot of fools in Iowa, who votes for a man who forgets "family" in Kenya as casually as he changes his socks, and who talks about his "granny" living without water or a toilet when he is a multimillionaire and lives in a mansion in Chicago, is uninformed and in denial. Would you want a candidate like that for a relative if you didn't know his last name? I don't think so. Of course not. Then why would you vote to put this joker in the White House?

Obama has fooled a lot of people during this presidential campaign. A lot of suckers have donated over $100 million to his campaign. Suckerrr.

But just look at his reaction to the anarchy in Kenya—total silence and disinterest—and you will know how Obama will treat the American People if he were ever in power. It's always all about Obama, all the time. What can you do for him, and what can he do you for? Look at the way he exploits his Kenyan relatives, and then ignores them when they are in danger. Look. Obama is the classic huckster pol that knows how to milk the people for every last drop. And then gives nothing in return.

I don't know about you, but if I had a "granny" that was living without running water and without a toilet, as Obama constantly reminds us his is, I would see to it that she got the comforts of life. Yesterday. Amazingly, Obama brags about his Granny's deprivation and the media cheers him on.

Obama and the media, sickos together. Perfect together.

I can hear the toilets flushing in the background.

Andy Martin Handicaps the Democrats in Iowa: Part Two

The Kiss of Kucinich: Obama makes a small slip with big consequences, bad ones

Will Kucinich's flying saucers be landing to caucus for Obama?

(CHICAGO)(January 3, 2008) When the media would challenge President Reagan after his endorsement by controversial groups, he had a stock answer: "They endorsed me; I didn't endorse them." Barack Obama should pay more attention to the Gipper.

A few weeks ago, Obama was encouraging college students to come back to college (in Iowa) early from the Christmas break, to caucus for him on January 3rd. The Chicago newspapers got wind of Obama's entreaties, and called him on seeming to encourage possible double voting. In Chicago, of course, we have a long tradition of "voting early and often." Had Obama learned from Chicago Mayor Ritchie Daley, or his campaign maven Tony Rezko? The senator denied encouraging illegal student voting. The matter dissolved.

Obama is not likely to escape as easily from his stumble on January 1st, when Congressman Dennis Kucinich, running for president to put forward an extreme agenda, "endorsed" Obama as a "second choice." Only for the Iowa caucuses. Instead of ignoring Kucinich, Obama made a classic error that will return to haunt him. Obama's mistake was in accepting Kucinich's "endorsement" and "honoring" DK for making the announcement of support.

The Chicago Tribune's "Swamp" reported that Obama responded to Kucinich's Iowa-only support in a statement saying:

"I have a lot of respect for Congressman Kucinich, and I'm **honored** that he has done this because **we both believe deeply** in the need for fundamental change," he said. "He and I have been fighting for a number of the same priorities — including an end to the war in Iraq that we both opposed from the start." (http://www.swamppolitics.com/news/politics/blog/2008/01/kucinich_obama_is_my_second_ch.html)

Iowa's crackpot caucuses encourage candidates to praise each other, because the Democratic caucuses (unlike the Republican caucuses which engage in "one candidate-one vote" process) are based on the European socialist system of voting with "second choice" balloting for candidates.

Under second choice voting, used by almost all social democracies in Europe, second place votes can be added to a first or second place candidate to determine the winner. In Iowa, supporters of candidates without enough representatives to reach 15% at any caucus can revote for candidates who will then meet the 15% threshold. So Clinton, Edwards, Obama & Co. praise each other, knowing a few second round, second choice, votes could mean the difference between winning and losing.

In 2004, Kucinich made John Edwards his "second choice" and may have propelled Edwards into a second place caucus finish. This time Kucinich's "kiss" of support may prove to be the kiss of death for Mr. Obama.

With Clintonian dexterity, Obama has carefully tried to triangulate away from the extreme left of the Democratic Party that adores him. Indeed, the Democratic blogosphere has begun to criticize Obama for being "too Republican."

Well, Obama has just jetted from being "too Republican" to landing on the lunatic fringe of the Democratic Party in one movement. Will Obama and Kucinich be encouraging flying saucers to land and disgorge potential caucus attendees? (Kucinich has stated he has seen flying saucers.) By being "honored" by Kucinich's support, Obama has aligned himself with the extreme left, in the party where he is striving to appear to be middle-of-the road. Like Dr. Strangelove's uncontrollable arm, Obama's congenital left-wing orientation has popped up when he least needs it.

Now Obama's opponents will be able to tar and feather him for making common cause with Kucinich and his band of loonies. Are Kucinich and Obama kissing cousins on the need for reform? That what they say. That kind of association is precisely what Obama does not need going into Iowa today, and New Hampshire next week.

Kucinich's "kiss" of common cause with Obama may prove to be a very costly the kiss of death in the long run. Obama has received the "endorsement" from hell. In return for meaningless support in one state, Obama has opened the door to allowing himself to be branded as an extremist by his more moderate front-runners.

There will be hell to pay as Democrats realize that Dennis and Barack are perfect together. "Mama, gas up the flying saucer. We're heading for Iowa to caucus for Obama. Kucinich told us to."

What a team.

Obama Wins Big,
and the National Media Miss the Story

How the Iowa "caucuses" cheat the actual voter

John Edwards, Andy Martin's projected winner, runs ahead of Hillary Clinton

Democrats surge in Iowa, and the bell tolls for Republicans; a bad omen for Republicans nationally

(CHICAGO)(January 4, 2008) Senator Barack Obama won an even bigger victory Tuesday night than the national media reported. As usual, in announcing the "big" story, the national media missed the even bigger story. But we have the real deal at ContrarianCommentary.com.

Before the caucuses began, media tried to explain how the caucuses work. Unfortunately they failed to offer a correct explanation of how the "voters" are actually translated into the "delegates" that then appear on TV as "percentages" of victory. Tonight Barack Obama was cheated out of an even bigger and even more astounding victory than the press reported. Here's why.

Unlike an election, where voters show up and cast a ballot that is counted—which is/was the Republican party's system in Iowa—the Iowa Democratic Party's (IDP) caucuses operate on a very different and much more confusing wavelength. The caucus system worked to Obama's significant disadvantage and understated the extent of his victory.

Prior to the caucuses, the IDP assigns a fixed number of "delegate votes" to each precinct. These "delegates" eventually go on to state convention where national convention delegates are actually selected. Here's the quirk. The number of "delegates" assigned to a precinct has no bearing on the number of people who actually show up to vote. Thus, if you win by an overwhelming percentage in any precinct, you still only get the assigned number of delegates. Moreover, if 20 people or 200 or 2,000 people show up in a precinct, the delegate number is the same. Ultimately, "voters" are not tallied, precincts are.

The national media were not reporting the raw vote for Obama; they were only reporting the "projected delegates" and assigning percentages based on those delegate numbers, not actual voter numbers. The upshot: Obama brought many more voters to the caucuses than were reflected in his delegate totals. In other words, he may have won "38%" of the delegates on TV screens, but he may have produced over sixty percent of the actual voters. The disparity between voters who show up, and delegates that are assigned by precinct, is a major reason why the caucus system should be abolished. And that is why, in reality, Obama won an even bigger victory than the delegate numbers that were used to calculate his percentage.

I am not an Obama fan, and I have always been skeptic of Obama's staying power and credibility. He was fibbing again in his victory speech, when he claimed to have provided "affordable health care in Illinois." He did nothing of the sort. It is precisely those types of fibs that will do him in if he maintains misrepresentations as a front-runner. But there is no denying Obama won a massive victory. And he drove a stake through the heart of Team Clinton.

Despite all of the polling that predicted Obama would win, my internal poll told me Edwards would/could win and I predicted he would. Not bad. He didn't come out on top, but he made a very strong, unexpectedly strong, showing and collected more delegates than Hillary Clinton. Some pundits stated after the vote that the race was now between Obama and Clinton, and that Edwards would soon be eliminated. I don't believe that.

Yes, Obama and Clinton have the national organizations, the huge piles of money, and the better media visibility. But in the face of these overwhelming odds, Edwards mounted a successful challenge, and survived. That was a massive moral victory for Edwards. He has every right to be proud.

Now here's the interesting part, and an explanation of why I think Edwards may still have a future. All three Democrats have now adopted the same message: "change" and "the middle class." But I feel Edwards articulates that message better than either Clinton or Obama. I liked Edwards' speech better than either Obama's or Clinton's. It was superior. Clinton's remarks were, as always, wooden. Obama's were rote. Edwards not only reads the American jury better than either of his opponents, he knows how to deliver a better closing argument. And he does. Can Clinton and Obama force Edwards out of the race by appropriating his message? I don't know. I know Edwards is a fighter and he will be a factor.

Now the bad news for Republicans. But first, a small explanation. I am also a candidate myself. A Republican. I have not endorsed any candidate for president. In order to avoid any conflicts of interest, or suspicion that I favor one Republican over another, I have generally avoided writing about the Republican presidential race. There are exceptions, but not many. I also make generic comments on the status of the Republican Party. I have chosen, instead, to be the Republican "expert" on the "opposition" Democrats; that's my role for now.

Tuesday night, the Republicans did not show well. The Democratic turnout surged and almost doubled the Republican participation. That's not a good sign for Republicans in November. The caucuses fulfill the equivalent of a primary election. They test voter enthusiasm. Both parties were well organized and had candidates who had the resources to produce voters. And still the Democrats turned out almost double the number of participants as the Republicans. Primary turnouts are usually a rough approximation of underlying party strength. In Iowa, usually a swing state, Democrats are energized by a factor of almost 2 to 1. That's not a good omen for November. Iowa may not swing to the Republicans if present trends continue.

Bottom line: Senator Barack Obama won an even bigger victory than the media suggested. His "voters" appear to have accounted for over 50% of the actual participants in the caucuses. John Edwards won a victory by running ahead of Hillary Clinton. And the three of them will fight on to the national convention in Denver. As for Republicans, they now have a catfight as well.

Is Senator Barack Obama "The New Martin Luther King"? Andy Martin Begs to Differ

Once again "mainstream media" are herded into exaggerated and unjustified conclusions

(CHICAGO)(January 5, 2008) Don't you just love the mainstream media? Or should I call them the "herd" media. One reporter suggests Senator Barack Obama is the "new Martin Luther King," and the whole herd rushes in the same direction. Another journo calls him a "new Robert Kennedy," and they rush off in that direction. As usual, ContrarianCommentary.com offers a more nuanced analysis.

Let me start by stating the obvious: Obama gives a good speech. On Iowa caucus night, however, I gave my vote for "most effective speech" to Senator John Edwards, not Obama and certainly not Senator Hillary Clinton. I usually refer to Clinton as "wooden." I'm being nice.

Why do I disagree with the herd about Obama? First, they are listening, but not seeing, what is happening. Second, Obama has yet to demonstrate the greatness of a truly powerful speaker. Finally, his "speech" is getting stale.

First, I am not a big television watcher. But on election nights I have to watch, to write, and so I watched. When Obama went on the stage to speak I was looking for something, but couldn't see it: a teleprompter. It wasn't clear whether there was prompter there. Only in watching reruns the next day was the presence of the prompter clear.

The teleprompter was an Andy Martin "gotcha" item. Whether I am on the battlefield or sitting on a couch, or even a bar, I look for the "gotcha" indication that betrays the true state of mind of the moment.

The prompter tells me a lot about Obama (sort of like a doctor diagnosing the patient, long-distance in this case). First, Obama was probably the last to speak Thursday night because he had people writing his speech. Second, and more importantly, he did not write his speech. Finally, someone wrote his words for him.

The teleprompter incident also explains for me a disconnect that some in the media have legitimately observed: that Obama delivers "great" speeches but does poorly in debates. Why? Because when he doesn't have people to write for him in a debate, his own words end up faltering. And so, Obama can deliver a speech, but he can't compose one on the fly. His words are someone else's.

Obama was not speaking from the heart in Iowa; he was speaking off a teleprompter.

I want to make clear that there is nothing wrong with using a teleprompter for long, complex speeches. But when you are supposed to be speaking "from the heart," and giving "thanks," you need to do it spontaneously and really speak from the heart. Obama can't do that.

Now, second, to Martin Luther King. King did write his own material. There is no evidence that King had a teleprompter, or that he had a flock of hidden speechwriters composing his speeches for him. King was the real thing. King's words have endured because they were so powerful; they were so powerful because he wrote them and because he delivered them spontaneously.

Third, I was struck on Thursday night by the staleness of Obama's speech. Maybe he thinks people in Iowa (or New Hampshire) are rubes and don't realize or remember, but they heard essentially the same speech four years ago in Obama's initial foray on national television at the Democratic National Convention. Same "cadences," too. The "blue state/red state/United states" line is getting old, and stale. I "hope" he comes up with something newer. But listening to Barry O I was struck how he has become a Johnny One-Note, giving the same speech over and over again. A stale speech is not going to get him into the White House. Just ask Hillary Clinton.

By the way, and parenthetically, now you know why Obama was never a courtroom man when he "practiced" law in Chicago. He's not really good on his feet. He could not handle himself in a trial court, only in an appellate tribunal—where arguments are scripted.

The bottom line: Obama is scripted, not spontaneous; he is an insecure speaker, not a confident one. His words are not his own. And these weaknesses are evident when he is forced to participate in the debate format. He cannot hold his own with truly confident candidates who deliver their own words, not someone else's. Like so much about Obama that we don't know, he is really a paper mache caricature, a Potemkin candidate, a creation of the people behind the screen who manipulate and control his public persona.

Obama may have fooled Iowans, and he may fool Granite Staters (though as an honorable Granite Stater, I doubt it; they didn't coin the "Yankee" phrase "agin'er" in New Hampshire for nothing). But don't let Obama fool you.

Barry, we hardly knew ye.

Or as Senator Lloyd Bentsen might have said if he were still alive, "Barack, I knew Martin Luther King. And you're no Martin Luther King."

[P. S. I write my own material.]

Whodunit?
Who Brought Down the 96-Hour Obama Dynasty?

Mainstream media dare not speak its name: the Internet

Obama says "Vetting has ended." Says who?

The "canned" candidate finally gets the can

Obama says he's going to talk "Chicago tough," again

Will Clinton's "crying game" work, again?

(CHICAGO)(January 10, 2008) In the Broadway hit and later award-wining movie "Mr. Roberts," the enraged captain of Roberts' ship runs amok when his beloved palm tree disappears. "Whoooo did it?" the captain screams. "Whoooo did it? Whooo did it?"

Whodunit?

Who brought down the Barack Obama dynasty? The 96-hour wonder. Was it Hillary Clinton's crying game? I don't think so.

The mainstream media dare not speak its name: the Internet.

Mainstream media have professed shock at the sudden decline of Obama from front-running victor in New Hampshire to also-ran. Not since president Truman's Chicago Tribune "Dewey Defeats Truman" headline has such a shocking event scalded presidential politics. So who did it?

Nothing so reflects the lack of connection to reality in the Obama campaign than the remarks cited in Lynn Sweet's

Chicago Sun-Times column Wednesday. (http://blogs.sun-times.com/sweet/2008/01/sweet_column_obamaville_caught.html)

Obama apparently believed "he was done being vetted." Sweet, a Chicago veteran, begs to differ. So do I. As if on cue, John Kass, another Chicago muckraker, popped up with his own anti-Obama sentiments: http://www.chicagotribune.com/news/opinion/chi-kass_09jan09,0,4588673.column.

And then there was a sort-of Obama defender, Washington Post columnist Michael Gerson, who ended up making my own case even better than I had, even if that was not Gerson's intention.

I was inundated with Obama's supports' criticisms after I pointed out Obama had used a teleprompter to say "thank you" to the People of Iowa. Gerson thought a canned speech was evidence of "well-crafted rhetorical ambition." Not in my play book.

I was also criticized because I said Obama's Iowa speech sounded canned, and stale. Was it ever. A TV dinner of political platitudes. Gerson confirms my instincts. He discloses that not only were Obama's remarks canned, they were canned before the caucuses even took place. "But a few days *before* his Iowa win, Obama called his speechwriter in Des Moines to say his victory speech…Obama's bright young wordsmith, Jon Favreau…" (http://www.washingtonpost.com/wp-dyn/content/article/2008/01/08/AR2008010803487.html?hpid=opinionsbox1)

So Obama canned his spontaneous and sincere victory speech days before he even won. Some sincerity. Some spontaneity. Gerson shows just how far removed the Washington Post and he are from reality when he congratulates Obama, when he should be castigating him. And, once again

ContrarianCommentary.com comes out smelling like a rose because we brought you the truth first, based on appearances and not based on an insider's leak from within the Obama camp. Obama's supporters should be quaking. Obama not only doesn't write his own speeches, he cans them days in advance. Canned sincerity? Canned spontaneity? Watch out for the Clinton can-openers.

I wonder if Obama canned his concession speech in New Hampshire days in advance. Or was that spontaneous? Mr. Favreau, are you talking?

Well, as president Reagan would say, "That's just not the way its done, sonny." And that from a cannery captain of the first order.

Obama got canned by the voters in New Hampshire. Big surprise and no surprise. And his reaction is, well, no surprise either. Obama is talking "Chicago tough" again. He said he "comes from Chicago politics," and "We're accustomed to rough-and-tumble." He better get ready for the real thing.

Obama's spiel has been stale for a long time. Now that he is at the top, the Clintons' long knives will come out. Obama's "dream house" was purchased with financing from a Chicago swindler and slum lord, Tony Rezko. Rezko's criminal trial is approaching next month. Rezko's lawyers say he fears "anti-Syrian" bias because of his parentage. What? An Arab in Obama's background? Not really.

Rezko was a notorious campaign influence peddler and purchaser. He was strictly business. And he did business with Senator Barack Obama, *after* his election to the United States Senate. To paraphrase president Bill Clinton, that's no "fairy tale."

In the Broadway/movie hit "The Music Man," the huckster Harold Hill eventually has to go legit. Will Obama eventually go legit? I'm not sure. I'm not sure he can. Wednesday Obama was at it, soliciting new campaign contributions. He's going to need the cash, for the long, drawn out battle ahead.

The Obama dynasty began on Friday, January 4th. It ended Monday, January 7th. Maybe instead of comparing Obama to John F. Kennedy and Martin Luther King we should be comparing him to the fictional "king" Ozymandias of Percy Shelly's poem. I do not for a moment suggest Obama's campaign is over. But as the campaign goes on, people are going to become as aware as I am that Obama's speeches are stale, and canned, and he keeps repeating the same old sizzle without ever delivering any real solid steak. Or should I say, "Where's the beef?"

In all of the drama of January 8th I believe the Internet received grossly insufficient credit. If the material which crosses my desk is any indication. Obama is far, far away from being vetted, either in the mainstream media or on the Internet.

Finally, to avoid crediting the Internet, mainstream media have sought to explain Clinton's victory based on her "crying game" the day before the election. Personally, I am doubtful. Crying is not a viable campaign strategy. It could work, once, but not again. It may even be sexist patronizing to suggest a woman won because she cried. No one knows for sure. But I put my chips on the Internet influence. Unseen, and unstoppable.

Next up: the Tony Rezko fiasco. Why did Obama ever take Rezko's money to buy a house? I'll "rough-and-tumble" on that one. Over a year ago, I pointed out desperate men change their tunes, and deliver the goods:

http://www.politicalgateway.com/main/columns/read.htm l?col=687

http://www.contrariancommentary.com/community/Hom e/tabid/36/mid/363/newsid363/116/Default.aspx

Rezko may be primed to deliver Obama to federal prosecutors. At a minimum Rezko's lawyers may call Obama as a witness. As Barry O would say, "I'm from Chicago." So am I. Which is why I have been questioning Obama's bona fides for 3-1/2 years.

Bring on the Clinton can-openers. Obama may be canned. But the presidential campaign obviously is not. It's wide open.

Andy Martin Explains Basis for Accusation that Chicago Influence Peddler Tony Rezko Paid Senator Barack Obama an Illegal Bribe in Housing Transaction

(CHICAGO)(January 11, 2008) Andy Martin will hold a Chicago news conference Friday, January 11th at 4:00 P.M. to explain the factual and legal basis for his claim that indicted Chicago influence peddler Tony Rezko paid and intended to pay a bribe to Senator Barack Obama.

"There has been a great deal of confusion over what Obama did and what Rezko did, and how their combination and action in concert to purchase Obama's home in Chicago constituted a federal criminal offense," Martin will state. "I am here today to clarify and explain the legal theories behind the accusations and behind their structured and coordinated real estate transactions.

"It is also critical to place the Rezko-Obama relationship in context. Obama sent letters on his Illinois State senate stationary on Rezko's behalf. Obama cannot take refuge in what federal courts call the 'Ostrich defense,' where Obama merely says he was 'boneheaded' and gets away with criminal actions.

"But while the machinations of Obama and Rezko may be confusing to a lay person, they are nothing out of the ordinary to experienced criminal and political investigators in Illinois," Martin will state. "I stand by my view that Tony Rezko is going to try to implicate Barack Obama in criminal activity as a means of escaping punishment for his own behavior."

Obama and the Boardroom:
Would Any Troubled Corporation Hire Senator Barack Obama to be a "Turnaround Artist" or CEO?

Clinton or Edwards? Not likely
Which Democrat would you trust with your money?

(CHICAGO)(January 21, 2008) The Democratic Party has three major candidates for president who say America is in a mess and they know how to fix it. OK. Which one would you hire?

Each of the candidates promises to be what in corporate–parlance is a "turnaround artist," someone who is brought in to clean up the mess of a prior management.

By looking at the presidential election as a corporate problem rather than a governmental one, we may be forced to confront the limited qualifications of the junior candidate in the race, Senator Barack Obama, and then look at the other candidates, Senator Hillary Clinton and former senator John Edwards, and disqualify all of them.

And, rather deliciously, we have a full plate of troubled corporations that have hired or are looking for new CEO's, from Merrill Lynch and Citigroup in New York to the collapsing Countrywide Financial in California. Let's use these companies as templates. Would any of these troubled businesses hire Obama to lead their turnarounds? Clinton? Edwards? I doubt it.

Some of my audience believes, incorrectly, that I have a personal agenda or personal hostility to Mr. Obama. That is not really the case. I live in Chicago and Barry O, as I call him, is being marketed as a "Son of Illinois," which is grossly misleading, considering that he is really a creature of Chicago Machine Democratic Party politics in this state. Has Obama occasionally been a maverick or independent? Of course he has, when it suited his personal interest in political advancement.

But once ensconced in the "management" of his law firm or the state senate or U. S. Senate, Obama has been a reliable management vote for the local establishment. Obama has never turned anything around.

And no, I am not a closet supporter of the "likeable enough" Hillary Clinton. Former Mayor Rudy Giuliani has noted that Clinton has never managed anything, not a business, not a state, nothing. As for Mr. Edwards, I have opined that he would probably be the Democrats' strongest candidate in November. Edwards, at least, has proven to be a successful trial lawyer. Being a good courtroom lawyer does require management skills. But all of them want to "manage" what they claim is the most troubled government in the world. Not so fast.

Back to Obama. Can you envision any troubled corporation hiring Mr. Obama to lead a turnaround? Would you hire him if you had troubled finances? Is "hope" a substitute for experience? I don't believe so.

And yet the Democrats argue we have a troubled economy. We have a troubled foreign policy. We have a troubled nation. Why would any voter hire any of them to be a crisis manger and turnaround artist if the United States was a corporation instead of a government? Would you trust your money to a company that hired Obama (or Clinton or Edwards) to turn around your investment? I don't think so. You would sell your shares.

Bottom Line: The Democrats fail the Boardroom Test.

Crusading Chicago Columnist Andy Martin Releases New Piece of the "Obamagate" Puzzle

Andy Martin explains why the Obama scandals continue to grow
"Obama is sweating," Martin says, "because there was no vetting"

(CHICAGO)(January 23, 2008) Andy Martin will hold a Chicago news conference Wednesday, January 23rd at 5:00 P.M. to release a new piece of the Obamagate puzzle involving indicted Chicago influence peddler Tony Rezko.

"Senator Barack Obama was never properly vetted by the Chicago media," says Andy Martin, "And as a consequence the national media accepted the default of Chicago's mainstream organizations. Disinformation continues to be released.

"Barack Obama was never a litigator. He was a lawyer who was hired to accommodate Tony Rezko. Thus the total number of hours he 'billed' on Tony Rezko deals is completely irrelevant and misleading. Ironically, local media previously sought to portray Obama as a shrewd lawyer; now he is being pictured as little more than a glorified paralegal who was under the constant watch of other attorneys, nothing more than arm candy. In order to deflect the truth abut Rezko, Chicago's media are now forced to shred illusions about his legal career.

"In October, **2006** I disclosed that the Obama-Rezko conflicts and criminal links were going to explode. The Chicago media suppressed the story, just as they have suppressed virtually all unfavorable information about Obama including questions about the confusion concerning his religion.

"Through the political process I am now being vindicated and the truth is coming to the fore. And all of the current 'disclosures' are merely a rehash of my prior analysis.

"Today we will release another piece of the Obamagate puzzle," Martin says. "I am pleased that all of my prior analysis and commentary has now been corroborated."

Obama Week 2008, Part One:
Barack Obama and the Myth of the "Two Democrats"

Why Clinton goes to the convention

(CHICAGO)(February 20, 2008) One of the conceits and condescensions of the Democratic Party and its cable TV cabal during the primary season has been that the Democrats have "two candidates" who are broadly acceptable to the Democratic base, while the Republicans have a front runner who is rejected by at least some of the Republicans' core constituency. The fallacy of the Democrats' belief may soon be exposed.

It is undeniably true that both Barack Obama and Hillary Clinton are, broadly speaking, acceptable candidates for most Democrats. How could it be otherwise? They have virtually identical views on the issues. Despite their "differences," the commonalities are overwhelming.

But the idea that Clinton and Obama are interchangeable candidates as presidential *nominees* is utterly wrong.

I began writing about Obama four years ago. I never expected to be writing about him four years later. OK, so what.

As the primary season moved into high gear I expected to efface myself, as the mainstream media (MSM) took over the job of questioning Obama and vetting his credentials. That hasn't happened. MSNBC, for example, has become an Obama foghorn.

The "chatter" I receive tells me two things: (1) MSM have not played the role they should have; (2) "Clinton" Democrats are not necessarily going to line up behind Obama when McCain is the Republican option.

In 2007 ContrarianCommentary.com sponsored "Obama Week," in which we devoted a great deal of analysis to studying Obama's qualifications and character. By popular demand we are now back with a 2008 version.

Obama & Co. have misinterpreted the mentality of the Republican Party. It is true that some talk show host cry babies have sought to agitate their audience by denigrating Senator John McCain and attacking him for old controversies. But in the long run the Republican Party is not run by talk show hosts, it is run from a pragmatic center that is focused on the work at hand, to win elections. In any and every election there will always be some members of one party that will migrate to the other organization. Rarely has this tendency been anything more than window dressing (Democrats for Nixon, anyone?)

Based on what I am receiving and seeing—because ContrarianCommentary.com is not only a news and opinion-producing organization, it is a news and opinion-receiving operation, many Clinton Democrats will vote for McCain in November.

If anyone doubts my thesis they need look no further than the New York Post for confirmation that my views are correct.

A Sienna College Survey found Senator McCain within striking distance of the democrats *in New York State*. See: http://www.nypost.com/seven/02192008/news/regional-news/true_blue_is_purple_98270.htm.

In New York?

Obviously, McCain is not the "old man" that Obama ridicules. McCain is drawing "Reagan Democrats," already. Even before Hillary is rejected (not to say that she will be). So who were the Reagan Democrats? Less educated, lower wage, Roman Catholics. According to pollsters yesterday, what has been Hillary's final "base?" Less educated, lower wage, Roman Catholics. In other words, Reagan Democrats have stayed with Clinton.

Where do these voters go if Clinton is rejected? The vast majority of them will go to McCain, not to the brie-and-Chablis Obama campaign.

As I told someone yesterday, the "Democratic Party has been having a conversation with itself; the real world will intrude on the day that the party's nominee has to start having a conversation with the American People."

Are Clinton and Obama interchangeable nominees? Not at all.

You read it here first. ContrarianCommentary.com

Bottom line: buyer's remorse among Democrats will set in the day primaries end and Obama claims a majority of the "pledged" delegates. Pledged to what? Defeat in November?

My advice to Hillary? Honey, talk it up. Tough it out. Take it to the convention. And tell it like it is. And start doing this tomorrow. Not on March 5th.

Obama Week 2008, Part Two:
"Yes I Can!"
[Explain to Richard Roeper of the Chicago Sun-Times Why Patriotic Americans Are Concerned about Barack Obama]

(CHICAGO)(February 21, 2008) Richard Roeper of the Chicago Sun-Times today poses a question to the "GOP right:" What's so bad about Obama? [http://www.suntimes.com/news/roeper/805525,CST-NWS-roep21.article]

Mr. Roeper deserves an answer.

Roeper poses a list of questions. I will answer each in turn. First, I would like to recharacterize Mr. Roeper's question, since it is not the "GOP right" that is concerned with Barack Obama, it is **patriotic Americans**.

Roeper question: Do you think Obama is "off the charts intelligent…?"

Andy's Answer: No one denies that Mr. Obama is an intelligent man. But "off the charts?" You're off base. There is no evidence that Obama has ever distinguished himself by his intelligence. He was a very mediocre lawyer who never argued a case in trial court, and shamelessly inflates his record as "fighting for civil rights in court." That's a fairy tale, with credit to former president Clinton. Obama's real skills flow from his childhood as an abused and neglected child, when he developed coping skills to survive and prosper in the hostile youth culture of his upbringing.

Obama appears to have been a protégé of indicted influence-peddler Tony Rezko, who arranged for Obama to be hired by Rezko's law firm. Smart? "Off the charts" intelligent?

Obama wasn't chosen to lead the Harvard Law Review because he was the brightest student. He was picked because he was the least offensive member of the board and the best politician.

Roeper question: "Is he a man of God?"

Andy's Answer: Mr. Obama's connection to the deity has been most confused. He began life as a Muslim, despite his desperate efforts to conceal that fact. At some point in his 20's or 30's he accepted Christianity, although the exact date of his Baptism remains murky. Because Christianity is an inclusive religion, where profession of the faith "includes" one in Christianity, Obama is a Christian today. I have no problem with that.

He belongs to a church that many find troublesome but I do not. Christianity is a big tent and there is room for "Black Christians" just as there is room for many other denominations. Jesus was an adder, not a subtracter.

But Obama's recent use of religion in South Carolina stems mostly from his attempts to deflect the attention I focused on his former religion beginning four years ago. Obama suddenly became a **"Super-Christian!"** and flooded South Carolina with religious material. I find Obama's battlefield conversion to muscular Christianity highly suspicious.

Roeper question: Is he a sincere person…?

Andy's Answer: I don't doubt Obama's "sincerity." But sincerity for what, apart from his own self-promotion? "Change" is actually a classic Marxist doctrine. When one looks at his Marxist mantra of "Change," and Obama's voting record—instead of his campaign trail claims—one finds a person who comes as close to a Marxist revolutionary as we have recently found in American politics. Is it any wonder that someone has reported an Obama campaign office in Texas had a picture of the Cuban flag and Che Guevara?

Roeper question: Do you think he is a man of strong morals…family values?

Andy's Answer: If this question is addressed to Obama's personal life, he appears to lead an exemplary family life. Yes, I would say he is a good husband, a great father and someone who embodies family values. No one has ever suggested otherwise.

Roeper question: If elected, would he surround himself with cynical hacks, or experienced, idealistic individuals?

Andy's Answer: Are you kidding? Throughout his entire political career Obama has knowingly surrounded himself with the most cynical and most corrupt hacks in America, Chicago's politicians. From the crooked Mayor Daley, through crooked Senator Jones, to crooked aldermen and others—not to mention indicted influence-peddler Tony Rezko—Obama has always wallowed in extreme sleaze. He is perhaps the sleaziest politician to make it to the presidential level in many, many years. [Can anyone suggest when someone with as sleazy a political background as Obama has risen so fast, so high?] An Obama administration would be chock full of corruption.

How could someone who had just taken office as U. S. senator in 2005 claim he made a "boneheaded" investment with Tony Rezko, when Tony Rezko financed the purchase of the Obama's home? How? Obama may be the greatest tap dancer in history, as shown by the way he has slipped away from his links to Rezko—with a pliant and somnolent Chicago media to do his bidding—but he can't tap dance away from the truth of his involvement with sleaziness and corruption in Chicago.

What if a corrupt lobbyist had helped John McCain buy a house? What if?

Bottom line: Obama has fallen in love with himself. And many gullible Americans, in fact almost a million of them at last count, have fallen in love with Obama. As Kris Kristofferson would say "Sunday Morning Comin' Down" is going to be a hard one. I pray the United States will not be victimized by this tainted and ultimately doomed love affair.

And that, Mr. Roeper, is why *patriotic Americans* feel so uncomfortable about Obama.

The Man Who Brought Down Barack Obama: 2008 Update
The Vindication of Andy Martin

Martin's columns ignited the firestorm that continues to envelop Senator Barack Obama

(CHICAGO)(March 3, 2008) They never laid a glove on him. Hillary Clinton has been punching Senator Obama, with not a lot of visible success. The Democrats who also-ran for president are also history, and could not land a glove. They were not in his league, either. Only my research and columns about Obama's religious heritage have stuck to the Teflon pretender for president.

The Democratic Party's left has pilloried me ruthlessly and relentlessly. DailyKos.com? I'm the bad guy. *The Nation* Magazine? I am the evil architect of a "right-wing smear machine." On and on it goes. But through all of this abuse, no one has ever questioned my underlying factual research about Barack Obama's religious history. Indeed, the media continue to get the facts wrong, so convoluted and confused have been Obama's evasions and explanations.

I began a worldwide search for information on Obama in 2004. The honyock Chicago media were asleep. While Chicago bills itself as a world class city, the city's media range from yokels to sycophants. Half the media were too lazy or incompetent to investigate Obama; they are the yokels. The other half were so starved for attention to Chicago that they kept concealing the truth in order to promote Obama's children's crusade.

Does the truth about Obama matter? It did. And it does.

First, let's set aside the left-wing's attacks on me: One, I accept that Barack Obama is a Christian today. I have written extensively on why that is the case, and why Christian theology accepts him. Two, I have no intrinsic problem with Obama's church; Christians come in many varieties and versions of theology. Three, I have never stooped to the "Barack *Hussein* Obama" gambit; it is so childish and so talk-radioish. Finally, I am not "anti-Muslim." Indeed, my columns on Obama have confused many conservatives, who see me as pro-Muslim, not anti. In fact, I am not pro or anti-Obama or pro or anti-Muslim. I just state the facts as I find them. My opinions are based on my facts.

Ironically, it was the facts I presented about Obama that started the wildfire. Over a year ago the mainstream media (MSM) claimed they had buried those facts. But the smoldering continued. Today's front page of the New York Post concerns Obama's religion, http://www.nypost.com. There is an extensively-reported story on Obama's denial of his Muslim roots in the Post, with factual errors, http://www.nypost.com/seven/03032008/news/nationalnews/smeared_o_has_cross_words_100255.htm.

And my prediction in 2004 that Jewish voters would become suspicious of Obama have also proven correct. The Post's Albany columnist Fred Dicker has a column on Jewish hostility to Obama (not yet posted online, maybe Tuesday).

So there you have it. Four years of accuracy.

Ironically, almost every column about Obama presents new factual errors. Today's Post story says Barack's father "was a Christian who converted to Islam." Not true. It was Obama's *grandfather* who converted, initially to Christianity and later to Islam. Barack's father and stepfather were always Muslims.

Obama's problem stems from a defect in his personality: he loves to please, he loves to dissemble, he loves to parry and avoid unpleasant truths. And these qualities have served him well in life. Bill Clinton caught heat for comparing Obama to Jesse Jackson. The real comparison should be to Cassius Clay/Muhammad Ali. Obama is a master of the rope-a-dope. He bounces off the unpleasant truths about his life, and his opponents have a hard time pinning him down. They keep chasing, but they can't catch up with his evasions and prevarications. And Obama always presents a sliver of the truth to confuse matters further and delay his day of reckoning.

In exposing Obama's lies I have also come to like the man. He seems very pleasant and he would probably make a good neighbor if I moved in next door to his mansion. I just don't want him in the Oval Office. Obama would be a disaster for America and a disaster for the world.

Although I am a columnist and editor, I was trained as a lawyer. My specialty was cross-examination. Evasion on the witness stand is fatal. Obama has never been examined by a competent cross-examiner. Tim Russert pretends to be tough but he is a powder puff questioner.

And Obama is shrewd. He avoids the Chicago media, who today are more familiar with his relationship to and machinations with the Chicago Democratic Machine. Obama prefers no media contact when he can get away with it, and national or regional reporters as a refuge from tough questions that might today come from some Chicago reporters.

On November 16, *2006* I exposed Obama's links to indicted Chicago influence peddler Tony Rezko. Again, no one was listening. In Chicago, where anything negative about Obama is *ver-*

boten, they pretended not to hear. But once again I made a public record of the extensive links between the two men. I also disclosed letters to the Grand Jury, Public Integrity Section and FBI. It took almost two (2) years for the truth about very close relationship between Obama and Rezko to be disclosed by the MSM. Obama and Rezko had gone house hunting together.

Once again, Obama had lied about the relationship for almost two years, and only confessed when federal prosecutors began to close in. Obama was doing business with Rezko even after Obama was elected to the U. S. Senate. His defense: I was stupid.

Obama could have put the Rezko story to bed in 2006 if he had been *loyal* to Rezko and admitted they were close friends; and that he was "pained" by the accusations. The truth would have immunized him. Rope-a-doping away from Rezko made Rezko stick to Obama's ongoing campaign.

Ironically, today I am the one, not Obama, defending Rezko against abusive treatment from the Department of Justice. I have no problem with Rezko being punished if he is guilty; I just object to violating Rezko's constitutional rights to obtain a conviction. If Obama had been fair to Rezko, he might have escaped future questions. By being evasive and deceptive he has laminated his future to Rezko's trial.

Is there more to come on Obama's Muslim roots? I don't think so. He comes from a devout Muslim family. His pseudo-"Granny" is an avid Muslim, and he worshipped at mosque when he lived in Indonesia. He did not become a Christian until his mid-20's. Those are the unavoidable facts which the media try so hard to avoid.

As for the Obama-Rezko relationship, Contrarian Commentary.com will have more exclusives in the days ahead.

Obama has never faced the "vetting" that Hillary Clinton said was essential. She was right. It is going to be a very painful experience for the Democratic Party if Obama wins the nomination.

And so, at the end of the day, it was Contrarian Commentary.com that ultimately lit the fuse that started the fire that will bring down Barack Obama. While we may appear to be only a Lilliputian force compared to the mighty Chicago Tribune and its new Emperor Zell, the TV networks and cable babblers, we got the Obama story right when they did not. By default, we became the engine that has driven the truth to the fore, and will eventually deflect Barack Obama away from the White House.

We eventually brought down Barack Obama. God Bless the Internet. And God Bless the USA.

Three Cheers for Carol Marin
Carol, Where Have You Been for the Last Four Years?

Andy Martin awaits more arrivals to the Obama squad

The truth about "Barry O" remains to be told. Dig in and dig away!

But be careful: the Obama family demands cash for interviews.
Even from the New York Times

(CHICAGO)(March 4, 2008) I first met Carol Marin thirty years ago. Where did the years go? She was new to Chicago television and at the start of her long stint at Channel 5. I vividly remember answering a call from her while driving on the New Jersey Turnpike some twenty years ago, in a snowstorm. Time flies. And snow melts.

But I have never thought of Carol as an "agitator." Until today, that is.

Washington Post columnist Dana Milbank refers to Marin as an "agitator" at an Obama news conference in Texas, a "visitor to the Obama entourage who accused the regulars of being too quiet." (http://www.washingtonpost.com/wp-dyn/content/story/2008/03/03/ST2008030303289.html?hpid=artslot)

Carol, honey, you stole my lines. Where have you been for the last four years?

The tabby cats in Chicago that masquerade as "reporters" have allowed Obama to inflate himself into a giant blimp that has begun to shadow the future prospects of the Democratic Party.

Obama has portrayed himself as America's new royalty, set to claim the throne in Washington and to bring "peace" to the world by disarming and destroying the only peace-making force on the planet, the U. S. Government. Imperfect it may be; I know all of its many imperfections; but the U. S. and the American people are still the last, best hope for peace on earth.

Unlike Russia, we have real elections, and we throw our tyrants out of power, not merely shuffle the names on doors. Whether one loves George Bush, or hates him, he will be out of office next January, not serving as America's "prime minister." A new president will take over and almost all of the Bushies will be history. Are you listening, Mr. Putin?

So welcome to the campaign. Carol. How's agitatin'? [I am afraid to say "Whassup?" for obvious reasons; I might be compared, unfavorably, to Bill Clinton. That's a column for another day.]

Milbank says reporters have begun to ask tough questions of Obama. What took them so long? I have news for them. Obama will be put on "lockdown" status. Yesterday (Monday) was probably the last time they will see an open Obama news conference until after the Democratic convention.

Listening to Obama speak when he is not reading from a teleprompter is an aggravating experience. Unlike the casual fluidity of his speech-reading, when Obama speaks without a script he is completely hesitant, hedged and unable to mumble more than a few words without more hedging and edging. He was that way Monday.

Back home, is a new day dawning in Chicago? Is some of the legendary rough-and-tumble of Chicago's journalism returning? Don't count on it. The Chicago Tribune has not yet committed any of Emperor Zell's co-owners and storm troopers to the Obama expose squad. And while Mike Flannery from Channel 2 managed to show up in Texas (an "agitator" for sure), the other TV stations were absent. No, I will remain hesitant until I see more evidence than just Carol Marin storming Obama's barricades.

Chicago media cover Obama as though he were the pope, and in return he exudes an air of infallibility and nonchalance. No more.

Way back in 2006 I reported that the links between Obama and Rezko were much deeper than known to the public. It took the "working press" fourteen (count'em) months to catch up with me, a mere Internet columnist, albeit one with the worldwide audience most Chicago writers lack.

On the other hand, if Carol keeps agitating, the Obama beat might just become fun. If Carol will keep agitatin' I'll make the sandwiches and bring a thermos.

Just to be sure we understand ourselves, the issue is not whether Obama is a Muslim today (he is not) but why he has made such convoluted statements for years about the religious heritage of his family tree. And why he continues to confuse the media about who his real relatives are.

"Granny" Sarah Obama is not his real grandmother. But she is sure a great prop. No wonder Barry Obama refuses to give Sara some cash to connect lights and running water. And, as Nick Kristof learned recently, Obama's "Granny Sarah" may lack electricity and plumbing, but she now knows how to demand cash for an interview. Ah, those Kenyans. They demand money even from Nick Kristof of the New York Times, a save-the-plant man if ever there was one. (http://www.nytimes.com/2008/02/24/opinion/24kristof.html?scp=5&sq=Kristof&st=nyt)

The whole Obama family now has their palms out. Or, as the late Mike Royko would have said about Granny Sara, she may not speak English, but she was a fast learner with her Latin: "Ubi est mea?"

Here's a more local assignment, Carol. Ask yourself why the hospital where Michelle works, located in a poor neighborhood, pays Michelle a third of a million dollars for "outreach" when that money could be spent either lowering fees for the "uninsured" or expanding treatment to the under-insured? Instead, they give Michelle Obama a third of a million dollars for a make-work job. In New York, they used to call such exploiters "poverticians," because they got rich serving the poor. Once again, the Obama family has had its hands out for years. Only Michelle is also likely now to go on lockdown status with the media as well. Maybe they will lock Barack in a cell next to Rezko until after the Democratic convention, to keep pesky reporters away.

The issue is not whether Rezko did a lot of favors for Obama, many still to be disclosed; he did. Rezko got Barack his first job at a law firm. But when the "going got tough" for Tony, Obama got going. So much for Obama's sense of loyalty. Obama learned more than he admits on the streets of Chicago; he's a taker, not a giver. The Daley family would understand.

Obama talks tough on the campaign trail, to the uneducated "regional" journalists or to college students in a state of rapture that would embarrass even Mike Huckabee's devotees. But back home in Chicago, he still sleeps in Emil Jones' bed.

And, if Obama had not been lying to the pliant Chicago media about his links to Rezko for more than a year, the issue would not have triggered an ambush on March 3, 2008. Obama may claim he has "judgment," but Hillary is right: other than a speech six (6!) years ago, what "judgment" has he shown?

If Carol Marin keeps up her tactics I may just have to serenade her with an old Sinatra song, recalling Chicago thirty years ago when we first met. It was a very good year.

Andy Martin on "The Day the Music Died" for Barack Obama

The Lion King begins to hear Hillary's roar; "end of the beginning" for Obama

Antiwar Obama purchased mansion with cash from Iraqi wheeler-dealer

"Michelle's Law" Dooms Her Husband

"Liar, liar, pants on fire" over NAFTA debacle

(CHICAGO)(March 4, 2008) Bye, bye Obama Pie. Yesterday, March 3rd, The Music Died for Barack Obama. It is not the beginning of the end, but it is certainly the end of the beginning (Churchill).

Hillary Clinton has suffered from what is probably the worst campaign staff in recent history. Slowly, that is being remedied. And if she listens to me, she will dump Penn & Co. and start with a clean sheet of paper. Nevertheless, Hillary's roar has become more audible. Obama can finally hear it. The free ride is over.

While I don't hesitate to criticize Obama, he deserves great praise for developing an extraordinary campaign machine. His campaign has been as efficient and effective as Hillary's has been inefficient and ineffective. But what happens when the two campaigns begin to match-up in competence?

Yesterday, it was clear that Obama fell to earth. With a thud. One of the subscribers to my e-mail list on Obama columns recently wrote me and said "It's over; take my name off the list." Well, obviously it wasn't over, and it isn't going to be over for a long time. He unsubscribed too soon. Maybe Obama himself had unsubscribed from his own campaign too soon. How can you explain yesterday? It was indeed a "kitchen sink" of disasters.

First, "Michelle's Law." Michelle has criticized Hillary by saying, "How could she run the government when she could not run her own household?" or words to that effect. Good point. Well.

How can Obama run the government when he can't run his own campaign? He was blatantly lying to the American people about a NAFTA meeting involving one of his senior advisers and a Canadian official. His limp excuse that his lies were based on "information I had at the time" is sheer nonsense. Michelle's Law disqualifies Obama from continuing his candidacy.

Second, not to worry. In Chicago, up is down and down is up. Especially when you are a co-owner and storm trooper for Sam Zell. Today the Chicago Tribune congratulated Obama for lying about NAFTA, and said "thank goodness" he was lying. And you wonder why corruption flourishes in the Windy City? People pass a lot of wind. The media are just as crooked and crackpot as the craven politicians they cover.

How could any responsible newspaper endorse lying? Well, in Chicago, they will do anything to keep Barry O's hopes alive. And maybe Sam Zell's as well.

I watched Obama's body language on Monday and it would be enough to blow up the screen on Bill O'Reilly's weekly body language séance. Obama's shoulders were stooped, his face dejected. He looked as though he had just lost the big game and his puppy had died as well.

Lynn Sweet of the Chicago Sun-Times, whom I castigated years ago for being an Obama sycophant, has morphed into an attack dog that kept barking as Obama exited the newsroom (what are they putting in the Sun-Times water coolers? Sam Zell's co-owners could use a bottle or two of the same juice.).

The NAFTA debacle was devastating to Obama. He claims to be honest, and he lied. He claims to be organized and have sound judgment, and his own advisers were lying to him. What a mess. "Liar, liar, pants on fire" is the only way to describe Obama's NAFTA disaster.

I should point out that Obama lies to us and insults our intelligence virtually every day. How often have you heard or read that Obama gave his anti-war speech in 2002 when he was "in a senate campaign." The obvious context is that Obama was a candidate for federal office and he was courageously speaking out on a national issue, at some political risk to himself. In point of fact, Obama was running for the Illinois *state* senate in 2002, and that body has nothing to do with issues of war and peace. The only wars fought in the Illinois senate involve battles between patronage armies, not real military forces.

But Obama and his fund raisers and supporters shamelessly misrepresent the context of Obama's antiwar speech in 2002 to suggest he was speaking during a campaign for the U. S. Senate. *He was not.* There was no risk to Obama speaking out against the war, no courage involved. Hyde Park, Chicago, where he was a candidate for the local senate seat, is probably as liberal as Cambridge Massachusetts, or Berkeley, California. And so, in small ways and not so small ways, Obama's entire persona is built on lies, lies and more lies. How many of them does he believe himself?

I have been screaming about Obama and Rezko since November, 2006. A long time. Of course, I also went to the Grand

Jury and the FBI. No secret. No one cared. No one believed. No one knew. Well, now, slowly, the truth is oozing out. And the truth is not a pretty sight.

The federal government is trying to "break" Tony Rezko. That's why Rezko is being tortured in a federal prison in downtown Chicago. I have condemned these practices. Will he break? As the late Senator Lloyd Bentsen might say to Rezko, "I know John McCain, and you're no John McCain. You'll break." In other words, at one extreme point, even John McCain broke in captivity. Rezko will break.

Over the past couple of months I have been providing insights into the progress of Rezko's federal case and, again, no one was noticing. But it's all there on my net postings to see. I have been involved in the federal court at 219 S. Dearborn for thirty-nine years (no, I'm not *that* old, but Jack Benny would approve, at least in my 39th year). I know how federal courts and federal prosecutors and federal judges operate. They are nasty people. But as the prosecutors ratchet up their torture of Rezko, the potential for an implosion and then explosion involving Obama also increases.

And, finally, the worst blow. Whether the numbers are crunched in the Rezko trial or outside the Rezko trial, it is now clear that Barry and Michelle bought their "dream home" in Kenwood with money provided by an Iraqi wheeler-dealer. The ultimate turn of fate. Obama opposed the war; then he had his own home financed by someone who was, depending on whom you believe, a Saddam stooge or a Saddam victim. Either way, an Iraqi financed the purchase of the Obama "compound" in Chicago. Yekkkh.

And this is the Democrats' "Mr. Ethics?"

Dear friends (as John McCain might say), it ain't pretty. I may have been a prophet Isaiah pronouncing to the unbelieving, but sooner rather than later the unbelievers are becoming believers. I am no longer a prophet without honor in my own house.

March 3rd was the day the music died for Barack Obama. By, bye, Obama Pie.

But fear not, I have a few more slices of Obama Pie to serve up before his trajectory hits the ground. Contrarian Commentary.com was first, and we will be the last, to provide accurate facts, information and interpretation about the Lion King of Illinois.

As for the great Emperor Zell and his co-owners/storm troopers at the Chicago Tribune, as long as they continue to congratulate Obama for lying there will be plenty of work for me to do in Chicago. Come to think of it, maybe I should order a bottle of their giggle juice from the Sun-Times. Bottoms up, Lynn and Carol? Just remember what mommy told you when you go home at night: don't violate Michele's Law. Look what happened to Barry O when he did.

There is a delightful Yiddish word to describe Obama right now: *bakakt.*

And, if I have any other subscribers who want to unsubscribe because the battle is over, just let me know.

Obama Expert Andy Martin Takes a Bow for His Investigative Commentary about the Charlatan Senator

Media critic Martin calls Chicago's bloated journalism enterprises "money losing media," not "mainstream media"

Investigative columnist criticizes the "money losing media" ("MLM") for continuing Chicago coverup on Obama

More to come from the crusading columnist

(CHICAGO)(March 15, 2008) For almost four (4) years I have been exposing the consummate political charlatan known as Barack Obama. From his bogus "autobiography" with concocted characters, to his links to the hoodlum Chicago political establishment, to his mendacious campaign tactics, I have relentlessly told the truth about Barry Obama. But there were none so blind as those who would not see; none so deaf as those who would not hear.

And the greatest deafness and blindness were found at the Chicago Tribune and Chicago Sun-Times. The Tribune acted like a small town mullet wrapper, boosting Obama as though he were a Chicago brand that was "good for Chicago." Every time Obama was trapped, he turned to the Tribune to bail him out with exclusive rope-a-dope interviews, photos, etc.

Likewise, because of the Sun-Times' urban audience, that newspaper was not anxious to publish the truth about Obama.

But the truth was there to see, in plain view:

http://www.politicalgateway.com/main/columns/read.htm
l?col=687; http://www.politicalgateway.com/main/columns/
read.html?col=688

Yesterday (Friday, March 14, 2008) Obama was back in full damage control mode. After dodging the MLM for months, if not years, about his links to Tony Rezko and Pastor Jeremiah Wright, Obama appeared to open up—if only for a brief interlude. It was all just another Obama illusion.

And once again, ContrarianCommentary.com will have new analysis and a new interpretation on what Obama disclosed—and didn't disclose.

I have no problem with people reading the MLM; honestly, I read them myself. I have a forthcoming column praising them for much of what they do.

But the reality is that in Chicago the MLM have long deceived their readers, and viewers, about the true character of Barry Obama.

Obama has started truth telling, bit by painfully reluctant bit. It's time for the MLM to do the same. Obama doesn't want us to know who he is. But ContrarianCommentary.com has been "whistle-blowing" for almost four years. And we will continue to do so. Keep it here.

And for these Obamaphiles who want to read some of our legacy material, a large number of columns prior to 2007 are still posted on PoliticalGateway.com. Thereafter, we began to blog at http://www.Contrariancommentary.blogspot.com, http://www.ContrairianCommentary.wordpress.com, and, of course, http://www.ContrarianCommentary.com. It's all there to behold. Why were the MLM concealing the truth?

On Pastor Wright, I have this to say. Probably 50 out of 52 weeks of the year I can be found in the pews of the Episcopal Church. I don't always agree with the clergy, and I did quietly leave a parish when the rector went beyond the mainstream with his theology. But whatever my occasional differences, I have never heard a sermon that was so divorced from reality that it had to be denounced and renounced.

Obama's claim that he has been a part of an institution for over twenty years, and yet had no awareness of the controversial claims being preached from the pulpit, is completely unbelievable, mendacious and probably a bald-faced lie. And this man wants to be president? He's running on judgment, intelligence and bringing us together? More to come in a forthcoming column.

It bears noting that even Friday Obama could not bring himself to tell the truth about Wright on MSNBC, CNN and FNC. No doubt Obama feared a Black backlash if he was candid with the media. Obama pretended and suggested that Wright's removal from Obama's campaign had something to do with Wright's "retirement." Oh, so it didn't have anything do with the incendiary sermons? Wright just left? He wasn't asked to leave? What rubbish. It's time for Obama to retire his lies.

Finally, truth be known, I sort of like Obama. As a neighbor. There is certainly lot to praise in him and about him. But there is also a lot to criticize. He may be a great American success story. But there is no way I would want him anywhere near the Oval Office. I have taken a great deal of ridicule and criticism for exposing Obama over the past four years. But I have taken the facts and truth where they led me. And I will continue to do so. I have over forty years of credibility as a public interest lawyer and advocate to maintain.

Amusingly, yesterday I received an abusive e-mail from a staffer at the Champaign-Urbana News-Gazette about my latest piece of investigative commentary. The News-Gazette first published pictures about me way back in 1965. Unfortunately, they didn't believe in me then, and some of them there apparently still do not believe me. A prophet is not without honor... But I will keep prophesying.

And, oh, Pastor Wright. Say it loud and say it proud! God Bless America.

New York Times Writer Credits Andy Martin with Exposing Senator Barack Obama's Religious "Roots"

NY Times Magazine article says "colorful Web columnist" Andy Martin first disclosed Obama's Muslim heritage

Martin says that the Times' attempts to portray Obama's Muslim heritage as a "rumor" are utterly false

(NEW YORK)(March 17, 2008) The *New York Times* Magazine for March 16th carries a column that credits "colorful Web columnist Andy Martin" with disclosing Barack Obama's religious roots. (http://www.nytimes.com/2008/03/16/magazine/16wwln-idealab-t.html?_r=1&scp=1&sq=Manjoo&st=nyt&oref=slogin)

The *Times* column seeks to portray Obama's Muslim heritage as a "rumor." The column goes on to make the false assertion that Martin's 2004 release "offered no proof."

Chicago-based Martin responded on Monday, branding the *Times* column part of Obama's religious disinformation operation.

"A column in Sunday's *New York Times Magazine* credits 'colorful Web columnist' Andy Martin with disclosing Senator Barack Obama's Muslim family 'roots,'" Martin stated. "That claim is correct. The balance of the column, however, is more Obama disinformation."

"First, the 2004 column is there to be read by anyone. I am adding the original release to these remarks. The *Times* claim that I offered 'no proof' is rebutted by the release itself. I did what no one else had done before. I developed international research both on Obama's family name (Barack, as a Muslim-derived name), and on the fact that both Obama's father and grandfather's were Muslims. No one has ever impeached my research. To claim otherwise is nothing more than Barack Obama's disinformation.

"To label facts as 'rumors,' and to claim that evidence of a family religious history is 'without proof' is nothing more than left-wing disinformation.

"Interestingly, way back in 2004 I offered and explanation of why Obama was hiding his religious history. He was afraid of a backlash from Jewish voters. That backlash materialized in 2007, validating by my predictive analysis in 2004. Now that Obama's mentor and pastor Jeremiah Wright's anti-Semitic statements have been publicized, we know what and why Obama was trying to conceal.

"I also suggested in 2004 Obama's book was a fraud. Obama later disclosed that his 'autobiography' had imaginary characters as major aspects of his 'autobiographical' narrative. To paraphrase Geraldine Ferraro, could a white guy get away with such chicanery? No way.

"Obama has been using religion and family as a scam for many years. He used Jeremiah Wright to create the illusion of Obama's Black Nationalist credentials, by attending Wright's church for decades. Obama tries to send a subliminal message of Black Nationalism to African-Americans through his association with Wright, and then issues cloying denials to the white media.

"He has turned the Muslim spigot off and on as it suits his interests. His 'granny" has been quoted in the NY Times as saying she is a devout Muslim, and then quoted by AP as saying she is a Christian. Well, what is she? What gives?

"While my subsequent columns since 2004 have clearly accepted Obama's avowals that at some point he began to profess Christianity, his relentless efforts to conceal his Muslim heritage have continued, right up to using a writer in the *Times Magazine* yesterday to brand his religious 'roots' as a 'rumor.' Obama started life as a Muslim. The exact date when he professed Christianity has never been disclosed. Obama continues to be deliberately vague.

"Obama has constantly tried to undermine me. He has used his allies at *The Nation* to smear me as the clandestine leader of a 'right-wing smear machine.' I am nothing of the sort. Now he has used the *NY Times* to resuscitate the false claim that my research was based on 'rumors.' Nonsense.

"Part of the problem in writing about Obama's religious beliefs, as well as his links to Chicago wheeler-dealer Tony Rezko, is that Obama constantly tries to rope-a-dope the truth. He has been dribbling out 'facts' on his religion and on Rezko for years. Each disclosure is labeled as 'final' and 'complete,' when they are nothing of the sort. How many 'final' disclosures about Rezko have we seen from Obama? I lost count. Ditto for religious explanations. Last week he was at it again, with another 'full disclosure' about Rezko. The interview left Chicago Tribune columnist John Kass still skeptical.

"I am very proud to have developed the original research, here at home and abroad in Kenya, on Obama's religious history. Likewise, I exposed Obama's Rezko connection fifteen months ago.

"But here are some questions for Mr. Obama, today:

"First, when was he baptized by Reverend Wright?

"Second, is there a baptismal certificate to document his alleged date of baptism? Most denominations issue certificates.

"Third, why won't Mr. Obama come clean and tell the truth about both his religious roots and relationship to Rezko? Why does he keep dribbling out the truth under duress?

Fourth, is his 'Granny," Sarah Obama, a Muslim or a Christian? Who is right? The AP or the New York Times? There are conflicting public statements.

"I have a great deal of respect for the Muslim religion. I believe in inclusiveness, not demonization. But when someone tries to hide his roots, rather than discover them, I am lead to question his candor and sincerity. That is why I have focused attention on Obama's Muslim heritage. Obama thought he could get 'protection' from his friends in the media and the truth would wither. I'm here to tell Barry O that the truth and the power of the truth are growing exponentially.

"Fifth, when is he going to make a full and complete disclosure of all of the imaginary characters he produced as real people in Dreams From My Father? As I stated in 2004, and again in 2007, the use of imaginary composite characters in an autobiography is absolutely fraudulent behavior that can lead to litigation.

"Sixth, why did Obama try to suggest on Friday that Reverend Wright left Obama's campaign because of Wright's 'retirement,' thereby suggesting that Wright's removal had nothing to do with Obama's disapproval of Wright's speeches and was simply linked to a 'retirement?' Another Obama rope-a-dope. Once again, Obama was trying to play the 'game' both ways, disowning Wright to please the white media while placating his African-American supporters by crediting Wright's 'retirement' as the reason for his removal.

"If Barack Obama had been as accurate as I have been in reporting the truth about his past, he would not be in the mess he is in today. I accused him of trying to fool the American people in 2004. I accuse him of the same conduct in 2008. I was right then, and I am right now," Martin stated.

Martin is in New York for media interviews.

Obama Expert Andy Martin Attack's Obama's Philadelphia Speech as "Reverend Wright Lite"

Martin says that Obama's radical "Hate America First" agenda is indistinguishable from Reverend Wright's

"Most hateful speech ever delivered by a serious candidate for president," says Martin

Martin says Obama cannot pass "the entourage test"

(NEW YORK)(March 18, 2008) Obama expert and Internet columnist Andy Martin will hold a 4:00 P.M. New York City news conference today, March 18th, to condemn Senator Barack Obama's Philadelphia speech as "the most hateful speech delivered by a serious candidate for president in the modern era."

"Obama's speech was 'Reverend Wright Lite,'" says Martin. "It was a sugar-coated version of Wright's 'Blame America First' oratory.

"In reality, Barack Obama *is* Reverend Jeremiah Wright. Now we know why they have been tight as ticks for 20 years. They share the same philosophy, the same ideology, the same theology.

"Barack Obama's attacks on American business could have been delivered in another era by Juan Peron, or today's Hugo Chavez. Economic problems? Blame corporate America? Blame accounting. Blame globalization.

"I have news for Barry Obama: Corporate America is what has lifted the African-American community out of economic despair over the past four decades. Corporate America has been the savior, not the bane, of Black communities. Likewise for cities and states and the federal government.

"Bad schools? American taxpayers are being bankrupted by exorbitant school taxes, higher pay, more benefits. School budgets are out of sight. But what do we see on playgrounds? I-pods, fancy shoes, and a collection of couture that is out-of-step with any avenue to economic success in this nation. Does Obama advocate higher taxes for what is a cultural and community failure?

"Barack Obama bared his real teeth today. His message was a message of hate, disgust, opposition. Yes, it was basted in the Constitution; and sugar-coated with his ritual claims for 'unity.' But then he blamed slavery and corporate America for today's problems. This man is out of touch with reality.

"As usual, Obama played to his children's crusade in the balconies with a litany of promises, attacks, and prevarications. Today Obama did what his critics have called on him to do: to outline his vision of America. Barack Obama's 'Amerika' is a land of hate, racism and surrender; and a talk-radio fueled backlash that Obama wants to eradicate.

"Obama stooped so low as to trash his grandmother, claiming she feared Black men and had made racist remarks. Disgraceful. Is that why he keeps her locked up? Anyone who would trash the very people that paid for his fancy schools and launched him on the road to success, and seeks to demonize his grandmother, is a demon himself," Martin says.

"Ultimately, Obama failed the 'Entourage Test.' Every president brings with him a group of close supporters and intimate associates who form the core and backbone of his or her administration. Obama's 'team' would be a 'Hate America First' team, filled with people that want to raise taxes and shift blame for the failure of urban communities. Reverend Wright is a vital part of Obama's entourage, and a big part of his baggage.

"Instead of using his speech to disassociate himself from Reverend Wright, as many had predicted he had to do, Obama brought himself closer to Wright and **validated** the pastor. Obama announced in advance this was 'his speech.' It will be his downfall.

"His statement that Blacks are two-faced, and say one thing at work and another at home, and that whites are similarly two-faced, is the most racially divisive remark in a generation.

"The Democratic Party should be ashamed of itself that Barack Obama is a serious candidate for president. Barack Obama had a chance to bring us together today and to reject Reverend Wright. He forfeited that opportunity. He validated and endorsed Jeremiah Wright's view of 'Amerika.'

"Obama's call to arms is a call to loot corporate America for more welfare, higher taxes, more special programs to undo the effect of slavery. More preferences, more preferential treatment. More self-pity and prevarication. A few weeks ago I called Obama a Marxist. Today he confirmed that accusation. Government and business are the enemy; Obama is the savior.

"Obama's remarks reeked of the very resentment and anger for which Jeremiah Wright has become notorious. These men are joined at the hip. After today, that much is clear. Barack Obama is not the Democratic Party's candidate for president. He is the Black Nationalist candidate for president."

Aftermath of the Speech, Part One:
Barack Obama is the Mau Mau Candidate for President

And, on Good Friday, Bill Richardson, an Obama Judas, reappears

(NEW YORK)(March 23, 2008) When I went to prep school in Britain fifty years ago the Mau Mau rebellion in Kenya was still very much in the minds of English schoolboys. Through arson, rape, plunder and murder the Mau Mau movement had brought Britain's East African empire into a state of eventual collapse. And killed schoolboys. I was not the only person impressed and influenced by the Mau Mau. Barack Obama Senior was a young Kenyan growing up in the thick of the rebellion.

Whether Barack Obama Senior was merely influenced by the Mau Mau (he was of the wrong tribe to join) or actively supported the movement is a matter still under investigation. Nevertheless, the Mau Mau left an indelible impression on the world. A few years latter the term "mau mau" even entered the American vernacular. And Barack Senior entered the United States. We are living with the aftermath.

In a classic book of social satire, Tom Wolfe in 1970 wrote "Radical Chic & Mau-Mauing the Flak Catchers," describing how the emerging "militant movement" in America was trying to threaten government agencies into capitulating to collectivist intimidation. Wolfe borrowed the term "mau mau" and converted the phrase into a gentler form of coercion, although many radicals in the 60's did use rape and arson as weapons in their arsenal of social deconstruction.

Today, Barack Obama, Jr. has become the Mau Mau candidate for president.

While on first glance that might seem an incendiary accusation, closer examination of the Obama campaign's latest tactics and the entire raison d'etre of Obama's candidacy confirm that Obama has successfully mau maued the mainstream media and is well on his way to mau mauing the Democratic Party into nominating him for president.

There is a certain amount of just desserts in having the Democrats formally and openly fall to a mau mau candidate. For the past third of a century Democrats have been moving steadily outside the mainstream of American life. Yes, Democrats are our neighbors; and as Obama reminds us we love them and work next to them at the office. But as Obama also reminded us in his recent Philadelphia speech, everyone, Blacks and Whites alike, are supposedly two-faced, and say one thing in public and another a the barber shop. Yes, he said that.

So too it is with Democrats. We love them in public, as the second major party, and deplore their surrender to collectivism and socialism in private. Or not so private.

To be sure, the Republicans have helped open the way to a successful mau mau insurgency by extreme elements in the Democratic Party. Republicans have mismanaged the economy, leading our financial system to the brink of collapse. We have mismanaged foreign policy, and mangled relations with friend and foe alike. Whether trickle-down economics really exists, many Americans who are struggling to survive believe the federal government is raining cash on the rich, not on struggling workers. The trickle is running backwards. Republican incompetence has provided a golden opportunity for the Democrats to take over.

And, ironically, in their hour of maximum opportunity the Democrats face the prospect of being mau maued into nominating Obama, the least-qualified and most radical candidate ever considered by a national party.

Why? Well, Hillary Clinton is a tough fighter. Good for her. She demands that her candidacy be taken all through the primary process and maybe even to the convention. What's wrong with that? What's wrong is that after two or three generations of anesthetizing American children with Nanny State notions of "No fighting" and "Can't we just learn to get along," culminating in the banning of dodge ball from school playgrounds, we now have a Good Friday Judas, Bill Richardson, demanding that Clinton stop fighting and surrender to Obama.

Or else.

The or else is that if African-Americans do not get "their" candidate, they will walk away from the Democratic Party. Tom Wolfe: meet Barack Obama. Blacks demand the nomination because they have been "loyal" to the Democrats. But haven't the Democrats been equally loyal to African-Americans over the past half-century? Haven't Americans as a whole showered trillions of dollars on "affirmative action," "model cities" and other give-away programs, none of which have done very much to improve the quality of life for the underclass? What has improved their quality of life is private industry and welfare reform. But Blacks now threaten to bite the hands of their benefactors and reelect a Republican in November. Well. The Democratic Party has become a party of special interest scorpions in a bottle. Yes, this does look like 1968 all over again.

Rather humorlessly, Richardson, who styled himself the first Hispanic candidate for president and was soundly rejected by Hispanics, stabbed the Clintons in the back on Good Friday. After they promoted Richardson to the cabinet and made him a national figure. Richardson enacted his own version of Passion by rejecting Clinton and endorsing Obama. Judas Iscariot would be proud. Richardson tried to mau mau Clinton into dropping out as a candidate. Brave man. Looking at Barry Obama and Bill Richardson is enough to make you love Hillary.

Obama's current demand for the nomination, coupled with the implicit threat that his supporters will walk if they are rejected, is a classic mau mau tactic. After seeking to explain away the racist rantings of his pastor Jeremiah Wright with the explanation that Wright is so 1960's, it seems that 1960's Radical Chic and Mau-Mauing are also back in style, courtesy of Obama and his supporters.

With their demand that Obama be nominated, or else, the Obama camp has descended into a caricature of the racist Dixiecrats who sought to intimidate the Democratic Party during the 1940's and 50's. Dixiecrats were wrong then, and Obamacrats are wrong today. The Dixiecrats lost. The Obamacrats will lose.

Politics is a contact sport, or so goes the cliché. But even in sports, there is something known as the good sport. Mormons did not threaten to bolt the Republican Party if Mitt Romney wasn't nominated. Catholics stuck with Democrats for decades before a Catholic was nominated after the Al Smith fiasco. But Blacks demand that the "first" viable African-American for president walk off with the prize—or else.

Where is this taking the Democrats? Down the road to defeat.

Americans are going to reject the Democratic Party not because Democrats are conducting a raucous primary process. No, truth be told people love a brawl. Rather, Democrats are likely to pay a price when they nominate a candidate who is never "in the room" when the real man in his life stands up and spews forth his attacks on Ameirka (in deference to Obama, we have renewed our use of the 1960's spelling as well). Democrats are going to be rejected because a party too weak and too militant to focus the mainstream is too weak to govern this fractious nation.

Americans are going to reject Obama because the Democratic Party has so marginalized the nominating process that Democrats rather rudely and proudly tell Americans that "Clinton can't win" because the party's nominating procedures make it impossible to defeat an early frontrunner due to proportional representation and delegate allocation, rigged caucuses, and manipulated primaries.

There is much to dislike in the Republicans' Darwinian presidential selection system, where winner-take-all primaries kill off contenders at a very rapid pace. But John McCain has acquired legitimacy, by winning. Even if Clinton keeps winning primaries, Obama got almost as many "net" delegates from Wyoming as Clinton got from winning Texas and Ohio. Even if she wins Pennsylvania, Democrats cloyingly tell us she won't "net" enough delegates to win. And so on. "Super delegates?" They're not real delegates at all. Democrats now tell us superdelegates are merely automatons who have to vote the way they are told. Is that democracy? Is that a fair process?

And just in case Clinton wins, or comes close enough to take it to the floor of the convention, where John Kennedy himself was nominated, Obama has issued a diktat that she can't win because the nomination "belongs" to him and his left-wing cohort.

Truly, Barack Obama Junior has become the Mau Mau candidate for president. Barack Obama Senior must be smiling. And so are the 1960's.

Andy Martin on Barack Obama
and the Nation of Islam

Andy Martin with more exclusive commentary on Barack Obama's religious roots. Martin discloses Obama's flirtation with the Nation of Islam in Chicago. Andy continues his penetrating analysis of Barack's "wander years" in Chicago.

(WASHINGTON, DC)(March 28, 2008) Barack Obama expert and Internet columnist Andy Martin told a Washington, DC news conference Friday, March 28th, that Barack Obama flirted with joining the Nation of Islam ("NOI") in Chicago before affiliating with Trinity United Church of Christ in the 1980's.

"Barack Obama's mid-1980's were a 'lost' period in his life," Martin told media. "Obama's 'wander years' lacked any spiritual or familial roots in Chicago. He eventually joined a Christian church, after abandoning the Islam/Atheism of his parents. But before formally committing to Trinity UCC, Obama 'church shopped' among other denominations and met with members of the NOI.

"NOI was in an expansion mode during that period, and Obama's 'street' experience had exposed him to the Black

Muslims. NOI was obviously interested in recruiting Obama as a member. Hew was an obviously attractive prospect. Obama met with members and expressed an interest on learning more about NOI based on curiosity about his own exposure to Islam as a child. Ultimately, Obama elected to join Trinity and pursue Holy Baptism at some uncertain date.

"Our research is continuing," Martin said. "All of this digging has been made much more difficult by the fact that Obama has never given any definite dates for baptism and membership at Trinity. Obama's recent reluctance to criticize Minister Louis Farrakhan is probably based on their initial contacts during the 1980's."

Andy Martin on Another Barack Obama Lie, Exposed
If Obama Will Lie About His Own Parents, What Won't He Lie About?

Martin says Barack Obama is confirmed as a pathological liar

Andy Martin asks: if Obama will lie about his own parents, what won't he lie about? Martin says that the Washington Post's latest admission that ContrarianCommentary.com was right to debunk Obama's lies about the Kennedy family connection more than a year ago show once again why Contrarian Commentary.com is one of the world's most respected sources of news and commentary. "People turn to us because we tell the truth," Martin says. "They mistrust the mainstream media because mainstream reporters are liars and cheerleaders for Barry Obama. Barack Obama is confirmed by the Post to be a pathological liar—one year too late."

(WASHINGTON, DC)(March 30, 2008) Last year Contrarian Commentary.com was criticized for exposing that Barack Obama's Selma, Alabama speech linking his father to a "Kennedy airlift" was a lie. It took the Washington Post over a year to catch up with the truth.

Today the Washington Post confirmed our claim last year that Obama lied about his father's history and the fabricated

link to the Kennedy family, see http://www.washington
post.com/wp-dyn/content/article/2008/03/29/
AR2008032902031.html?hpid=topnews.

In passing, the Post also confirmed another Obama lie that
we have been exposing for four (4) years. Obama has always
portrayed his father as a lowly "goatherd," suggesting his father
was some barefoot hick who miraculously landed in America.
We exposed in 2004 that Obama's father Barack, Senior came
from an affluent, educated, successful family. As today's Post
story makes clear, Obama's father boasted about "his wealth."
Barack Obama, Senior was not a poor peasant as his son has
falsely portrayed him.

If Obama will lie about his parents, what won't he lie about?

Barack Obama is a pathological liar who will say and do anything to advance his political ambitions.

If anyone wonders why young people especially, and readers in general, are abandoning the mainstream media for
ContrarianCommentary.com, you need look no further that the
Washington Post's fiasco in being one year behind
ContrarianCommentary.com on the truth about Obama. We are
very proud to have led all media in bringing the world the truth
about Barack Obama, years before competing media admitted
we were right and they were wrong.

Although we don't always agree with the way our research
and commentary is used, we are driving the Obama campaign
to defeat. We do not pretend to influence everyone. Not at all.
But we have influenced a sufficiently significant segment of the
electorate with our reporting that Hillary Clinton remains viable
and will continue to be so.

That is why we are also preparing to sue the New York Times
and a clown writer for Salon.com, Farhad Manjoo, for falsely
accusing us of publishing "rumors" about Obama that have

been "debunked." It is the mainstream media that have had to eat crow, and debunk themselves and their own lies. We continue to lead all media in exposing Barack Obama. With the truth.

Andy Martin on Barack Obama and "the Philadelphia Speech + Two Weeks"

Obama delivers the single most disastrous speech in recent political history

Mainstream Media continue to spin Obama as a savior when he is really a disaster

In a two-part commentary Andy Martin analyses Barack Obama's disastrous speech in Philadelphia. The Mainstream Media and their racialists/poverticians may think Obama hit a home run. Andy Martin says the speech was a disaster that will eventually doom Obama's candidacy. **That's** why we are called **Contrarian**Commentary.com

(CHICAGO)(April 7, 2008) Two weeks ago (March 18th) Senator Barack Obama gave his celebrated speech on "race." The Mainstream Media's (MSM) profuse praise for Obama's remarks was way off the mark. Moments after Obama stopped speaking I offered a critical and contrarian interpretation. Those initial views proved to be accurate: http://www.contrariancommentary.com/community/Home/tabid/36/mid/363/newsid363/184/Default.aspx.

The MSM have tried to convince the public that Obama hit a "home run" in Philadelphia. On the contrary, I believe Obama misspoke. His flawed strategy and calculated but clumsy and callous confessions did fatal damage to his campaign.

Sometimes it takes more than a day for the true impact of words to sink in. People need to reflect, review, reconsider. That is why I believe the long-term impact of Obama's declarations will prove toxic to his candidacy.

We originally planned to do a "Speech + One Week" column, but Obama material keeps cascading into the offices of ContrarianCommentary.com. We are now going to publish two columns (this one and part Two) that present a significantly different point of view to the MSM catechism on "Obama in Philadelphia." We divide our "Speech + Two Weeks" into two parts: first below, the ongoing calendar/timetable disaster Obama created for his campaign. Tomorrow, how Obama blundered into Black Rage; and the White Backlash to come.

First, the timing aspects of Obama's disastrous speech.

As we will argue in the "Black Rage" columns to come, Obama is a sophisticated and obsessive control freak. He has manipulated every aspect of his adult life, very successfully to date. And so when he faced national outrage over the venomous sermons of Reverend "Jeremiad" Wright, and questions over his silence in the pews for twenty years, the senator reached for his obvious and traditional weapon: a controlled speech.

Although MSM'ers will tell you Obama has "improved" in extemporaneous or unprepared speeches, listening to him is very taxing. He hems and haws and hesitates with every sentence. His performance in debates has improved from abysmal to mediocre or passable. By contrast, Obama's prepared and choreographed speeches, from the 2004 Democratic Convention to date, are masterpieces. Fundamentally, Obama is an accomplished entertainer, not a political leader. That's why his scripted moments are so moving, and why he is so quotidian in everyday conversation.

Obama went into his Philadelphia speech expecting to finish off the Reverend Wright controversy. He failed. Abysmally. He was done in by the clock. There was a gap in news coverage before the Pennsylvania primary, and he fell into the hole.

Obama's conceit ignored the "open" month ahead and apparently miscalculated that the period between his speech and the Pennsylvania primary would be filled with new issues and events. He was wrong. The Wright controversy continues to grow. Hillary Clinton's Tuzla through the tulips is already fading. But the poisons Wright unleashed in the pulpit have been compounded by the toxins released by Obama's own words (Part Two).

Why are my views so different from those of the MSM? Fundamentally, "reporters" are "journalists," not opinion columnists or investigators. Most reporters go to journ school, and work with a pad and pen or laptop during their media lives. Many advance up the ladder to Washington or New York perches. They are competent at what they do, well-intentioned, and generally decent persons. But almost all of them are liberals through and through.

My own commentary credentials flow from a lifetime "in the arena," which began with a background in English, not journalism. I am sometimes ridiculed for having run for office against corrupt or incompetent officials. There is no other crucible but an election to searingly experience how people react. You pick up the phone, answer a voter, and experience firsthand how raw public opinion can be. That is why in January, 2007, when the MSM'ers said the issue of Obama's religion was "done," I said "Not at all." My own lifetime of experience in the real political world exemplifies why my instincts both in Iraq and on the campaign trail have been so radically different from those of "reporters" or the newly coined "commentators."

Obama has not been helped by his "supporters." Lord, save us from our friends. Trinity Church UCC has now sought to impose restrictions on the media, hardly a sign of people who think they are succeeding in getting their message out to the general public. Worst of all, Obama's racialists want to hijack May's "Trinity Sunday," one of the great holidays of the Christian Church, as a day for discussions on "race." (http://www.chicagotribune.com/news/local/chi-trinity. 1apr04,0,2238591.story)

Trinity Sunday is the first Sunday after Pentecost and celebrates the Holy Trinity, Father, Son and Holy Spirit. It is not a day for blabbering on about "race" in America. By trying to make race the preeminent issue, Obama's racialist endorsers, whom he kept locked in the closet for over a year, have finally escaped and are now running wild and endangering his campaign's stability. In one sense Obama is just getting just deserts. He says he sat quietly in the pews for years while malignant accusations were preached against whites and against America. Now his theological crazies and their fellow travelers are hijacking his campaign and turning off Americans by trying to make race the major issue. Race is not even remotely a central issue in the 2008 election.

Politicizing Trinity Sunday by trying to make it a racial discussion day can only turn off Christians across America. A real Christian, a strong leader, would say "Don't do that." But true to form, Obama has remained silent. The tub-thumping of Obama's sympathizers is going to continue at least through the Pennsylvania primary, when "reporters" will finally have something new to write about.

Rather than taking race out of the campaign, Obama's Philadelphia speech made race his bedrock issue, the one topic that will survive into November. He lost control. The conductor no longer directs the orchestra, all because his understanding of the post-Philadelphia calendar was flawed. The one time Obama should have used a Watergate-style "modified limited hangout" to deal with the Wright crescendo, he didn't. He put faith in the power of his speechifying to calm the Wright-infested waters. And he left a whole month for the waters to be roiled over and over again by friend and foe alike.

Bottom line: Obama blundered, and gave what will prove in retrospect to have been one of the most disastrous speeches in American political history, the turning point in his campaign. Obama, who worked so hard to evade race as an issue, now finds himself captured by the controversy. And hostage to the concept. Sorry, Mainstream media. You won't sell Obama's spin to the American people this time. The backlash is building. Would someone please save Barack Obama from his "supporters?" And from himself?

Andy Martin Asks Whether a Posting/Blog on BarackObama.com is a Real Posting

Martin says the posting is insulting and objectionable and, if an actual posting, should have been removed long ago

Who is monitoring BarackObama.com for abusive materials?

Andy Martin receives an e-mail and checks BarackObama.com. Andy doesn't believe what he sees, but the post has apparently been there for nearly two months. Who is responsible?

(CHICAGO)(April 7, 2008) On Sunday, April 6th we received an e-mail linking us to BarackObama.com and a community blog. (http://my.barackobama.com/page/community/post /shaesmith/CsNZ)
Here is what we found:

Field Slave/Obama Supporter:
"I seen a way to freedom and power. C'mon go with me. I figured out a way to the promise land - that place Martin and Malcolm spoke of. There's hope and possibilities out there for us. There some white folks I know say they gon help us get there. The time is now – right now. Come On..."

House Slave/Clinton Supporter:

"Massa Clinton been good to us. Git on 'way from here Obama. You gon cause problem fo us all!! Didn't Massa Clinton give you food and shelter all these years. Where you gon take us? You never been nowhere but right here on dis plantation wit us. This here fine living. We don't know where you trying to go. They gon kill you. Then how us gon survive? Aint no white folks gon hep you. Get on way from here Obama. Gon now...git"

Looking at from this historical perspective . . . who was right????

That this posting may have been on Obama's web site for over a month is disturbing to ContrarianCommentary.com. Is it as disturbing to you? Does anyone at Obama headquarters monitor blogs (as we monitor our blogs) to remove objectionable postings? Or is the foregoing posting acceptable to Obama headquarters? Is the posting possibly a hoax? It is hard to say.

Referring to Senator Obama as a "fields slave" and Senator Clinton as a "house slave" would appear to offend most Americans.

The Obama campaign owes voters some answers.

Obama: Hicks in the Stix are Nixed
Obama is the First Anti-American Presidential
Candidate in U.S. History

*Small town support for the military, turnout in 2008 elections
show reverence, not bitterness, for America*

"Obama is not a true Christian," says Andy Martin

Martin demands that Obama end his "secret campaign"

(CHICAGO)(April 12, 2008) Chicago-based Obama expert and Internet columnist Andy Martin will hold a 1:00 P.M. Chicago news conference Saturday, April 12th, to condemn Senator Barack Obama for suggesting that small-town America is "bitter" about America and that Americans "cling" to "guns" and "religion" as an outlet for their bitterness.

Martin will also demand that Obama end his "secret" campaign in which the presidential candidate uses meetings that are closed to the media to raise money from wealthy liberals by privately disparaging ordinary Americans.

"In listening to Obama depreciate and disparage small town America," Martin will say, "I am reminded of the New York tabloid headline about 'Hicks in the Stix.' Obama has denigrated small town America. In Obama's eyes, Main Street in Middle America is 'Macaccaburg.' Obama believes ordinary Americans are the real Macacaas.

"While others are focused on the politics of Obama's outrageous comments, I want to zero in on what his remarks tell us about his religious beliefs and values. And I want to demand that Barry Obama end his 'Secret Campaign,' where he attends fund raisers at the homes of wealthy liberals and depreciates American values and out constitutional rights.

"Obama seems to think that people turn to religion out of 'bitterness.' That has not been my experience. Christians are optimistic people, not bitter. Maybe Obama and his soul brother Jeremiad Wright are bitter, but America is an optimistic nation.

"For Obama to suggest that people turn to Christ and attend church out of bitterness devalues every Christian around the world. Obviously, after converting from Islam and after twenty years of the distorted racist theology of Reverend Wright, Obama still has no conception of Christian theology. People do not seek Christ out of bitterness; they seek His church out of grace. Obama may be a 'Christian' out of political expediency, but his remarks in California reflect contempt for the Christian message.

"Fundamentally, Barack is the first Anti-American candidate for president of the United States. He has been running down America in secret séances with wealthy liberals. Now we know why Obama and is wife hold closed-to-the-media fund raising sessions with wealthy contributors. They want secrecy so they can spew out their message of hate and contempt for the American people. They want secrecy so they can run a public campaign of piety and concern for American values, and a private campaign of elitism and condescension and contempt for the United States. The Secret Campaign has now been exposed for what it is by the 'San Francisco Tape.' The Secret Campaign must end. Obama must open fund raisers to full media scrutiny. Senator Clinton must do the same.

"Lynn Sweet of the Chicago Sun-Times was the first, I think, to make an issue of Obama's 'secret' campaign schedule and Michele's closed campaign appointments. Sweet also pursued Obama's secrecy to southern California mansions where Obama delivered his 'real' message to wealthy, anti-American liberals in Hollywood. Now Obama is spreading his virus to northern California.

"I demand that Barry and Michele end their 'Secret Campaign,' and stop holding clandestine meetings with wealthy contributors, where this pair stomps on Americans and ridicules our values. We now know from the San Francisco Tape that Obama uses these secret meetings with elite contributors to give liberal extremists the 'Real Obama,' and to deliver his real message of 'hate and contempt for Amerika.'

"For Obama to suggest that small town America is 'bitter' is really a reflection of his own bitterness, and his wife's bitterness. With all they have been given, this couple expresses a sense of arrogance and entitlement that is truly amazing. And very un-Christian. They especially condescend to the very people that have been bamboozled into voting for Obama in the primaries. His message seems to be, 'Thanks, sucka.'

"Small town America` is the backbone of our military. Small town Americans reflect patriotism and optimism, not bitterness.

"Liberals are bitter because they want to devalue America and adopt defeatism as our foreign policy. Small town Americans are not prepared to disown this great nation. Only the wealthy, elitist supporters that Obama meets in secret salons share his despicable plan for the destruction of the United States.

"Four years ago I began to strip the bark off Barack Obama's phony image, his distorted message and his shameless ability to denigrate even his own family for political manipulation and advancement. In the four years since then, the mainstream media have barely begun to catch up with ContrarianCommentary.com.

"Americans are slowly coming to know the 'true' Obama that I first exposed way back in 2004. I have fought against the efforts of Chicago newspapers to whitewash Obama and to conceal all of his corruption and condescension. This man is someone who has been coddled all of his life by the establishment, and his payback is to run as their 'elitist' candidate for the White House. Obama says in his defense, 'I'm in touch.' I' agree. Obama has been 'putting the touch' on the American people for the last four years."

Chicago's Number One News Analyst and Obama Expert, Andy Martin, "Takes a New York Bow" for Repeatedly Predicting the Extent of Obama's "Tony Rezko Problem"

*Martin predicted Rezko trial would embarrass Obama;
new lies by "Barry O" about Auchi doom his candidacy*

Andy Martin made prescient Clinton directive

*"How do we get it so right, and Chicago media get it so wrong?"
asks Andy Martin*

(NEW YORK)(April 15, 2008) Chicago's Number One media analyst, Obama expert and Internet columnist Andy Martin will hold a 4:00 P.M. New York City news conference today, April 15th, to condemn Senator Barack Obama's latest prevarications and "lapse of memory" as reflected in the Tony Rezko trial.

"In November, 2006," Martin will note, "We stated that Obama had far more extensive links to Rezko than he was acknowledging. At the time Obama was saying Rezko was 'someone he knew.' Obama was lying. On February 22nd, we said that Obama had clay feet and told Hillary Clinton to 'take it to the convention.' (http://www.contrariancommentary.com/community/Home/tabid/36/mid/363/newsid363/161/Default.aspx)

"In other words, we were the first analysts to predict that a future Obama implosion would open the way for Clinton to wage a convention fight, and that she should. (Not to mention we told her to dump Mark Penn.)

"On February 22nd, we again stated Obama was lying about the extent of his relationship to Rezko. (http://contrariancommentary.blogspot.com/2008_02_01_archive.html)

"On the first day of the Rezko trial, we said 'The worst is yet to come for Obama:' http://contrariancommentary.blogspot.com/2008_03_01_archive.html; Andy Martin on Barack Obama and the Rezko trial, Day One Friday, March 07, 2008.

Andy Martin looks at the first day of trial for Barack Obama's fundraiser and confidante Tony Rezko. Martin says Rezko could walk from the criminal charges he faces in Chicago; federal prosecutors presented a dispirited opening day of evidence and argument. Legal expert Martin analyzes the complex issues involving the presidential candidate and his former supporter. Andy says the worse is yet to come for Obama. (http://www.contrariancommentary.com/community/Home/tabid/36/mid/363/newsid363/171/Default.aspx)

"How do we constantly get it so right and Chicago's competing media always get it so wrong? When Obama issued a news release saying the Rezko trial was 'not about him,' we said it was on March 7th:

Indeed the case is very much about Mr. Obama.

The Chicago media have sold the nation the biggest pig-in-a-poke in recent political history. They have sold Obama as the great savior, the Teflon "hope," when Obama is merely just another glib Sammy Glick, who challenged the Chicago Democratic Machine until he got his own slice of the pie, and then quietly slept with Emil Jones and the other slimy machine hacks in The Party.

If there was such a tort (legal wrong) as journalistic malpractice, all of Chicago's media should be put on trial and charged with defrauding the American people about Barack

Obama. They wanted him to win, because he was a good story, and a great local story, and they engineered his ascent while fully aware of the cancer behind the curtain.

"Obama recently went to the Tribune and Sun-Times and promised to make a clean breast of 'everything.' And he lied all over again. How did he just manage to forget he had been an ornament at a Rezko soiree at which the guest of honor was one of the richest men in the world?

"Can anyone seriously believe that both Barry O and Michelle Obama forgot meeting one of the richest men in the world, after their lifetime together cultivating wealthy personages? Can anyone suggest Obama's staff did not 'prep' him with the fact that questions about Auchi would come up at the Trib and S-T? Mr. Axelrod was silent?

"Once again, Obama lied to the Chicago media, and these media in turn unquestioningly accepted his lies and brandished them to the world as part of the sordid 'truth' they have been peddling about Obama for the past four years.

"Hillary was pilloried for forgetting something that happened 12 years ago in Bosnia. Obama says he forgot he met Auchi four years ago, and now pleads bad memory. Whose memory is worse?

"Barack/Barry Obama has been lying to the American people for four years. He is on the brink of lying himself into the Democratic Party's presidential nomination. As someone who has been associated with the Republican Party, I am delighted to see Democrats preparing to go over Niagara Falls in an Obama. As an analyst/columnist with a reputation for fairness, accuracy and integrity, I am duty bound to sound the alarm, once again, and to warn the American people that Barack Obama is a fraud and poseur who has no business being in a presidential campaign. Keith Olbermann are you listening?

"Obama has now fooled over one million 'contributors,' and he is on the brink of fooling the entire Democratic Party. Whoa," Martin will state. "I predicted the worst was to come, and it has arrived. Obama's 'dream house' was financed by money provided by an Iraqi wheeler-dealer that Obama says he forget he ever met. How convenient. How pathetic. Stay tuned to ContrarianCommentary.com, not Chicago's media, for the truth about Obama."

Catfight!
Obama and Wright Take Off the Gloves

ContrarianCommentary.com was the first to disclose the Obama-Wright-Farrakhan mutual admiration society

(NEW YORK)(April 29, 2008) One week before the Indiana and North Carolina primaries, Senator Barack and his former pastor Reverend Jeremiah Wright have taken off the gloves. Yesterday, Wright called Obama a "politician." Today Obama said he was "denouncing" Wright and said Wright was "outrageous, appalling" and made Obama "angry."

Obama obviously condemned Wright to stem the hemorrhaging to his presidential campaign. But Obama's remarks are going to provoke a retort from Wright; we appear to be in the midst of an escalating catfight.

But there is also back story here. What is interesting about the exchanges of the past couple of days is how the latest disclosures by Wright validate my news conference in Washington on March 28th. At that time I disclosed the hidden links between Obama and the Nation of Islam (NOI): http://contrariancommentary.blogspot.com/2008_03_01_archive.html.

Once again we beat the mainstream media (MSM) with exclusive information that Obama had sought to camouflage. We exposed the old links between Obama and the NOI.

Yesterday, Wright offered effusive raise for Minister Farrakhan, thus reflecting that Obama, Farrakhan and Wright were much closer than the public record had ever appeared and something of a mutual admiration society.

Will Obama's denunciation allow the presidential campaign to concentrate on "you," or "us" and not on Wright, as Obama has been asking? Not on your life. In February, 2007 we offered a psychological profile of Obama and predicted that his mask would eventually crack. The mask is falling away. Although Obama said today he is "not a theologian" and is unfamiliar with "[Black] liberation theology," how could he be so innocent after two decades in the pews? How could he not have been aware of Wright's great admiration for Farrakhan? How could Obambi have been so innocent?

Obama is unfortunately caught in a catfight he can't win and Wright can't lose. That is why we can almost guarantee more and more conflict and finger-pointing. The more the MSM publicize Wright, the more his stock will rise in the African-American community as an authentic voice of Black rage. Obama was right about that, all Wright. But since Obama already had 90% of the African-American vote he can only lose support; Wright's ranting can only polarize the electorate further.

For the past four years ContrarianCommentary.com has been ahead of the MSM in disclosing the truth about Barack Obama. The revelations of the past couple of days confirm how, once again, we were right on the mark in Washington last month.

Where do we think Obama's campaign heading? Early this morning, long before his afternoon news conference, we predicted that he is going to lose both North Carolina and Indiana. Our prediction is looking pretty good right now. DNC Chairman

Howard Dean said "one of the candidates" has to withdraw in June. Increasingly, and surprisingly to some but not to us, it looks likely Obama will become the one facing pressure to step down. Because he won't withdraw, and Hillary Clinton should not withdraw, the donnybrook is going to continue.

We are hoping to be able to report from the campaign trail in North Carolina or Indiana between now and May 6th.

On May 7th, the Democratic race will be a new campaign. Obama will be wounded, Clinton will be surging and the irresistible force will meet the immovable object.

The Obama Implosion
African-Americans Turn on Obama
as Racial Polarization Increases·

(NEW YORK)(April 30, 2008) On Monday, April 28th (dated April 29th) we posted our survey results predicting Hillary Clinton would win both Indiana and North Carolina. (http://www.contrariancommentary.com/community/Home/ta bid/36/mid/363/newsid363/198/Default.aspx)

As usual, we made a very good call. Of course, we were then inundated by threatening phone calls from pro-Obama wackos in North Carolina, as well as abusive and insulting e-mails. Within hours our predictions were validated by Tuesday's events.

We can now predict that the "Obama implosion" has begun.

There are two fundamental and related reasons why Obama is not going to be the nominee of the Democratic Party. Dick Morris of Fox news disagrees. Morris is wrong.

First, the "birds of a feather" argument. Although our exposure of Obama's money laundering was completely eclipsed by the Wright imbroglio, the facts surrounding Obama's money laundering and "legal fees" for no work are as solid as a rock. Once the Wright matter quiets down, Mr. Robert Blackwell, Jr.

will have his day in the sun. The Blackwell story is too explosive to go away. It links Obama to financial manipulation and "honest graft," which are the antithesis of what he claims to stand for. (http://www.contrariancommentary.com/community/Home/tabid/36/mid/363/newsid363/196/Default.aspx)

We will be doing a Chicago news conference on Mr. Blackwell and his bogus "legal fees" to Mr. Obama at a later date.

The "birds of a feather" commercial will be devastating when it appears. Here's the 60-second spot (I am also a TV producer):

Barack Obama says he made a "boneheaded" decision when he engaged in a structured financial transaction with Chicago influence-peddler Tony Rezko (picture please). What did Obama do to earn $112,000 from Illinois politician Robert Blackwell, Jr., and why did Obama disguise his so-called "legal fees" on state disclosure forms? Bill Ayers has never apologized for bombing the U.S. Capitol and Pentagon. Obama says the mad bomber is still his friend. (picture please, with simulated explosion) And, finally, Reverend Jeremiah Wright. Obama says he "knew nothing" about Wrights malignant philosophy and anti-American obsession. For twenty years. Obama & Friends. "Birds of a feather." Why is Obama always apologizing? Always saying "I didn't know? (sound bite) Can you really trust Obama with the safety of our nation?

In other words, no one has to single out Reverend Wright alone. He fits nicely in a commercial collection of all of Obama's unsavory associations. Birds of a feather? Democrats would have to be birdbrains to nominate Obama.

The second reason why Obama is beginning to implode is that he has managed to anger both Blacks and Whites. Mary Mitchell, a Chicago Sun-Times reporter who adores Obama was very downbeat and negative today. "Obama shouldn't have held a press conference to deal with Wright," she said. (http://www.suntimes.com/news/mitchell/923055,CST-NWS-mitch30.article)

Mitchell suggests Obama has burned his bridges to Trinity United Church. Mitchell says Obama "open[d] up a can of worms," and that Obama's remarks were a "sad day for Black America." Other columns in the Sun-Times criticize Obama from the opposite perspective, for "too little, too late." Obama was also criticized for a lack of passion. Indeed, Obama seems to forget that he is not addressing a classroom of eager beaver law students. Mike Dukakis' campaign died another day during the 1988 debate when he "Obamaed" a question about an attack on his wife Kitty. Too cool, too calm is stone cold dead.

In North Carolina, where we predicted a win for Clinton before Obama's speech, the Sun-Times reports that North Carolina's first black House Speaker "'see[s] a permanent fissure now' between black and white Democrats." I don't know if Obama has a pet at home but, if he does, he should watch out. Even the dog may give him a kick. The bottom line: many African-Americans will be horrified that Obama threw Wright under the bus to save himself with white America.

What Obama never understood, and what the followers of his pied piper crusade never understood, and what I did understand when I told Hillary to "take it to the convention" on February 20th, http://www.contrariancommentary.com/community/Home/tabid/36/mid/363/newsid363/161/Default.aspx is that national politics is a very rough game indeed. I will always remember the subscriber to our Obama e-mail list who sent me an e-mail and said to take his name off the list, because the battle was over. On February 6th. It wasn't. And on February 20th I gave Clinton a go-ahead for Denver which has proven prophetic.

Is the battle over now? Not on your life. But the slow decline of Obama's pied pipery has begun. Before, I could see what lay ahead and the mainstream media (MSM) could not or would not. With each passing day, the invisible becomes more visible and soon it will be inevitable. There is a reason we call ourselves the #1 political blog of the 2008 campaign. A proven track record no one else can match.

You will know Obama is toast when Rush Limbaugh adopts Barack's cause. Limbaugh, of course, has been just as inaccurate and ineffective as the MSM's he decries. Hillary is rising, because her campaign was never dead. Not because Limbaugh wanted to revive it. I won't begrudge Rush his bigger bankroll if he won't begrudge me my better crystal ball.

Where does it all end up? Are you kidding? I wouldn't hazard a guess right now. Stay tuned to the #1 blog in America for regular updates and analysis. We'll be in the campaign until the last dog dies. Just ask Barack Obama if you don't believe me.

How Obama Botched the Wright Episode
"Barry O" is No Negotiator

Why ContrarianCommentary.com is America's #1 political blog

On the eve of the Indiana and North Carolina primaries, Andy Martin calls Barack Obama a "failed candidate." Martin analyzes what is now known about the battles between Obama and his former pastor Jeremiah Wright, and condemns Obama for "negotiation malpractice." Andy also explains why ContrarianCommentary.com is America's #1 political blog.

(NEW YORK)(May 5, 2008) Barack Obama has been criticized for saying he wants to "negotiate" with the Iranians, and the North Koreans and other adversaries of the United States. Sadly, he failed the test of "negotiating" with his own pastor, "Jeremiad" Wright. The Obama-Wright fiasco is also a Chicago/Mainstream Media (MSM) fiasco. But the entire episode demonstrates why ContrarianCommentary.com is the undisputed #1 political blog of the 2008 campaign.

A few minutes after Obama's "Philadelphia speech" we published an instant analysis critical of the performance: http://contrariancommentary.blogspot.com/2008_03_01_arch ive.html.

We called Obama "Reverend Wright light."

On April 7th, two weeks later, we presented a more detailed interpretation of Obama's Philadelphia speech that was contrary to virtually all of the MSMs conclusions: http://contrarian-commentary.blogspot.com/2008_04_01_archive.html.

We stated:

His flawed strategy and calculated but clumsy and callous confessions did fatal damage to his campaign... That is why I believe the long-term impact of Obama's declarations will prove toxic to his candidacy... The one time Obama should have used a Watergate-style "modified limited hangout" to deal with the Wright crescendo, he didn't. He put faith in the power of his speechifying to calm the Wright-infested waters...

Bottom line: Obama blundered, and gave what will prove in retrospect to have been one of the most disastrous speeches in American political history, the turning point in his campaign. Obama, who worked so hard to evade race as an issue, now finds himself captured by the controversy. And hostage to the concept. Sorry, Mainstream media. You won't sell Obama's spin to the American people this time. The backlash is building. Would someone please save Barack Obama from his "supporters?" And from himself?

At that time, the full extent of Reverend's Wright's internal frustration or the reasons for his anger were unknown. The facts concerning Wright's humiliation by Obama in Springfield in February 2007 had been concealed by the senator. Obama was sitting on a time bomb. He lit the fuse in Philadelphia. Now that we know more of the facts, Reverend Wright's explosion is much more understandable. We also know that Philadelphia was the trigger to Wright's attack last week. Finally, we know that Obama is no negotiator. On the contrary, he is a complete incompetent.

Please note: I have written numerous columns in the past highlighting Obama's incompetence as an attorney and his flatulent misrepresentations that he was a "civil rights litigator," which is simply untrue. Obama was a ham-handed lawyer who found a patron in and a job through Tony Rezko. That he pretends to be competent to "negotiate" with foreign leaders is a joke.

And sadly, the joke lives. In yet another Chicago media coverup and embarrassment, the Chicago Tribune on May 4th urged Indiana voters to support incompetence and vote for Obama. The Tribune continues to live in a dream world, totally divorced from reality, and still praises the "remarkable speech in Philadelphia." (http://www.chicagotribune.com/news/opinion/chi-0504edit1may04,0,3206628.story)

This column is not a Tribune-bashing story (more of that to come) but, nevertheless, is it any wonder the Tribune is hemorrhaging readers and revenues when it practices incompetent and fraudulent journalism parallel to Obama's incompetent politics and negotiation malpractice?

In February, 2007 when he announced, we now know Obama humiliated Wright by keeping him locked in the basement of the Old State Capitol while white politicians introduced the candidate. If I had been in Wright's place, I would have been seething too. Wright's reaction was not a case of "Black rage." This was a case of human outrage, and an instance where Obama's timidity coupled with his incompetence created chaos. Bringing Wright to Springfield, and then hiding him in the basement was disgraceful behavior for a man who had been labeled the candidate's "father-figure." Disgraceful.

Had Obama been as much of a negotiator as he claims, he would have seen the Wright sound bites for what they were, an extremely irritating distraction but something that ultimately concerned Reverend Wright and not Obama. That is why in my prior analysis I said he faced a situation where a Nixonian "modified limited hangout" was called for.

Obama, of course, wanted to go for the dramatic. And play to the MSMs. He succeeded in bamboozling the MSMs, as the Tribune's latest editorial embarrassingly indicates. But he totally failed to manage the volatile Reverend Wright. I don't usually agree with Chicago Sun-Times columnist Mary Mitchell, because she has been a blind Obama partisan. But her recent writing has done more to place Wright's behavior in context than any other journalist. (http://www.suntimes.com/news/mitchell/930244,CST-NWS-mitch04.article)

If you want to know what happened, read Ms. Mitchell. The only missing link that we do not yet have is the date when Wright got wind of the fact he was going to be disgraced by Northwestern University. My guess: Wright scheduled his attacks after he was told Northwestern was planning to revoke his honorary degree. (Please note, that's a guess. Northwestern announced its action after Wright's Washington performance; common sense suggests universities do not move that quickly, and that the stab-in-the-back must have been in progress before that.)

Wright thus faced a "Captain Carpenter" situation. It is a maneuver I am familiar with, because I have faced similar challenges in the past. "Captain Carpenter" was a famous West Point athlete who found himself in Viet-Nam, surrounded and overrun by the enemy. With no hope of extraction or escape, he called in strikes on his own position. The tactic worked, and the enemy scattered and withdrew. In my mind, a "Captain Carpenter" operation is one where you are surrounded and have no option but to bring down the artillery on yourself as the only way to survive.

Reverend Wright saw his entire career being destroyed by Obama's campaign for national office. There was no escape. Obama had gone on national television in Philadelphia and "defended" Wright by disowning him politely. Then Northwestern probably hinted that it was reconsidering Wright's honorary degree. Wright snapped. The result was the effective demise of Obama's presidential hopes. At the National Press Club in Washington.

If Obama had been as good a negotiator as he thought, and as good a judge of character as President Bush said he was when he looked into the eyes of the Russian Dictator Vladimir Putin, Obama would have anticipated the danger he faced with Wright and done everything to neutralize the fallout. He could have acted quietly, and he could have worked the line without tearing up Wright's reputation and claiming he had never heard any of Wrights controversial sermons.

Obama clearly provoked Wright to counterattack. Obama tried to lie, professing ignorance of Wright's theology; he insulted a man that he had previously led into a basement for "prayer" in secret because he was too fearful of being seen praying in public with his "father." For shame. Obama misjudged the man.

Last year, we published a "psychological profile" of Barack Obama. Go back and read it. (http://www.contrariancommentary.com/community/Home/tabid/36/mid/363/newsid363/79/Default.aspx)

We understood and presented a profile of Obama that is consistent with all of his hesitations and machinations since then. "Barack" Obama is still controlled by "Barry" Obama. He is a man trapped inside himself.

If Obama had handled Wright properly, and handled himself properly, there would have been no need for the

Philadelphia speech. Mary Mitchell makes clear in her comments that Reverend Wright has not changed over the past 20 years; indeed Obama refers to Wright's fiery tongue in his own book, published over a decade ago. Mr. Obama has changed. Sadly, Mr. Obama is not any better a "negotiator" today than he was as a fledgling lawyer. He is an intelligent man, who lacks the very street smarts he claims to possess.

Seen in context, Wright's actions were very human and very understandable and very predictable. Faced with the same betrayal, many people would have acted the same way. I do not agree with Wright's theology; but I find it hard to disagree with his reaction to Obama's ingratitude and condescension.

And, not to put too fine a point on it, it was only ContrarianCommentary.com that predicted on April 7th the Philadelphia speech would become "one of the most disastrous speeches in American history." Who knew? We knew.

We got it right. No one else did. Is it any wonder that we are the #1 political blog in America?

Question: would anyone now like to tell me Obama's Philadelphia speech was a masterpiece? Or tell me Obama is competent to negotiate with dictators when he could not negotiate with his own pastor? Obama is guilty of "negotiation malpractice." Obama is a failed candidate. And this man wants to be president? Be real. Or read the Chicago Tribune's fantasies and fabrications masquerading as "editorials."

Well, to throw the Tribune a bone, we both agree that Obama's speech was "remarkable." After all, that speech destroyed his candidacy. Pretty remarkable.

An Explosive Analysis of the Relationship Between Barack Obama, William Ayers and Venezuelan Dictator Hugo Chavez

Fox News' Hannity & Colmes hypes a nonexistent "exclusive" on Ayers and misses the big story

Mainstream media hysteria has overlooked the Chicago Annenberg Challenge link between Obama and Ayers

(NEW YORK)(May 6, 2008) This is a three-part story: [1] Hannity & Colmes bogus "exclusive" involving Senator Barack Obama's crony William Ayers, the "mad bomber" of Weathermen fame; [2] an understanding of why a "second look" is always essential in studying transient campaign issues, especially those discussed fleetingly on television, and [3] our "explosive" look at William Ayers, his ongoing relationship to Venezuelan dictator Hugh Chavez and their potential connection to Senator Barack Obama. Fasten your seat belts.

Although a great deal has been written about Obama and Ayers, the most critical link between the two men has been ignored by the mainstream media (MSMs).

First, Hannity & Colmes' bogus "exclusive:" On May 5th Sean Hannity said he had an "exclusive" picture of William Ayers stomping the U. S. flag. We had the picture and the story at 2:06 P.M., along with Hannity and everyone else, and put the information aside for this story. Others may have chosen not to use the material, but that in no way made the information "exclusive" to Fox News. I happen to think that Sean has done a very good job of "outing" Obama and his confederates. Sean cheapens his success when he tries to claim imaginary "exclusives." He should know better.

Second, one of the things we pride ourselves at ContrarianCommentary.com is that we do analysis and interpretation better than anyone else in the media.

Broadcasters operate under extreme difficulty in a presidential campaign. The people on the screen are usually chosen for appearance and affability, not investigative experience or writing ability. Questions are initially prepared by "researchers," often young and lowly paid, and then thrown out in a debate, as they were about Ayers in ABC's now-celebrated debate. Obama gave ABC answers that were evasive and incomplete. But because a debate is not an inquisition, the opportunity for follow-up is usually very limited. And the ability to follow up can sometimes be critical to understanding the issues.

A story isn't just a story. It is a set of facts that constitute an independent reality. How to get at the "real" reality? Not always so easy. Sort through facts to get to the core information? Often not so clear. It takes investigative experience to cull the wheat from the chaff. That's what we found in the case of the relationships between William Ayers, Hugo Chavez and Barack Obama. So, here goes.

Third, what did the MSMs miss, and what did Chicago's pathetic print media cover up? The chronology of the aftermath of ABC's confrontation with Obama over Ayers is instructive. Once again, some media, notably the Chicago Tribune, made a concerted effort to mislead and intimidate the viewing/reading public. On April 18th the Tribune ran an editorial attacking ABC for using "guilt by association" involving Obama and Ayers.

(http://www.chicagotribune.com/news/chi-0418edit
3apr18,0,7443216.story)

On April 18th, Lynn Sweet of the Chicago Sun-Times tried to pooh pooh the Ayers controversy by suggesting that the Obama-Ayers link was widely known in Chicago, and accepted. That was simply untrue. Sweet's claim that Ayers' past had "never bothered anyone" was misleading. (http://www.sun-times.com/news/sweet/901879,CST-NWS-sweet18.article)

Sweet, however, disclosed another piece of the Ayers-Obama puzzle, the link between Michelle Obama, Ayers and her husband. Yes, this information was on the net; but no one had ever gone looking for it. Or connected the dots. Perhaps in a telling admission of the low quality of Chicago journalism—which I have been insulting for its lackluster coverage of Obama—Sweet also involved "local political reporters [and]…the editorial boards of the Sun-Times or Tribune" as part of the conspiracy of silence.

Is it any wonder we have repeatedly beaten Chicago's print media on the Obama story, or that Chicago print coverage of Obama has been a joke and embarrassment to American journalism?

On April 19th the Sun-Times led with more asinine and incendiary coverage of Obama-Ayers. (http://www.suntimes.com/news/elections/904015,CST-NWS-ayers19.article)

The Sun-Times quoted Ayers' brother calling questions about William Ayers' past a "pathetic red herring," and referring to Obama's "alleged ties to *so-called* terrorist Bill Ayers…" Rick Ayers called any inquiry into the Obama-Ayers relationship "the most base version of McCarthyism." Well. Brotherly love and loyalty may be endearing, but Rick Ayers acted like a complete nincompoop in trying to conceal his family's sordid past—and questionable present.

A law professor, Steve Diamond, has done what appears to be excellent research on the Obama-Ayers connection. (http://globallabor.blogspot.com/search?updated-max=2008-04-25T06%3A43%3A00-07%3A00)

I have analyzed and interpreted Diamond's facts for some of my conclusions in this column. Diamond's April 22nd chronology offers perhaps the best time line and explanation for the decades-old close association between Obama and Ayers.

First, Obama was hired at a law firm where Ayers's father controlled the major client. Obama's sponsors also were associated with that law firm. Second, Ayers sponsored Obama for leadership of the Chicago Annenberg Challenge ("CAC"), a $50 million grant program. Here, I think we strike pay dirt in understanding the longstanding close links between Ayers and Obama. Obama did not just wander into Ayers' home when Obama decided to run for the state senate. The two men had an intimate prior working relationship through Ayers' sponsorship of Obama for head of the CAC.

The 1996 state senate fundraiser at Ayer's home was not a door opener or an introduction between the two families; it was a continuing extension of the links between Ayers and the Obamas.

In classic Chicago style politics, Ayers armed Obama with $50 million to distribute to local schools. Talk about a "door opener." Thus, when Obama tried to evade ABC's questions about Ayers by saying he was "eight years old" when Ayers was bombing buildings, Obama was trying to deflect attention from the real links between the presidential candidate and the mad bomber.

Obama's Annenberg role is discussed at length in an Education week article. (http://www.edweek.org/ew/articles/2007/03/07/26politics.h26.html)

Ironically, MSM attention has focused on Obama's "board" service with Ayers, as well as the odd speaking engagement, and totally ignored the fact that Obama was Ayers' Potemkin (front) as leader of the Annenberg Challenge. In other words, Ayers used Obama as a front man to control the disbursement of CAC's $50 million patronage fund. Pretty close relationship, wouldn't you say? Pretty powerful, too. And, so, presto, properly analyzed and interpreted, we now know that Obama was a tool, or pawn, or stooge, of William Ayers as Ayers controlled the Chicago Annenberg Challenge from behind the scenes.

Sean Hannity has been sitting on a blockbuster story and, because of the limitations of cable TV, has entirely missed this "explosive" relationship as well as other potential future eruptions involving Obama.

Where do we go from here? There are three aspects that make the Ayers/Obama relationship a massive political issue, now in the primaries and later in the fall if Obama wrests the nomination from Hillary Clinton.

First, there is the Rezko/Obama/Ayers pattern of deception and concealment. When Rezko was indicted, Obama pretended Rezko was an obscure factor in his campaigns. Rezko got Obama his law firm job after law school, financed his campaigns and helped him buy the "Obama Mansion" in 2005. We now know Obama was blatantly lying (as I disclosed in November, 2006) about Rezko.

Obama has adopted the same deceptive tactics about Ayers, with his "red herring" that he was "8 years old" when Ayers was a mad bomber, when in fact it is the Ayers/Annenberg/

Obama relationship that shows the longstanding relationship between the two men.

Second, while Ayers may have achieved "respectability" in a city controlled by a crooked mayor and that has long admired organized crime figures as the apotheosis of municipal manipulation, most Americans would find the "Chicago Way" grossly offensive. In most towns, associating with mad bombers would be a matter for shame, not pride. Ayers, moreover, has never apologized, has always been defiant, and continues to be a leading world proponent of fascist revolution.

The Ayers connection with Venezuela's dictator Hugo Chavez has also not surfaced in the MSMs. It is a time bomb waiting to explode. We make the connection today for the first time.

Chavez' alleged associates were indicted in Miami for trying to funnel illegal campaign cash to Argentina. Can Chavez be planning similar machinations on behalf of Obama? Only Chavez and Ayers know. The fact that Ayers is totally unrepentant, and continues to associate with vicious dictators who espouse violent revolution, makes the Ayers/Obama/Chavez connection one with long legs through November. The fact that a Chavez stooge recently pleaded guilty to participation in the Venezuelan campaign cash scheme raises the bar in so far as possible Venezuelan intervention in the U.S. campaign is concerned. (http://www.miamiherald.com/775/story/506633.html)

Well, I could go on, but you get the point. Barack Obama's links to unsavory people such as William Ayers raise not only historical questions about his past poor judgment and serving as a lackey and front man for unrepentant violent revolutionaries, but also provide concern for the present and future, that Ayers' associate Chavez may attempt to reprise in the United States the same kind of clandestine cash operation in support of Obama that Chavez was caught financing in Argentina. "Oh, what a tangled web they weave."

Obama isn't as dumb as he claims, and he's a lot more slick, and crooked, than he admits. A lot more than the MSMs have told Democratic voters.

Barry Obama, meet William Ayers and Hugo Chavez. MSMs, meet the "secret life of Barack Obama." Democrats. Is this the man you want to be your candidate?

Obama Faces Pincer Movement from McCain and Clinton
"Presumptive Nominee" for Democrats is Surrounded

Clinton's "nutcracker" strategy will keep Obama endangered until Denver convention

(CHICAGO)(June 4, 2008) I have not yet ordered my Senator Hillary Clinton nutcracker (http://www.amazon.com/gp/product/images/B000UB0004/ref=dp_image_0?ie=UTF8&n=284507&s=kitchen) but she did a nut cracking job on Senator Barack Obama Tuesday.

Obama finds himself under siege by a pincer movement with Clinton on one flank and senator John McCain on the other.

The utter fraudulence of anointing himself as his party's candidate was brought home by Obama's loss in South Dakota. Clinton surprised her opponent by winning a victory in a state Obama was expected to hold. Hillary forced an embarrassing split decision on Tuesday.

Not surprisingly, the mainstream media (MSNBC, CNN, Fox) missed the significance of the night. There was blather about Obama's brilliant speech and McCain's lackluster remarks. OK. Let me start by stating the obvious: Barack Obama is the best after-dinner speaker in America today. He is a true Toastmaster.

390

But Obama's "speech" was just another tried and true rehash of his 2004 convention oratory. He has been recycling 2004 ever since then. Yes, it worked against the early Clinton in January and February. But Obama was trashed by Hillary in the later states. Despite Obama's speeches and crowds he was not able to prevail in later primary states. And the latest primary of all comes in November.

The significance of Tuesday was not the speech making. Rather the fact that Clinton is still in, and McCain is on the attack, placed Obama in a pincer movement on his first night as a putative nominee. McCain launched his attack on Obama's nonexistent record, and Clinton cited her record as a reason she is the best candidate to run against McCain.

The day began with reports Obama would claim victory. Clinton parried Obama with a "conference call" in which she announced her availability to be a vice president. In her speech she congratulated Obama for running, but not for "winning." And she grabbed a primary night victory for an even split on the last day.

When analysts look back on Clinton's campaign they will see that she was poorly served last year by the hangers on and "regime remnants" of the Clinton White House. It was only when Hillary took command that her campaign began to click. Obama won caucus states where affluent voters could show up at night and "vote" in what are essentially doctored and rigged insider elections. Clinton won primaries. Obama's loss in South Dakota suggests he could not repeat today many of his earlier caucus victories. So Democrats are stuck with a nominee who ran downhill for the last half of the primary season. Not a great start.

In February I advised Hillary to "take it to the convention." That is still my advice. She should take up the cause of party reform, and seek to abolish both caucuses and proportional voting. Some of the results were absurd: Obama won delegate pluralities in tiny states, while Clinton could not achieve any traction in the big states where she prevailed. Is this democracy? Obviously not.

Democrats need to tilt their campaign process more towards rewarding primary winners, and not favoring majorities in tiny states. The current process of allowing "red" (i.e. conservative) states to dominate the Democratic Party's nominating process with caucuses and unbalanced primaries (e.g. Texas) places the Democrats in danger of choosing an unrepresentative nominee. The entire operation is illogical.

Finally, while Obama may believe he is the nominee he is only a very provisional choice. In reality he has only staked his claim, an uncertain claim at that. Obama is at the mercy of muckrakers and opposition researchers between now and the Denver convention. The reality is that he has delegates who are temporarily committed to him but are not legally bound to support him if he continues to run downhill over the summer.

Post-purchase anxiety may cause Democrats to wonder just who they have nominated. Obama's flacks can talk all they want about history. But history teaches us that "historic" candidates often lose.

Will Hillary be offered the Vice President's slot? Can't say. Would she accept? I think she would. Is Obama going to have it easy now that he is the nominee? Not on your life. The pincer movement has just begun. And it is going to pinch.

Better order a Hillary nutcracker before they go out of stock. You may still need it. Walnuts anyone?

Chicago News Conference:
Obama Supporters Begin Smear Campaign to Block Andy's Martin's Obama Book Sales

As Andy Martin's Obama book reaches pre-publication blockbuster status, Obama media flacks launch new personal attacks on the powerhouse Internet columnist

Andy Martin demands apology from Obama and his butt boys in the left-wing media, may sue "The Nation" magazine for AIPAC accusation

(CHICAGO)(June 7, 2008) Legendary Chicago Internet columnist and muckraker Andy Martin will hold a news conference Saturday, June 7th to denounce Barack Obama's smears against Martin, and to demand an apology for the personal attacks of Obama's lap dogs in the left-wing media.

"Wow. My book went on sale on Wednesday, and by Friday Barry Obama's attacks dogs were smearing me. I must be more feared by the Obamanuts than even I realized. I may not be the 'Most Powerful Name in News,' but Obama & Co. are treating me as though I am 'The Most Powerful Columnist on the Internet,' and an author whose blockbuster new book is going to help bring down the Obama charade. 'The Nation' says Obama's speech to AIPAC was a response to my Internet columns and e-mails.

"Obama's lies are obviously intended to deflect sales of my book. I am flattered. His flacks at 'The Nation' have previously called me the mastermind of a 'right-wing smear machine,' seeking to elevate my cosmic danger to Obamanuts. Now they have recycled their smears in the wake of the outstanding pre-publication sales of my new book. Thank you Barry O. You keep attacking me, and I will keep selling.

"We may have to up the print run by another 100,000," Martin will state. "I stand by what I have written, and I will stand behind everything in my new book: Barry Obama is bad for America and, by inference, he will become a colossal disaster for the Democratic Party. And nothing Obama's supporters at The Nation write is going to deflect me from my appointed rounds: telling the truth about Barack Obama and his crusade to destroy America."

Andy was the first columnist, in 2004, to write about Obama's fraudulent book "Dreams From My Father," and to expose all of Obama's lies in that book.

Andy is the author of Obama: The Man Behind The Mask. Details on Martin's book can be found at http://www.OrangeStatePress.com. Advance orders from Orange State Press. Available everywhere in days. Because of the overwhelming pre-publication demand, orders will be filled by date of order.

New York News Conference:
"Yes, Barack Obama was a Muslim"

*Obama author Andy Martin counters Barack Obama's
new Web site denying Obama was a Muslim*

*"Yes, Obama was a Muslim," says Andy Martin. "Barack Obama is
lying again. This time, he won't get away with it*

(NEW YORK)(June 13, 2008) Legendary Chicago Internet columnist and Obama author Andy Martin will hold a New York news conference Friday, June 13th to announce a new blog intended to counter Senator Barack Obama's new web site that denies Obama was a Muslim. At the news conference Martin will also issue a surprise challenge to Senator Obama.

Martin's book, **Obama: The Man Behind the Mask,** is now in pre-publication sales and goes to the printer within days. See http://orangestatepress.com.

Martin is universally credited with first exposing Obama's Muslim heritage in 2004. Andy has been attacked as the mastermind of a vast "right-wing smear machine," a charge he vehemently denies.

"Apparently desperate, Barack Obama announced Thursday he has begun a web site to fight 'rumors,'" Martin will state. "To be sure, some of what is said about Obama is exaggerated or untrue. I refuse to publish a great deal of anti-Obama material that crosses my desk. But much of what Obama characterizes as 'rumor' is true. Obama has been lying about his family and his religious past his entire life. This time he will not get away with his lies."

See: http://blog.washingtonpost.com/thefix/2008/06/obama_tries_to_fight_the_smear.html; http://my.barackobama.com/page/content/fightthesmearshome/.

"Obama says in large print and underlines 'Senator Obama has never been a Muslim, was not raised a Muslim, and is a committed Christian," Martin states. "Two thirds of that claim are bald-faced lies. The last third, about Obama's Christianity, has never been adequately documented. Most people who are baptized have a Baptismal Certificate. I call on Obama to release his Baptismal Certificate or record. Many Americans do not believe that sitting in the pews, listening to Reverend Jeremiah Wright's racist jeremiads for two decades qualifies anyone to be a 'committed Christian.' Committed racist and America-hater, maybe.

'Most importantly, by denying his Islamic roots, Obama unfairly and unnecessarily stigmatizes Muslims. Despite current controversies, Islam is one of the world's great religions. No one can pretend otherwise. Not even Barack Obama.

"I have asked the State of Hawaii to release Obama's birth certificate. If Obama really wants to clear the air, let's see what religion was listed on his birth certificate. Obama was never much of an attorney so he may not be aware of the 'adverse inference rule,' but if he fails to disclose his birth certificate and refuses to allow me to purchase a copy directly from the state, the American people are entitled to draw the adverse inference that the birth certificate says Obama was a Muslim at birth. How about it, Barry?

"Some people claim Obama was not even born in the United States. I express no opinion on that claim. But it is out there. (http://www.usafricaonline.com/news.html)

"I do know that Obama's relentless evasiveness feeds the wildest claims about him. If Barry Obama would stop lying about himself and start telling the truth, instead of 'denying' the truth, he would be better off. He is a lousy crisis manager.

"But back to Obama's Muslim roots.

"What is the undisputed, **factual** basis of the claim Obama was a Muslim?

"First, his father Barack Hussein Obama, Senior, was a Muslim from the day of his birth to the day of his burial. His grandfather was also a devout Muslim. 'Barack' is a name with Arabic origins. The woman he falsely tries to pass off as his real 'granny' is a devout Muslim. Virtually all of his Kenyan relatives appear to be Muslims.

"Second, under Muslim law, Barack, Junior, became a Muslim at birth. See: http://www.csmonitor.com/2008/0519/p09s02-coop.html.

"Third, the Christian Science Monitor writer states 'According to Islamic jurisprudence, children of a Muslim father – even an apparently non practicing one, such as Obama's father, and irrespective of the mother's faith – are automatically Muslims. Most Muslims around the world agree: A child of a Muslim father is a Muslim. Period....That's why Obama is bin Laden's dream candidate.'

"Fourth, Obama himself, and his sister, have admitted they occasionally attended Mosque with his stepfather Lolo Soetero in Jakarta.

"Fifth, Obama's mother or stepfather registered him as a Muslim at public school in Jakarta. The actions of his parents speak louder than Obama's belated denials.

"Sixth, as I disclosed at a Washington, DC news conference in March, Obama had close ties to the Nation of Islam and flirted with joining that religious denomination. He considered joining the NOI as an adult.

"Did Obama change his religion and abandon Islam? Apparently he did. He had a First Amendment constitutional right to do so. In this country. But that abandonment raises a new series of questions, as the CSM article makes clear. Will Muslim nations recognize Obama's religious renunciation?

"The bottom line: I have sent a check to Hawaii to order Obama's birth certificate. I challenge him to send me a letter approving release of the certificate to me. If he refuses to do so, I will assume he is possibly doing so to cover up the religion disclosed on the certificate.

"Second, Obama should take down his bogus Muslim-denial site, and come clean with the American people. He should say 'My father was a Muslim. I was born into that faith. When I was old enough to choose for myself, I was baptized into Christianity on (insert date and produce baptismal certificate). I accept Jesus Christ as my Lord and Savior.' Anything less is more of his habitual evasiveness.

"Obama is trying a Watergate-style 'modified limited hangout.' It won't work. Indeed, his new site is going to backfire on him. This time he is not going to get away with lying, or misleading, or fibbing, or dissembling. The truth will prevail, and the truth is, Barack Obama **was** a Muslim," Martin will state.

Martin will unveil his new blog that is intended to counter Obama's own web site: http://barackobamawasa muslim.blogspot.com/.

Martin, an adjunct professor of law himself, plans to issue a surprise challenge to Obama at the news conference.

Andy is the author of Obama: The Man Behind The Mask. Details on Martin's book can be found at http://www.OrangeStatePress.com. Advance orders from

Orange State Press. Available everywhere in days. Because of the overwhelming pre-publication demand, orders will be filled by date of order.

New York News Conference:
"Barack Obama was a Muslim," Part Two

Obama author Andy Martin accuses Barack Obama of "smearing the truth" about Obama's childhood religion

Martin challenges Obama to sue Martin for defamation on "Muslim" issue

Andy says Obama is blatantly lying to the American people

(NEW YORK)(June 16, 2008) Legendary Chicago Internet columnist and Obama author Andy Martin will hold a New York news conference Monday, June 16th to charge that Barack Obama is "smearing the truth" about Obama's childhood religion. Martin will challenge Obama to sue Martin for defamation.

Martin's book, **Obama: The Man Behind the Mask**, is now in pre-publication sales and goes to the printer June 18th. See http://orangestatepress.com.

Martin is universally credited with first exposing Obama's Muslim heritage in 2004. Andy has been attacked as the mastermind of a vast "right-wing smear machine," a charge he vehemently denies and for which there is no proof.

"Barry Obama flatly denies that he was ever a Muslim," Martin will state. That is simply not true." (http://my.barackobama.com/page/content/fightthesmearshome/)

"I challenge Senator Obama to sue me for defamation if he truly wants to perpetuate the myth that he had no ties to the

Muslim religion. I will waive all of the traditional First Amendment defenses ("Public figure," "actual malice," etc.) and will interpose only one defense in support of my claims: truth," Martin will state at his news conference.

Martin, a former CUNY adjunct professor of law, says Obama is lying to the American people. "Obama has concocted this 'Fight the Smears' web site to propagate propaganda and false information. It is one of the most cynical ploys in American political history.

"Frankly, in opposition to every mainstream media, I think the 'Smears' site will prove to be a disaster for Obama.

"Already an Israeli internet magazine has produced a purported article—which I have been unable to verify at the Jerusalem Post—claiming that Obama's brother says his brother was a Muslim and that Obama comes from a Muslim family:

Malik Obama confirms his half-brother Barack grew up a Muslim (http://web.israelinsider.com/Articles/Politics/12918.htm).

Is Barack Obama a Muslim wolf in Christian wool? (http://web.israelinsider.com/Articles/Politics/12745.htm)

"But an earlier article by the highly-respected New York Times columnist Nicholas Kristof says more to me and, I believe, most common sense, clear-thinking adults: Obama admitted to Kristof that Obama was in 'Koran study classes.' More critically, forty years later, i.e. almost forty years after leaving Jakarta, **'Mr. Obama recalled the opening lines of the Arabic call to prayer, reciting them with a first-rate accent.'** (http://select.nytimes.com/2007/03/06/opinion/06kristof.html?_r=1&oref=slogin)

"Where did Mr. Obama learn to pray in Arabic, and develop a 'first rate [Arabic] accent?' At the Nation of Islam in

Chicago? Or in Jakarta where he was a Muslim student for sure?

"I am reminded that some Jesuit Catholic priests say 'give us a boy until he is 7, and we have him for life.' (http://forum. catholic.org/viewtopic.php?f=81&t=35646&sid=a7f55a506c1b 8be8a8500d510a809153)

"Forty years later, Obama retained a 'first-rate accent' in Arabic and could recite a Muslim prayer. They had some pretty good religious teachers in Jakarta. And Obama was not a Muslim during his childhood? The Muslims had Obama until he was 9 or 10. They beat the Catholic test.

"Once more I want to stress two principles that I have stated so often:

"First, I do not question that Obama is a Christian **today**. But Obama has always tried to obscure his childhood religion by thumping his chest about his current religion. Christianity is an open religion, he was free to join, and he did. I have always accepted that principle.

"Second the issue is not whether Obama was a Muslim until he left Jakarta around the age of 10. The evidence is overwhelming that he was; that evidence was best extracted by Nick Kristof.

"The issue is that Obama blatantly lies and tries to reinvent his past, because he is afraid of retaliation for his childhood religion. I think he would get more votes if he told the truth, certainly more than he is going to lose by telling a lie. Muslims vote too. The issue, therefore, is not 'religion' in fact, but his relentless pursuit of propaganda and disinformation to obscure what that religion was up to the age of 10.

"Obama was never much of a lawyer, and he never tried a lawsuit in court, but even from his Harvard student books he should have learned that dissembling and evasion are crucial to credibility. When Obama lies about the truth, the fact that he is willing to lie is a critical aspect of his character.

"Obama's entire 'Fight the Smears' web site is itself a smear of Islam, and a smear of the truth. Obama uses his 'defense' of smears to propagate smears, and to produce relentless lies and disinformation. It is on that basis that I challenge him and his fitness to sit in the Oval Office.

"I also challenge Obama to sue me for defamation concerning my claims about his religion. The only defense I will offer is 'truth.' I don't care what religion his mom and dad and step dad chose for him; I do care that he lies about those objective truths and facts, and continues to do so brazenly and blatantly. No one can read Kristof's 2007 column and come away believing Obama's lies. He studied the Koran, and he still speaks Koranic Arabic with a 'first-rate accent.' How many non-Muslims can recite Islamic prayers the way Obama can?

"Contrary to what Obama claims, this Internet author is propagating the truth about Obama's religious past, not 'smears' and not 'lies.' I have no interest in publishing false information. Obama is the liar, plain and simple. Stop it Barry. Or sue me."

Andy is the author of **Obama: The Man Behind The Mask.** Details on Martin's book can be found at http://www.OrangeStatePress.com. Advance orders from Orange State Press. Available everywhere in days. Because of the overwhelming pre-publication demand, orders will be filled by date of order.

CHAPTER NINE

Obama Begins His Presidential Campaign

No sooner had Barack Obama won the Democratic Party's presidential nomination in mid-June, 2008 than his campaign began to manifest peculiar aberrations.

One of Obama's first decisions was to set up a "FighttheSmears.com" web site to deflect and defeat alleged "smears" against him. Whether "fighting smears" gave credence to these disputes was an open question.

Moreover, much of what Obama continues to consider a "smear" is merely a difference of opinion over his convoluted and contradictory life story, or his somewhat opaque manner of expressing himself.

In my opinion, Obama's goal was not really to fight smears; rather he is seeking to manipulate and control the truth, so that only Obama's version of the "truth" will be acceptable, and all other inconsistent versions would be branded as "smears". Any conflicting or differing interpretations of what Obama had said or done would thus become *ipso facto* "untruthful" and be damned as "smears."

Not surprisingly, I challenged Obama's "Fight the Smears" tactic and immediately condemned it.

Finally, on a lesser matter, I found that Obama did manage a competent national campaign office.

So where does that leave us? The bottom line?

Obama has proven to be a supremely capable and organized campaigner in the primary election season. He won the nomination because he was better organized than his opponents, and had a better organizational concept to guide his efforts. If he continues to operate in a very orderly and organized fashion, and if Senator John McCain does not become more like Obama and less like his own somewhat erratic primary operation, Barack Obama will be the next President of the United States.

We await the fall campaign, and will be reporting on Obama and McCain as they battle for the White House.

Mainstream Media Slobber over Obama's "Fight Smears" site

Andy Martin says mainstream media slobber at Obama's lies and desperate move to fight "smears" with new Web site

Martin claims the mantle of the most influential columnist in America

"The Internet rules," says Andy Martin. "We are fighting Barack Obama's disinformation, and winning."

Is opposition to Obama orchestrated from an underground bunker in midtown Manhattan?

(NEW YORK)(June 13, 2008) There were floods in the Midwest Thursday evening, but the water overflowing the river banks was a trickle compared to the mainstream media's slobbering over Barack Obama's desperate attempt to "Fight the Smears." (http://my.barackobama.com/page/content/fight-thesmearshome)

From fashionable Fox News on the right to MSNBC on the loony left, the verdict was unanimous: Obama's confession that his campaign strategy for the past two years had failed was greeted with approbation and enthusiasm. "Fighting smears" was the message of the day and the media duly swallowed that sardine whole.

Is it any wonder the power of Internet-based journalists is growing? When no one in the mainstream media stands up and offers a dissenting opinion or a contrarian take on Obama's desperate "anti-smear" gamble, there is something drastically wrong with MSM coverage of the campaign. (Sean Hannity claims he is not part of the "mainstream media," but Fox News is absolutely part of the pack.)

Four years ago I disclosed that Barack Obama was fighting to conceal his family's religious roots in the Muslim faith. Because some conservatives consider me a sympathizer with Muslim causes, there was initial confusion when I was identified as the source of the Obama disclosures. But I have no pro or anti-Muslim agenda. "Just the facts, Mam'm." I just place the facts in the record and let readers decide. For my integrity and independence in digging out the truth about Obama I have been vilified by almost everyone.

And Tuesday night there they were, the mainstream panjandrums such as Chris Matthews (he of the "wet leg" when Obama enters a room) pontificating "Obama was never a Muslim" and words to that effect.

As is so often the case when the mainstream media are united in their incompetence and mendacity, the truth was exactly the opposite of that being preached on TV.

Obama's "Fight the Smears" site is not an attempt to debunk lies or "smears." Rather, the site is a confession of failure; a very risky gamble and one that I strongly feel will boomerang and blow up in his face. Obama is trying, once again, to conceal the truth with bombastic attacks on anyone who dares publish the facts about his religious roots and prior history of unpopular remarks (more on these remarks in a subsequent column).

I may be the only columnist in the United States who publishes the truth, but here it is: http://www.BarackObama WasaMuslim.blogspot.com/.

Why are the media concealing the truth and depriving their viewers and readers of truthful information?

First, they are slobbering over the fact that Obama might just become president. So they are already genuflecting to their future king. The media toads are already toadying.

Second, the mainstream media dropped the ball on Obama's religious roots. The truth that Obama tried so desperately to conceal did not originate in the Washington Post or New York Times. The truth originated with my newspaper, ContrarianCommentary.com and its predecessors. Mainstream media are always incensed when they are scooped on a story, especially when the scooper is a *pisher* publisher, not the mighty Chicago Tribune.

Third, the truth hurts. The truth hurts because Obama has said for the past two years that he would ignore and suppress the truth about his religious roots and hope it would go away. I have not gone away; the truth has not gone away and the percentage of Americans who suspect Obama is lying has steadily risen into the low teens. In other words—and may I take a bow on this one as the most influential columnist in any media today—my original research has been disseminated and regurgitated (not always accurately) to such an extent that the power of the truth has completely overwhelmed the ability of the mainstream media to suppress the facts.

My name does not appear under the masthead of the New York Times or the Washington Post, but I have gained credibility because I publish the facts and they refuse to do likewise. Fox News passed over me as an analyst for the Iraq war because I was too honest and too independent. I went to Baghdad and broke more news and criticism on the incompetence of the American mission than anyone else but John McCain.

The Nation, a leftish magazine, has published two attacks on me as the orchestrator of a CapitalOne-advertisement-style vast underground "smear machine." Since when did telling the truth become a "smear?" I invited The Nation's publisher to visit my secret bunker deep under midtown Manhattan, where we orchestrate the disinformation that confuses virtually everyone from ethnic groups to our own adversarial mainstream colleagues on the surface. Perhaps that will fulfill her fantasies about how we operate.

The reality is far more modest. I may not be as powerful as The Nation suggests, but I am willing to claim that ContrarianCommentary.com has been right more often than not during the 2008 election cycle. That's why Obama is running scared. He knows I am in hot pursuit.

In our Obama "war room" at ContrarianCommentary.com we are flooded every day with negative information about Barack Obama. We publish only a tiny fraction of the material we receive. Sometimes I am criticized for what we don't publish. But can anyone point to any errors we have published about Obama? I don't think so. We do our own independent due diligence before a story or an accusation appears. I have never written that Obama attended a "madrassa." Others added that embellishment.

Likewise, I have never said that Obama "is" a Muslim. Obviously he is not. In our First Amendment republic people are free to worship as they please. Even if they worship at the altar of Rev. Jeremiah Wright.

Fourth, the mainstream media are in steady decline. The Chicago Tribune is now being run into the ground by a man whose prior claim to fame was that he made a fortune evicting helpless poor people from trailer parks. He jumped from mean-spirited evictions to mean-spirited attitudes towards his own reporters.

I follow the story where I know it leads. And after 40 years in the courthouses of Chicago, I know my way around the sewers of that city.

When I reported in November 2006 that Obama's ties to indicted influence peddler Tony Rezko were far more extensive than he was admitting, the mainstream media yawned. Who was right, and who missed the story? When Rezko's trial began I said more about Obama would come out. There was testimony Obama was acting as arm candy for Rezko during his 2004 senate campaign; Obama said he "didn't remember" meeting one of the richest people in the world.

Obama went through years of denials, evasions and prevarications, and the full truth about Tony Rezko is still not known.

But we will have new insights in **Obama: The Man Behind the Mask**, which goes to the printer in days.

To my loyal readers and those who join us every day, I say, "welcome." To my competitors, I ask, "How many websites is Obama going to have to put up to counter our writing before you admit that Obama's strategy has been an abject failure, not the wonderful idea to 'fight smears' you were suggesting in unison on June 12th?"

And for Senator Obama, I have a promise: we will do our best to publish only true and accurate charges and opinions about you, because we know that it is precisely the truth about yourself that you fear the most.

In the meantime, if anyone else would like to visit the mythical secret command-and-control bunker deep under midtown Manhattan, please contact us for a guided tour. Just remember, we are a hell of a lot more influential than our competitors up on the surface. And if you don't believe my claims, or think we are exaggerating our influence, just ask the Obama people. They know we're telling the truth. They just put up a web site to "stop the smears," which in reality is a web site to control the truth and deprive voters of the facts. Maybe Obama should have called it the "StopContrarianCommentary.com" site.

Luckily, our readers and the American people are smarter than the mainstream media. Which is why the Internet rules.

Can McCain's People Organize a Campaign? Obama's Can

McCain's presidential headquarters is ham-handed; Obama's flows smoothly

Obama wins one from Andy; McCain better wake up and open up

(NEW YORK)(June 17, 2008) It is not often I give Senator Barack Obama a point; but when he deserves one, he gets it.

Today I had reason to contact both Obama's and Senator John McCain's national headquarters. The responses could not have been more different. Someone needs to teach McCain how to run a national campaign, or hire someone who does.

I called Obama's office first, worked my way through the phone tree, ("press 6") and someone promptly and crisply answered. I asked for a fax number, and she gave it to me.

Whether Obama's people like or dislike my communication, later today they will receive a fax. End of discussion. Obama's national office ran efficiently. Very impressive.

Then I called McCain's national campaign headquarters. It took forever for someone to answer the phone (try it). The first time I called I pushed buttons to get to someone's extension. No one answered. No one returned the call.

The second time I called I pushed the button for the press office, and some idiot munchkin answered. (Luckily for him, I did not ask for his name or it would be here.) McCain's Munchkin said they do not release a fax number, "to keep it open for incoming and outgoing faxes." Oh really. I pointed out that it was unusual for a national campaign to be run as a clandestine operation, especially by someone working in the press office.

Then the munchkin told me to write a letter to McCain's post office box.

I got nowhere. The munchkin was made of pure tree stump.

I tried asking for the person's e-mail address that I wanted to contact. "On, no," the munchkin said, "We can't give that out either. Maybe we can give you a general e-mail address and I'll try to see he gets it."

"Not good enough," I said. At that point I had had enough and wasted enough time talking to the idiot in McCain's press office at national headquarters.

I hope McCain upgrades his national staff. If he can't do a better job of communicating with the outside world and responding to people who contact his office, his campaign will lack the heft to go forward after Labor Day when the real hand-to-hand combat with the Democrats begins. As for the McCain munchkin with the secret fax machine and secret e-mail address? He is probably looking out the window. Watching the grass grow.

McCain may have experience on his side. But if his national headquarters is any guide, he sure doesn't have competence. Maybe it's time for a smattering of the legendary McCain temper at headquarters.

Andy is the author of Obama: The Man Behind The Mask. Details on Martin's book can be found at http://www.OrangeStatePress.com. Advance orders from Orange State Press. Available everywhere in days. Because of the overwhelming pre-publication demand, Internet orders will be filled by date of order. To purchase book: http://www.OrangeStatePress.com.

Conclusion

Beginning in 2004, I read and reread "Dreams From My Father," Obama's pseudo autobiography with invented events and persons.

The more I read "Dreams," the more revealing I find Obama's words back in 1990's when the book was written and originally published.

"Dreams" is Obama's Mein Kampf. He portrays himself honestly—brimming with confusion, rage, alienation, suspicion, and abandonment. These qualities are still present in his psyche, even if they have been papered over for purposes of political advancement.

What clearer warning could Americans want? Barack Obama is a dangerous personality. He would be a disaster as president.

And, as if to confirm my fears and suspicions, Obama began his fall presidential campaign with a new TV ad, a veritable field of dreams. This time the title was not "Dreams From my Father."

This time the title should be "Dreams from Obama."

Obama's New TV Commercial Enters Candidate's "Fantasyland"

Obama's first TV commercial invites viewers to join him in "Fantasyland"

Is Obama the product of "strong families and strong values?" "Give me a break, says Andy

(NEW YORK)(June 20, 2008) Obama has released his first TV commercial of the general election campaign. It is an excursion into Obama's own Fantasyland.

Obama says "America is a country of strong families and strong values. My life has been blessed by both." Unfortunately, the claims about himself are fantasies. Obama's family life was not "blessed" (nice Christian term, that) by either a strong family or strong values.

In the next line of the ad he goes on to claim "I was raised by a single mother..." Obama's mother was anything but an exemplary parent. And she appears to have been the first source of his anti-American values.

As an 18 year-old, Mrs. Obama became pregnant by a married foreign student. Such behavior hardly reflected a strong family or strong values in 1960. Indeed, Obama himself admits his parents may never have married, which is why no marriage license/certificate has ever surfaced (we are looking for one). Any marriage would have been a crime in Hawaii, because his father was already married and would have become a bigamist.

In other words, Obama has been living a lie about his parents his entire life, and he knows it.

Strong values? Mrs. Obama appears to have hated America as much as she disdained American boys as social contacts.

Mrs. Obama dragged her son to Indonesia, to live with yet another foreign father, and then dumped him back on her parents when Barry became a 10 tear-old and obviously more difficult to manage. After returning to Hawaii to complete a post-graduate degree, Mrs. Obama-Soetero-Dunham then spent much of the rest of her life in Indonesia.

Obama has made a point of the fact that his mother collected food stamps, at a time while he was attending an expensive private academy. "Ripping off the man" sounds more like it. Obama's mama was some drama.

Obama's grandparents, whom he loved and disdained at the same time, were solid people. But only so far. Did Obama receive religious values from his grandparents? Sadly, no. They were atheists or agnostics or something in between. But what they were not is church-going people. Hardly representative of "Kansas values." Obama was left to wander through adolescence with the confused and incomplete faith tradition of Islam, until he finally accepted Jesus Christ at some unspecified point later in his life.

David Brooks in the New York Times today has an essay on "The Two Obamas." (http://www.nytimes.com/2008/06/20/opinion/20brooks.html?ref=opinion)

One of the "Two Obamas," the coldly calculating opportunist who is on the brink of capturing the White House, did not come from either a solid family or solid values. Rather, in his disoriented and disorganized young life, "Barry" Obama learned to take what he wanted, and to put himself first, last and always. Obama is the product of a seriously dysfunctional family and a grossly confused and conflicting set of values. The values he spouts in his new TV ad are those written by his TV image makers, not the ones he learned in his early years.

In "Dreams From My Father," Obama's marvelous novel (not "autobiography") of his early years, Obama admitted that he was forced to create fairy tales and live in a dream world about his father and his life. He also says his mother encouraged those imaginary excursions. She herself also had a hard time living in the real world (America) or making normal social contacts with American men.

Obama is still living in his fairy tale bubble today. Moreover, children who are abandoned by one parent, or both parents as in Obama's case, develop fantasies and coping mechanisms to deal with the misery of their reality. Their frustration and alienation is overwhelming. And permanent.

Obama developed a very powerful fantasy world to deal first with a father who abandoned him, and then a mother who abandoned him; he is still living with and in those childhood delusions. Later he had to confront the reality of a father who was a drunken rake and bigamist, and who fathered eight children by numerous women. "Strong family and strong values?" Give me a break.

Obama is asking the American people to join him in a "Fantasyland" constructed of his own childhood imagination and images. We should decline the invitation. The consequences of accepting Obama at face value will not be a fantasy. It will be a "long national nightmare."